The Higher Illiteracy

The Higher Illiteracy

Essays on Bureaucracy, Propaganda, and Self-Delusion

Gene Lyons

The University of Arkansas Press
Fayetteville 1988 London

Copyright © 1988 by Gene Lyons
All rights reserved
Manufactured in the United States
92 91 90 89 88   5 4 3 2 1

DESIGNER: Nancy Burris
TYPEFACE: Linotron 202 Palatino
TYPESETTER: G & S Typesetters, Inc.
PRINTER: McNaughton & Gunn, Inc.
BINDER: John H. Dekker & Sons, Inc.

The paper used in this publication meets the minimum requirements of the American National Standard for Perma-
nence of Paper for Printed Library Materials Z39.48-1984. ⊚

LIBRARY OF CONGRESS CATALOGING-IN-PUBLICATION DATA

Lyons, Gene, 1943–
    The higher illiteracy: essays on bureaucracy, propaganda,
and self-delusion / by Gene Lyons.
        p. cm.
    ISBN 1-55728-003-7. ISBN 1-55728-004-5 (pbk.)
    I. Title.
PN4874.L963A5 1988   87-34013
814'.54—dc19   CIP

311736

*For my mother Helen A. Lyons, and in memory of
my father, Eugene A. Lyons, Jr.—who made it possible.*

Acknowledgements

"The Artificial Jewboy," From *Moment: The New Magazine for America's Jews*, Vol. 1, No. 4 (October 1975) pp. 33–48.

"The Higher Illiteracy," Originally published in *Harper's Magazine*, Vol. 253, No. 1516 (September 1976) pp. 33–40.

"Publishing the Backwoods Genius," *The Nation Magazine*, Vol. 223, No. 16 (November 13, 1976) pp. 501–503.

"The Little Magazine: Grow or Die," *The Nation Magazine*, Vol. 225, No. 3 (July 23, 1977) pp. 85–6.

"Good Fiction, Plain and Fancy," *The Nation Magazine*, Vol. 225, No. 13 (October 22, 1977) pp. 405–8.

"Report on the Fiction Collective," First published in *Triquarterly*, Fall 1978, pp. 635–47.

"*Harper's* Bizarre," *The Nation Magazine*, Vol. 226, No. 1 (January 14, 1978) pp. 24–7.

"The Famous Breadloaf Writer's School," Originally published in *Harper's Magazine*, Vol. 260, No. 1557 (February 1980) pp. 75–80.

"Why Teachers Can't Teach," First appeared in *Texas Monthly*, Vol. 7, Issue 9 (September 1979) 122–8, 208–20. Reprinted with permission.

"The Other Carters," *The New York Times* Company (September 18, 1977) pp. 14–6, 76–100. Reprinted by permission.

"Inside the Volcano," Originally published in *Harper's Magazine*, Vol. 254, No. 1525 (June 1977) pp. 41–55.

"Invisible Wars," Originally published in *Harper's Magazine*, Vol. 263, No. 1579 (December 1981) pp. 37–52.

"Repealing the Enlightenment," Originally published in *Harper's Magazine*, Vol. 264, No. 1582 (April 1982) pp. 38–40, 73–78.

"Politics in the Woods," Originally published in *Harper's Magazine*, Vol. 257, No. 1538 (July 1978) pp. 27–38.

"Why I Live Where I Live," First published in *Esquire*, Vol. 99, No. 1 (January 1983), pp. 96–9.

Inklings, Excerpt from *Inklings* by Geoffry Wolff reprinted by permission of Random House, Inc./Alfred A. Knoff, Inc.

"Dulce et Decorum Est," by Wilfred Owen, Reprinted by permission of New Directions Publishing Corp.

The author owes profuse thanks to the following people for helping make various of these essays far better than they would have been without their advice, editorial help, patience, and friendship: to Paul Burka, William Broyles, James Fallows, Michael Kinsley, Lewis Lapham, Pam Maffei McCarthy, Deborah McGill, Michael Mewshaw, William Novak, Linda Obst, Elizabeth Pochada, Philip Roth, and Annalyn Swan. To Miller Williams for suggesting the idea of this book, Brenda Zodrow for holding my feet to the fire until it was done, and Bertram Barnes for his editorial diligence. To Cheryl Henry for typing the manuscript. And always, to my wife Diane, for everything.

Contents

The Higher Illiteracy

Introduction

> But when a Man's fancy gets *astride* on his Reason; when Imagination is at Cuffs with the Senses; and common Understanding, as well as common Sense, is Kickt out of Doors; the first Proselyte he makes, is Himself; and when that is once compass'd, the Difficulty is not so great in bringing over others; a strong Delusion always operating from *without*, as vigorously as from *within*.
>
> —Jonathan Swift, from "A Digression concerning the Original, the Use and Improvement of Madness in a Commonwealth" in *A Tale of a Tub*.

The successful propagandist, Swift knew, is his own first victim. That being so, a writer introducing a collection of his own essays on the theme of language, bureaucracy, and self-delusion had best deceive neither himself nor his readers as to what he's about. Specifically, then, the sixteen essays in this book were written over an eleven-year period for eight different magazines. Concerning topics as unrelated as my own New Jersey childhood, Mexican culture and politics, the Breadloaf writer's conference in Vermont, teacher education in Texas, wildlife management in national parks in Wyoming and California, and the U.S. Army's gas warfare plans, they were reported and written as occasional pieces—with no thought given to collecting them until quite after the fact.

3

Yet this book is called *The Higher Illiteracy*, not *Gene Lyons' Greatest Hits*. Nor even *The Artificial Jewboy*, after the book's lead (and earliest written) essay—a tempting title indeed to one who learned in four years as a *Newsweek* reviewer some cynical appreciation of how books get noticed. (Not to mention, to anticipate just a bit, the futility of writing by committee.) I do hope that the autobiographical aspects of that essay, limited in focus though it is, will give some satisfaction to readers curious about the opinionated fellow who wrote the rest of the book. To have called it that, however, would have been misleading—implying as it does a kind of purely literary coherence the book hasn't got and doesn't aspire to.

In putting it that way, I don't mean to slight either "The Artificial Jewboy" or "Why I Live Where I Live," the essay written ten years later that more or less completes it. (I am indebted for this insight to my friend Jim Moses—an Arkansas Jew to whom much of the first essay reads like a transmission from Eastern Europe.) And a good thing it is too, as "The Artificial Jewboy" has no conclusion of its own. Yet if it contains more sentences that make me wince than the rest of the book combined, I have found them irreparable short of a total re-write. And as readers who grasp the not terribly subtle parable formed by the two essays can doubtless appreciate, I couldn't possibly do that today without altering the essay almost beyond recognition. So it stands as is, an odd and ambitious hybrid, both its strengths and weaknesses perhaps a result of its obvious imaginative debt to Philip Roth— without whose encouragement and practical help it wouldn't have been written, much less published. Suffice it to say that Roth is a brilliant novelist, and that I am not. Yet if I weren't proud of it, it wouldn't be here at all.

So *The Higher Illiteracy* it is, and for two very good reasons. Historically speaking, if it isn't too absurd to speak of one's own work in those terms, it was in that piece—given its title by Lewis Lapham of *Harper's* magazine—in which the congenital skeptic responsible for the tone of these essays located his voice. Also, in making what amounted to his resignation announcement from The Department (English), that same fellow hit upon the subject that in one way or another animates every essay in this book: the contemporary intellectual disorder Orwell in *1984* called "collective solipsism."

Now citing Orwell can be a tricky business. To many, myself included some of the time, he is a secular saint. During my years writing for *Newsweek*, for example—remembering clearly the sneering aside in my title essay to "the metaphysical netherworld of the weekly newsmagazine feature"—I kept a photograph of Orwell at his BBC microphone on a shelf next to my desk. Of course he had the excuse that there was a war on; broadcasting propaganda, much of it of a purely literary nature, was "doing his bit." But then my work for *Newsweek* only occasionally touched upon the obsessions of the magazine's real power brokers. Even then my editors were normally able to persuade what are called inside 444 Madison Avenue "The Wallendas"—high-flyers, you see—that book reviewers are expected to be a bit eccentric. Also that nobody important reads them anyway.

Some may find it amazing, as I certainly did, that it was editorial censorship of the essay below called "Natural Regulation" that forced me to resign. (The pureed version of same appeared as an unattributed sidebar to a cover story of July 28, 1986). "They're afraid of it," a sympathetic colleague assured me. Afraid of the National Park Service? "Let's put it this way," he said. "The Washington Bureau is full of people who, when they say 'we,' don't mean *Newsweek*, but the government." It struck me that I thought of both entities as "they." It was time to leave.

But I digress. The point about Orwell isn't so much to emphasize my purity of motive, nor to claim his posthumous imprimatur. The calendar year 1984 produced enough "Why St. George Is on My Side" articles to last us all a lifetime. Orwell wrote essays; I write essays. We share a concern with language and truth. Orwell had little faith in the competence and good will of the authorities, and neither have I. I can think of no other significant points of resemblance. Indeed, if forced to name a literary inspiration for my particular brand of impudence and idealism, it wouldn't be the hero of "Homage to Catalonia" at all. Better the curious investigator of my own essay "Invisible War," "a humble Gulliver in the Grand Academy of Lagado . . . visiting the resident experts in their variously appointed cubicles." (That's Lemuel Gulliver, folks—a fictional character, and a credulous ninny at that.)

The Orwellian apocalypse has not arrived on schedule—as its creator never imagined it would. 1984 was a satire, not a prediction. (The literal-minded often confuse the two. Even Orwell mistook Swift's Houyhnmhnmland for a utopia.) Yet even if we in the West have to date been spared the omnipotent, omnivorous state that devoured poor Winston Smith, the danger to individual freedom posed by self-aggrandizing bureaucracies public and private seems to me greater every day. In putting it that way I mean to distinguish my point of view from that of the intellectual survivalists of the extreme right—who lampoon all public agencies save the military, but express only reverence for banks, insurance companies and multi-national corporations. (Imagine the fun if reporters could dig around in, say, the Prudential Insurance Company's files as they can the Texas Education Association's.)

Furthermore, contemporary life is literally unimaginable without large bureaucratic entities. Science, here defended against religious fraud and political opportunism in "Repealing the Enlightenment" is bureaucratic in its very essence. The university, implicated in several of these essays, is in its way—as John Barth has devoted an exceptionally long, brilliant and tedious novel called *Giles Goat-Boy* to showing—the Ur-bureaucracy of our age. At least in theory, it divides, subdivides, parses, and categorizes the sum of human knowledge into schools, colleges, departments, disciplines, specialties, graduate and undergraduate programs, upper and lower division courses—the whole lot.

Yet, whatever their nominal missions, all large organizations are subject to what I think of as the iron laws of bureaucratic inertia. As summarized in "Why Teachers Can't Teach" they are three: "to grow, to protect [themselves] from competition, and to ward off outside scrutiny." Central to all three is the invention and propagation of jargon, a word nicely defined in the *American Heritage Dictionary* as follows: "The specialized or technical language of a trade, profession, class, or fellowship; cant." Now there, it seems to me, is the most significant semi-colon in the dictionary.

The purpose of "Newspeak," Orwell wrote in an appendix to *1984*, was

to make speech, and especially speech on any subject not ideologically neutral, as nearly as possible independent of consciousness. . . . A Party member called upon to make a political or ethical judgement should be able to spray forth the correct opinions as automatically as any machine gun spraying forth bullets. . . . Ultimately, it was hoped to make articulate speech issue from the larynx without involving the brain centers at all.

Basically, that's what he meant by "collective solipsism": the extirpation of irony, the loss of our ability to distinguish between the necessary technicalities of the specialist and the pre-fabricated gibberish of the brain-dead functionary. That the several essays in this book that are devoted to literary subjects deal only tangentially with formally organized bureaucracies seems to me secondary. There are hundreds of university English departments. But when it comes to the question of teaching freshman composition, they speak as one. (Though there has been a wondrous reform since my essay and others like it appeared. English departments now harbor creatures designated as "comp specialists," those who have written dissertations on how to teach freshmen to write. Hence nobody else need bother themselves about it. And certainly not the comp specialist, who has graduate students of his or her own to supervise.)

In short, cant, jargon, and the temptation to erect intellectual castles in the air (complete with dungeons for heretics) exist where you find them—whether in the endless corridors of the Pentagon or the lawn chairs of the Breadloaf Writer's School. The only known antidote is the individual crank with his mocking, gibing voice. Whether mine is a high and lofty calling I leave to readers to determine. It does seem to suit my nature, and I have had, over the years, a great deal of malicious fun writing these essays. My hope in putting them between covers is that readers will share it.

The Artificial Jewboy

Judaism gives the world no peace, it bars slumber, it teaches the world to be discontented and restless so long as the world has not God; it stimulates the movement of history.

—Jacques Maritain

You exhibit here what I have termed contradictory Judaism. . . . Because you believe at one and the same time that Jews are unique and that they are not. Thus you would be offended if a Jew told you the Jews were chosen by God, but you would also be offended if a non-Jew told you they were not.

—Walker Percy, "Love in the Ruins"

The outrage, the disgust inspired in my parents by the gentiles, was beginning to make some sense: The goyim pretended to be something special, while we were actually their moral superiors. And what made us superior was precisely the hatred and the disrespect they lavished so willingly upon us.
Only what about the hatred we lavished upon them?

—Alexander Portnoy

A young man maturing as I did in the Eastern provinces of our country during the Fifties—that period in American life which lasted from 1948 to 1967—and aspiring to that form of endeavor that has been called "The Quality Lit Biz," particularly one whose entrance into the trade required the crossing of ethnic and class barriers, has had to learn to cope with Jews. Such were the conditions of my growing up that intellectualism itself, that peculiar amalgam of restlessness and inertia most often rather smugly called "the life of the mind" during those years, first appeared to me as an almost exclusively "Jewish" phenomenon. At the times and places I was taught there was an unfailing, if often unspoken, association of those key words expressive of the highest values in life and art: "literature," "tragic," "ironic," "human," "moral," "symbol," "organic," and "Jew."

The intensive cultivation of morality, Jewishness, and literary intelligence as virtual synonyms has been noted elsewhere, perhaps most revealingly in Norman Podhoretz's *Making It*. Besides giving credence to the terms I am using by calling his version of the literary establishment a "Jewish Family," Podhoretz is irritatingly accurate in discussing the cultural synthesis of the generation that taught my own. An understandable reaction to the Holocaust and Stalinism—and to what seemed the failure of ideology—resulted in the guilty enshrinement of the Jewish intellectual by many gentiles and the simultaneous celebration of America as a land of freedom and plenty for almost all resembling what Pope called "the isthmus of the middle state."

Scarcely are these words on the page than I feel compelled almost as a matter of reflex to disavow anti-Semitism, for my education has been such that one simply does not speak of these things. So overpowering is the moral authority of the Holocaust, so tangible are the achievements of many of the men and women I may seem to be slighting, and so pervasive the mythos of Jewishness, that one hesitates before them. By way of avoiding semantic backflips and apologies that sound all the more insincere for their repetition let us imagine that a novel had appeared in 1957 in which a greedy Shylock of a landlord raised the rent on an humble Italian shopkeeper until that man was forced out of business in order to make room for a more profitable tenant. Let us further imagine that said Shylock had out of remorse gone to work for nothing, operating the Italian's pushcart when he fell ill, in the process falling in love with his Jew-hating "shicksa" daughter, and being gradually won over by their simple and heartfelt faith to the hope everlasting and a merciful Jesus, converting to Roman Catholicism on the last page. If such a book were published at all, there is little doubt that it would have been denounced as a clumsy slur, its degree of literary merit an index to its danger, and its appearance brooded upon as presaging some dark turn against the Jews by the American public. What is more the protestors would very likely have been correct.

Why then was I not as a young Catholic from the lower orders made at least uneasy by Bernard Malamud's *The Assistant*, the plot of which I have not parodied but simply turned inside out? Why did it move me as a work of literature expressive of Universal Truth rather than as the contrived exercise in ethnic self-indulgence that it is? Partly because the contrivance was not cheap. Malamud is a skillful literary artist and intended, I am sure, no slur. Occasional bows in the direction of St. Francis of Assisi are taken in the novel, although hardly vitiating its central force. Then too, casual bias against Catholicism is so pervasive in American culture that it is hardly noticeable, particularly to those ex-Catholics like myself who partly share it. More important than any of that, though, was that like Malamud's Frank Alpine I was on my way to becoming an Artificial Jewboy and I was not alone. Let me explain:

I first became aware of Jewishness as an issue in the fall of 1952, when I was nine years old. My family lived on Magie Avenue in the Elmora section of Elizabeth, New Jersey, a gritty third-rate industrial city bordering on Newark and just opposite Staten Island. Because it was free I went to Public School 12, two blocks east of my home instead of St. Genevieve's school two blocks west. Only months before I had made my First Holy Communion, a sacrament received on a gloriously appropriate spring day entirely out of character with my memories of Northern New Jersey. Walking home that morning in my white suit, black and white saddle oxfords and floppy bow tie, hair water-parted and admiring God's daffodils is the only glimpse I have had, then or since, of a state of grace, and to a fading glimmer of what it is people are after when they enter churches.

In early September of that year my father had brought home a

11

1953 DeSoto sedan, powder blue with a semi-automatic shift to replace our 1946 Chevy. It was our first new car. We were the recent owners of a 19" Dumont console television set, also our first. I admired my father, a handsome freckle shouldered Irishman whose uniformed pictures bear a striking resemblance to Mike Riordan of the Capitol Bullets, with uncritical abandon. The Old Man had played semi-pro baseball and football, as well as having been the center (at 6'2" and 215 pounds) of a Prudential Insurance Company basketball team which won the New Jersey State AAU championship but which the company had declined to send to the Nationals. One of our famous family legends concerns his thrashing of three men, including his older brother Jim, who tried to hold him down and make him drink whiskey. He once played the fourth quarter of a football game at fullback after dislocating his shoulder in the third and having his teammates pop it back into place. I thought that my mother, a redhead whose maiden name was Sheedy, was the loveliest woman in New Jersey.

My father favored Adlai Stevenson in 1952, as he has favored all Democrats since the first time he voted in 1932. As one would imagine, so did I. Had P.S. 12 been polled, however, Stevenson would have lost badly, in spite of the lower middle class origins of most of its students. With schoolboy clarity it had been decided that soldier Eisenhower represented right-thinking masculinity and Stevenson the sissy vote. There was a song, borrowed from Disney's "Snow White": "Whistle while you work / Stevenson's a jerk / Eisenhower's got the power / Whistle while you work."

It was no surprise one afternoon when Jeffrey Choate, son of the high school football coach, a solid Eisenhower man, and possibly the only WASP I knew well, apprehended the Owings twins between two garages with Mitchel Greenberg, a nearsighted classmate who was being urged through the agency of a twisted arm to recant the Stevensonian heresy and admit that he liked Ike. Greenberg's tearful threats of retribution from various agencies of civility from the school principal through the police were doing him no good. If anything they caused his tormentors to twist that much harder.

It took no special courage to dispatch Bobby and Billy, a pair of runny nosed palefaces whose inquisitory zeal was matched only

12

by their lack of status. Choate and I were the fastest runners and the best baseball players in the third grade, and we were in a good position to stand up for Fair Play. We knew that as long as we could play ball we could indulge our noblesse oblige as we chose, even when rated at a distance as "Jew lovers" and "fairies."

Whether out of gratitude, curiosity, or simple friendship Greenberg soon invited me home after school for cookies and milk. I remember only a cool, dark house that smelled funny, a very solicitous mother, and a Stevenson poster prominently displayed in the front window. The friendship never developed, perhaps because the poster made me uneasy and perhaps because it showed. Being for Stevenson, it seemed to me, was merely correct. But putting a visible sign of one's apostasy in the window was odd, betraying an unhealthy balance in the importance of things. Maybe Greenberg was asking to have his arm twisted. Why else, I wondered, would one openly advertise separateness if one were not strong enough to defend oneself?

It is best not to overdo it. My characterization of the incident may well be retrospective. It is very unlikely that I was as unprepared in the ways of the world as I have represented myself and had not been prepared to see Greenberg as both victim and subversive by the general culture. Much more significant in terms of my youthful judgment would have been the fact that Greenberg was a Yankee fan, a form of treason understandably shared by Italians (Raschi, DiMaggio, Rizzuto, Berra), but when combined with his weakness it made Greenberg a loser with a tendency to fawn over winners in the style of Mel Allen, whose Jewishness, incidentally, was not apparent to me until much later. Greenberg must have known it. That is the only way I can account for outbreaks of Yankee worship among Jewish kids around New York in the early Fifties. The Yankee Image was synonymous then with Wall Street and the *New York Times*, the essence of pin-striped arrogance, and if my father taught me nothing else he taught me mistrust and dislike for that crowd, as well as the fear that, like the Yankees, they could not be beaten. How the team managed that image with louts and rustics like Berra and Mantle I do not know, but it is worth recording that in later years when his anti-Semitism was sharper (or just more obvious to me) my father used to call the latter, with heavy sarcasm, "Mickey Mandele." In any case I never went back to Greenberg's house, and perhaps more aware of my parents' attitudes than I can consciously recall, I never invited him to mine.

Greenberg was not my first Jewish acquaintance, just the first whose identification as such was problematical. From 1948 until 1952 I had spent at least two hours of every day in the home of Judy Peckerman, the daughter of a house painter and seltzer salesman on my block who had provided his family with a television set. From the time school let out until Howdy Doody was over at 5:30 and we all went home for dinner, every kid on the block—most of them Celtic Papists like me—could be found in front of the little round screen in the Peckerman living room ruining our eyes together. Judy also had a two-car garage cluttered with cases of empty chrome-fauceted seltzer bottles, the better to imitate Clarabelle the Clown with, and a large abandoned wardrobe chest inside of which she, Peggy MacNamara and I exhibited to each other our private particulars and pissed into empty Dutch Boy cans to demonstrate their use.

A regular feature on those afternoon children's shows from Channel 13 in Newark was a public service announcement on behalf of brotherhood, a cartoon in which a smug blonde trapeze artist swung back and forth refusing the grasp of successive minority partners until he fell, as the announcer cried, "Oh Joe, you schmo." Yiddish and all, we children received this as the gravest of truths, and on our block at least, I believe that we practiced it. If I knew that Judy was a Jew, or if she attached any significance to our Catholicism, I cannot recall it. Once again though, while it may be faulty memory, I do not remember her coming to my house.

Contrary to popular myth there was no hint of anti-Semitism in my Sunday school devotions at St. Genevieve's. My pre-communion training, what there was of it, stressed the belief that while only Catholics could enter the Kingdom of Heaven, Jews were to be respected as possessing an erroneous but deeply held and coherent tradition. Since I have noticed that theological anti-Semitism is often stronger among my co-religionists who attended parochial schools, it may be that the brotherhood stratagem was self-consciously assumed for public school students. But

I doubt it. *The Assistant* notwithstanding, we were deemed in no immediate danger of becoming Jews. Such a conversion would have been mere pathology, like coming down with leukemia instead of polio. Closer at hand was a more insidious trap for our immortal souls: Protestantism.

Perhaps Simon Daedalus is right, and the Irish never persecuted the Jews because they never let them in. But there is also the fact of a common enemy on both sides of the Atlantic: the WASP. It is difficult not to feel foolish writing this down in 1975, and people outside the east coast may be forgiven treating it as a hopeless anachronism, but against all reason and most statistics Irish Catholics there still see themselves essentially as landless peasants in a system run by and for their hereditary oppressors, an attitude they continue to share through the parish church with their fellow ex-peasants of Eastern and Southern European extraction—and which all of them share with increasingly equal dubiousness with the Jew. Still vivid in my mother's mind is her stepfather's excuse for his besottedness: signs reading "Irish need not apply." Active among my father's resentments is what he saw as the anti-Catholic bias of the Prudential Insurance Company, only very recently reported to be giving way.

So when the Jew is discussed in those circles it is with ambivalence. His alleged clannishness, like his other qualities, is a two-sided coin. Jews will stick together to defraud the simple Christian; but no Jew will allow another to go hungry. If he is an arrogant, self-seeking schemer, he is also a Real Go-Getter. Grass Does Not Grow Under His Feet. For every disloyal intellectual and potential subversive there is a Smart Jew Lawyer, who knows the value of a good education, and is the only kind to have when you are in trouble. The same goes for doctors. So far as I know neither of my parents has ever gone to a gentile doctor for anything important. What is equally important I think is that perhaps because he cannot—anyone can spot one—the Jew does not as soon as he gets a few dollars ahead become a Republican and begin aping the gentry. And he is good to his family.

Behind all of this lies the suspicion that whatever else Jews are, they are serious people, little given to frivolity and waste. Although I have always found my grandfather's curses against the

English dated and my father's largely rhetorical, they are emotions that persist. I can recall quite vividly volunteering in a Sunday School discussion of religious tolerance that my best friend was a Presbyterian, and basking in self-congratulations because I forgave him in this world the sure knowledge that he would suffer an eternity of punishment in the next. To this day I continue to harbor an irrational mistrust and distaste for all varieties of Protestantism, and secretly regard the lot of them as self-seeking or deluded simpletons of the Pat Boone-Charles Colson variety, whose zeal for public righteousness masks the shallowest and most crocodilian morality.

In December of 1953 my family moved permanently to the largely gentile suburb of Chatham. Unlike so many others, though, we did not move west as a result of postwar prosperity so much as in search of it, purchasing a huge four-apartment investment of a home in what my mother, who hates it to this day, considers the remote provinces, twelve miles from the house she was born in, and my father more affectionately calls "the sticks," although it is scarcely more rural now than the Bronx.

My mother's objections to this migration might have been settled by a classier set of neighbors, although they would have terrified her, but the economics of the thing landed us smack in the middle of the only Jewish neighborhood in town, a sizeable tract known as the Chatham Colony Association. And such a neighborhood. These were not your upward mobile, country clubbing, assimilationist type of Jewish persons. They were first and second generation Russian and Yiddish speaking immigrants, former ghetto dwellers and long time ardent Zionists. We had purchased security at the expense of respectability. We had actually made a downward move to the suburbs, leaving a stable lower middle class environment to settle with a tribe of "friggin' Sheenies." Adlai Stevenson was all you got, you should live so long.

The Chatham Colony Association was founded in 1922 by a group of Polish, Russian, and German immigrants seeking to establish a cooperative community on Socialist principles in what was then the remote fastness of the Jersey woods. By the time we arrived, however, the membership was aging, many having died or moved away, their children having long since departed and the old left to keep up fifty year old houses on wooded plots that they had cleared themselves by hand when the experiment was new.

Perhaps because they were so identifiably Old Country and poor, no Jewish families ever moved in when houses were vacated or lots sold. The old Colony was dismantled piecemeal to support its often bewildered and angry members as an increasingly wealthy suburb grew up around them, rendering their existence in what remained to many of them a half-foreign country yet stranger and more inhospitable every year. Our arrival itself meant the transfer of another acre and what had been built as a school and teacher's residence to gentile hands. So instead of the Collinses, the McNamaras, the Murphys, and the Walshes, much of my adolescence was spent as yardboy, egg and newspaper deliverer, general factotum, and confused observer of the Switzens, the Eisenschers, the Katzes, and the Coffets.

In my business relations with the community I learned to be worked hard and paid as little as I would take, a bare necessity for most of my employers that I, learning the ways of the great world, was often moved to attribute to sheer Mockie stinginess. The work that I did, raking and mowing, burning great piles of oak leaves, cleaning basements, garages and gutters of years of accumulated trash, shoveling snow, clipping hedges and digging vegetable gardens, was work that most of my better off companions at school did not do at all, let alone for hire. The process by which I was paid less than I wanted (and more I am sure than I was worth, being a notoriously reluctant and inefficient worker), was called "Jewing down," a phrase my mother uses with either approbation or scorn depending upon who is the Jewer and whom the Jewee. (She is herself a formidable mistress of the art, I might add, a ferocious bargainer who never pays the announced price for anything without a battle.)

As desperately as my parents wanted respectability there was something comforting about living among poor Jews, for in no case were they in a position to condescend. Besides which in their foreignness they were apt subjects for Aesopian fables of moral instruction. Although it was half-believed that all of our neighbors had vast sums hidden away and were smuggling bags of loot to

17

Israel, their outward need was evidence of yet another truth: the Jew in his greed was like the farrow that ate the sow, and the departed children of the elderly, having robbed their poor parents of life and goods, were leaving them to die in shame while they wintered in Miami. Two needs were thus taken care of. Jews without wealth were accounted for, and a powerful moral lesson was imparted: Don't ever leave home, my parents were telling us, do you want to be like a Jew? That the whole works conflicted with other fables of Jewish existence and was internally inconsistent anyway never bothered them, although being as literal minded as I was, it gave me no end of trouble.

As I write, moreover, I am in danger of falling into another kind of sentimentalizing fiction. By no means all of our neighbors were poor. Although most lived modestly, at least a few made trips to Israel, others to Europe and Russia, and some wintered in Florida, Arizona, or California, perhaps with their children. For all I know the others didn't have children, or lost them. And except for one proud woman whose son was a "big television producer" and who drove a Cadillac, none of us had any idea where those children were or what they did for the most part. When the Cadillac went by we sometimes shouted "Jew Canoe," as soon as it was out of range.

Our gentile neighbors were halfway specimens like ourselves: an alcoholic lawyer whose wife took in boarders and typing, and whose sons (as my mother never let me forget) ate Clark Bars and drank Pepsis for breakfast; a machinist whose wife conducted an open liaison with the town's garbage contractor (he arrived in his truck); Chatham's second string dancing teacher, who conducted classes in her living room and whose husband was permitted inside the house only to stoke the furnace; a laborer and his wife whose two room shack smelled of gin and garbage (the wife was never once seen out of doors in ten years). That kind of thing. By coincidence there were several boys my age or my brother's, and we shared two things. Fascination that sometimes edged over into revulsion for our strange neighbors, and a common social stigma derived from living near them; a stigma which grew all the stronger as the suburbs spread and the woods and fields filled up with executives and their kin. Having lost the sharp definitions of the city I only half comprehended, as we all did, what was going on. Without the sustaining categories of city life, I simply floated. From my father I learned to reject the smug and successful, from them I learned to reject my father, and from the Jews around us, I am now convinced, I learned how to maintain my dignity even as I half accepted and partly rejected the vicious anti-Semitic stereotypes of which my parents were intimately and my classmates cooly convinced.

My father's Jew hatred, like his nigger phobia, seemed to grow more pronounced as his own feelings of failure and my mother's barely submerged hysteria closed in on him. In 1956, by which time it was plain he was not going to make his fortune with the Prudential, he sunk his life's savings and all he could borrow, together with what remained of his belief in himself, nurtured by all those years of athletic triumph and personal charm, into a Dairy Queen franchise on a badly chosen country highway in Wayne, twenty miles from our home. As he had been with the Prudential (we had a painting of the Rock of Gibraltar in our living room) he became a Dairy Queen believer, a very Morris Bober of the soft ice cream trade. He could talk butterfat content for hours, extolling the merits of the Dairy Queen product over all competitors. How someone could actually put Carvel ice cream in their mouth was beyond his comprehension. I spent frustrated hours sweating over the spigot, the old man bellowing instructions over my shoulder in a fruitless attempt to perfect the trademarked curl that had to go on the top of every three ounce cone. I never saw, myself, what difference it made. I was not cut out for the retail business. By moving to the suburbs we skipped a generation in my family. I should have been a hustler and my own kids punks like me.

Whatever, we never made it to Easy Street. Instead of working from Easter to Halloween and going south for the winter, my father spent the next ten years putting in sixteen to eighteen hour days all during the warm months, commuting home from "The Pru," grabbing a sandwich and heading for the "D.Q." on the run, never making anything more than ten dollars a day he could skim off the top. It ended only when his cursed avaricious Kike of a landlord refused to renew the option on his lease so he could do it for ten more.

Whatever he thought of the "miserable Jew bastards" when the vapors were on him my father was unfailingly polite and helpful towards our elderly neighbors and became a community favorite. Sensing a soft touch, many of them came to count on him for tasks my brother and I were too young to do. Without public complaint he hung shelves, unclogged pipes, moved furniture, played taxicab, and lifted things. The phone would ring at dinnertime, my sister would shout "It's one of the Jews"—all had heavy accents and depended upon them for identification, beginning conversations *in medias res:* "Lyons, in the attic is such a business with squirrels I couldn't sleep. You could fix it?" Whatever he was doing the Old Man would drop it and go. Katz had a stuck door; Sach's car wouldn't start; Switzen wondered was he maybe going by the train station. "Meesthair Lynz," Fanny Sachs once told me, "is a good man."

No one in that community ever called my mother a good woman, less because of anything she did or said, I think, than the discomfort that is written so plainly on her face in the presence of anyone more distant than a first cousin. Her own childhood was a mixture of *Studs Lonigan* and *The Playboy of the Western World*, and she retains a sensibility as close, I am sure, to that of a nineteenth century Irish peasant as exists on the North American continent. Her stepfather Bill Connors was almost a parody of the gentile barbarian one reads about in Jewish novels. To survive he worked intermittently on the railroad; for entertainment he drank and hit things, among them his family. Well into the Forties (and his fifties) one of his favorite pastimes was storming into a bar like Popeye in *The French Connection* backed by his friends or his sons and lifting the biggest "nigger" he could find off the ground with a savage and usually unprovoked uppercut, whereupon he would hock a ginder of tobacco juice upon the floor and leave cursing. He got his ass kicked a few times, but never, I am told, without leaving his mark. It was for him the bitterest of ends that when cancer of the colon finished getting him at the age of seventy-eight three years ago he was the last white man on Broadway in Elizabethport, wasting away in a wretched, falling down frame house surrounded by the "jigaboos" that he loathed as visible evidence that his more theoretical adversaries, John Bull and "Ikey and Sam," had won in the end.

It is said by mother's brothers that she married my father primarily because he was the only man she knew that Bill Connors was afraid of. It seems that one night in 1935 he was drinking on the front porch when my father brought her home from a date and offered some suggestions that were coarse. It required her three brothers to prevent his going to work on Pop with his fists.

At the same time the Dairy Queen was failing the domestic sign of my father's inability to move us into the suburban mainstream was the Chatham Colony Association's only public enterprise, the most ramshackle swim club in Northern New Jersey. Over a period of years the members had converted a swampy pond on a back corner of their property into something resembling a swimming pool by damming one end with a cement wall, digging an artesian well and dumping in granular chlorine at odd intervals from a rowboat. At a time when everyone else in town was joining country clubs and taking up golf, my brother, sister, and I wheedled eighty bucks out of the Old Man for a season membership at "The Colony," which had water the color of light coffee, bullfrogs, and a tarpaper shack for a dressing room, through the plywood walls of which Barry Edelman and I drilled scores of peepholes. (A bolder voyeur than I, "Edel" once packed a lunch and spent an entire day sitting quietly in the open rafters over the Women's dressing room, which could be reached from the Men's side.) Even more significant in our gentile paradise, "The Colony" drew carloads of Jews without money from the hot streets of Newark, Elizabeth, Irvington, and Union. A few families from New York summered in flat roofed bungalows on the community property, serene in what they considered "the country." No tennis, golf, volleyball, or swim team. No cabanas, no sandwiches, no liquor. Even the showers didn't work. Just overweight, and some not so overweight, lower middle class housewives with their hair as often as not in curlers playing Mah Jong, Canasta, and Bridge under the trees while their children pissed in the water and shat on the dressing room floors. On weekends the husbands arrived to sit chewing cigars and reading the *Newark News*, dressed in sleeveless undershirts, bermuda shorts, and crepe-soled web sandals with calf-length black socks.

Fortunately for all of us, the pool was located at the end of a dead end street next to a power line right-of-way and most "Chathamites," as they are designated in the town's weekly paper, did not know it existed. Had it been more public I do not doubt that attempts would have been made to get the County Board of Health to shut it down. For me, lurching through adolescence in a suburb only slightly less caste-ridden than Calcutta, the pool was a multiple blessing. In order to avoid my father's self-defeating pride it was necessary that I continue to be only subliminally aware of class differences. The pool helped by providing me ready access to people to whom I did not have to feel inferior, both because of their faith and their social position. And not only was I introduced to that mysterious form of oriental sensuality known as the Jewish girl, but by mutual consent I was able to keep my infatuations a secret. Whether copping a feel off Bambi Edelman in the murky waters or dry-humping Ruth Kantrowitz against a tree in the woods I was safe from detection. And so were they.

I only wish I knew more than I do about the subject of Jewish girls and gentile boys, and hope that some scholar more learned in the ways of the world will appear to enlighten us. For now I offer these few comments: in my experience Jewish girls seemed on franker terms with their desires and less concerned with maintaining about their flesh an aura of mysticism than their *shicksa* counterparts. But then like a photographic negative of Alexander Portnoy's, my limited erotic experience during the period of adolescence was confined largely to *shicksas* who didn't and Jewish girls who *did*, or more frequently *almost did*, or *did everything but*. I wonder if Philip Roth is aware how badly all of us with murky class origins wanted the archetypical young snub-nosed cheerleader he calls Thereal McCoy?—the kind of girl who knew the value of a good body and a fresh face and was not about to be pawed or spurted upon by anybody who couldn't afford her. To this day the sight of a girl like that in a tennis dress triggers in me contradictory impulses of near-homicidal desire.

More matter of fact and less hysterical about it all, Jewish girls did not seem so anxious to make one pay for what one was getting. This because there was a sometimes tacit and sometimes spoken assumption that we were not in it for the long haul. But then I only went out with the kind of Jewish girl who goes out with gentiles. When Ruth Kantrowitz and I were caught in a moderately compromising position on her grandmother's back porch we suffered politely the old woman's Yiddish accented lecture on tradition and the individual *goy* because it was less upsetting for her to fear that her son's daughter might marry a Christian than that she simply liked to do what she was doing.

It was Ruth who introduced me to the idea, later to become familiar, that Jewish girls would be far more willing to play You Do It For Me and I'll Do It For You with one of us than with one of their co-religionists because of the lack of long-range prospects involved. More likely an explanation, I think, was that these were summertime games away from home where one's "reputation" could not be affected. In the 1950's that consideration would have been far more important than anybody's religion. For all of this petting and pawing, incidentally, I never in my life actually showed up at a Jewish girl's house for a date; we are speaking here of ad hoc arrangements. It strikes me that most of what I know on the subject is on a level with the kind of tribal superstition that created the complementary myth that Catholic girls screwed like minks because they could confess it all, but invariably became pregnant because they forbade the use of rubbers. Nice logic there. When "Edel" showed up at the pool one day with a naked family portrait that his father had taken, he at the age of eight on one knee, sister Bambi at six on the other, mother's pelt luxuriant in the foreground, it occurred to me to wonder whether it was that they were Jews—or simply mad. For all of the cross-religious carrying on that was conducted in parked cars all over Northern New Jersey during the period, we stayed as ignorant about each other as so many stone age savages sharing a rain forest together.

So from the seventh grade until I left New Jersey permanently after college I spent most of every day at the Colony pool, exchanging with solstice gentile friends for Jews, and passing, as time went on, from member to lawn mower and drain skimmer, and from there eventually to head life guard. I retained at each step all of my former duties, so that when I achieved my loftiest position with the organization I was performing (or rather malingering) at everything from teaching lifesaving to digging Kotex pads out of the toilet. Had my duties required anything short of conversion to the faith of Abraham I am sure I would have grudgingly performed them. Anything to stay out of the Dairy Queen. If my father was going to sink he could man his own lifeboats.

Imagine my surprise then, when I began to learn that Jews

were prejudiced against *us,* and prejudiced in ways that could not have been better designed to contribute to my own secret conviction that I was a foundling unrelated by blood to anyone with whom I lived. That my mother's family was an almost parodic example, and my father's not far removed from what most Jews seemed willing to think that we were, did not lessen my discomfort at gradually discovering that we Christians, and we Irish Catholics in particular, it seemed, were held to be drunken undereducated philistines, Jew-haters to the core, and prone to random outbursts of insensate violence. What civilized habits we attained, such as literacy, were held to be a thin veneer over a spirit only slightly advanced since the time when our ancestors painted themselves blue and worshipped totems. Explicit in Grandmother Kantrowitz's lecture, in fact, with me sitting right there trying to tuck my shirt in, was that there was no logical attitude for gentiles and Jews to take toward one another except mutual suspicion and dislike. I even suspected that there was a foreskin hidden in there somewhere, although like everybody else I knew I had been circumcised at birth. It reminded me of the time that Mrs. Kaplan from down the street had stood on the sidewalk in front of our house shaking her cane and shouting that my brother and I were "little Nazi pigs" for wrestling and hollering on our front lawn, leaving us bewildered and abashed and providing impetus for a twenty year grudge between my mother and her. In any case a *goy* with a book, I learned, was considered a contradiction in terms and was to be approached gingerly, like a trained bear in a tutu. Even if this theory was advanced most openly by people whose idea of literature was *Exodus* or *Only in America* it hurt. Those were my ideas of literature too. Where was I supposed to learn any better? So far as I know, neither of my parents has ever read a book.

My relationship with Eddie Zarin, fellow lifeguard, was a case in point, and a premonition of more complicated relationships to come. For five consecutive summers we spent most of every day together. Although we attended the same college (Rutgers) and lived only ten miles apart, our friendship, if that was what it was, was confined to working hours only. Unathletic and given to plumpness, at least in my strenuous sense of what was athletic,

24

Zarin had an abhorrence of physical labor that made me seem energetic by comparison, and devoted astonishing amounts of time to avoiding it with a barefaced chicanery that was almost ingratiating in its openness. He would scheme for days to be sure the lawn was mowed on his day off—usually dropping a hint to our aged employers that it was looking ragged as he went out the gate the night before. When there was garbage to be collected or chlorine drums to be unloaded Eddie would usually be deep in conversation with one of the old ladies at the front entrance, of whom, as the only Jewish lifeguard, he was an assiduous favorite. He had a way of knowing (small cousins) which of the bathrooms had been befouled by a child and would volunteer to clean the other before anyone else knew what was up. When the rest of us complained he would urge us to straighten things out with the handful of Christian mothers in the place, because obviously no Jew would do such a swinish thing. Zarin drove the rest of us to fits by beating everyone at an improvised handball game we had invented by mastering chops, spins, lobs, and undercuts while I lost three points to two setting him up for soul-satisfying smashes. He boasted, but would never try to prove, that he could beat me in the same way at basketball, which was more my game, although we both knew he couldn't, since I was by then my father's size and fairly good at a sport more suited to sheer physicality.

What's more if my description of Zarin seems tainted with barely disguised anti-Semitism of the cheapest kind, it should be clear that Eddie not only cheerfully accepted these terms, he invented them. Implicit in all our dealings over a five year period was the often repeated assertion that *as a Jew* Zarin was shrewder, more cunning, and fundamentally saner than we coarse louts who were so stupidly vain as to hoist one hundred pound chlorine barrels to our shoulders and carry them through the grounds for the sole purpose of showing off our muscles. If I were enough of a *putz* to strain my goyish back it was fine with Eddie, and would only serve to confirm his already low opinion of my intelligence. Zarin never let us forget that he was paid twenty dollars a week more than the rest of us for the same job, that he had been given it as a kind of scholarship for a nice Jewish boy, and that the goyim were expected to do all the work. Furthermore, although he flirted with probation the whole four years we were at Rutgers together and had not yet graduated when I left, he treated his intellectual superiority as an unchallenged matter of fact.

For all of that I could never bring myself to dislike old Zarin, for while his chauvinism was sometimes annoying it was also simple, essentially amoral, and at bottom comic in a way that is very nearly sad.

Shall I begin with Beethoven, with chess, or with physics? Or shall I simply observe that in arriving on the campus of Rutgers— the State University for my freshman year I was for the first time in my life confronted with persons far beyond my intellectual depth—almost my comprehension, as it seemed at the time—and who treated my obvious inferiority with patent, if kind, condescension. Here were young men of lower-middle-class origins like myself who shared, or at least were conversant with, my own cultural enthusiasms—Jerry West, Willie Mays, Chuck Berry—but who were simultaneously able to distinguish by ear between Mozart and Stravinsky, to discuss the merits of various openings in chess, who seemed to know a lot of history, and not only had heard of relativity theory but professed to understand it. Do I need to say at this point that these young men were Jews?

Whenever I read, in this autobiography or that article, of the formidable intellectual influence upon various individuals by the eminent Scholar and Professor X, I am puzzled and suspect either exaggeration or sycophancy. I arrived at college with a mind possessing all the density and rigor of Silly Putty, and was too inexperienced to do more than sit with my mouth agape taking notes in the presence of any of the real luminaries of the Rutgers faculty. Until I hid out in a gentile jock fraternity house at the end of my sophomore year my real teachers were all students—and almost all Jews.

Like every suburban high school in America, Chatham's had touted itself as one of the finest in Christendom and prided itself on sending virtually all of its graduates to a college of some description or other—even those so pitiably unprepared that they could not cope with the remotest academy of monosyllabic theology in West Virginia. Everyone had to go. Only persons so unfortunate as literally to drool on their desks were exempted from the

universal shove, although those of us whose parents were sufficiently *déclassé* were permitted to exercise a certain degree of free
choice. I rejected one or two well-meaning teachers who tried to
make a project of me (one by getting me to read Saki)—not, like
Norman Podhoretz for fear of being made a "facsimile WASP,"
but out of resentment that my frantic attempts to look, dress, and
sound like somebody on the "Ozzie and Harriet Show" were so
transparent. No wonder I never got anywhere with Thereal Mc-
Coy: in the interest of saving a buck my mother had convinced me
(at least until I was sixteen) that Vaseline Hair Tonic and Vaseline
Petroleum Jelly were the same product in slightly different form.
My white buck shoes were wing-tip models handed down by my
father. They had leather heels with nails that sounded like taps
echoing down the hall.

I stayed confused and resentful all the way through high school,
even at the games I played, with the result that the athletic world
lost one of the great slow, short New Jersey forwards who fill the
ranks of every third-rate small college basketball team in the east.
When I sat down with the Head Guidance counselor in September of my senior year I was advised to give it up and learn a trade,
or at best to try for a Junior College in New Mexico. Only relatively spectacular College Board scores and a sympathetic Polish
football coach who dabbled in guidance because he was considered too dumb to teach Social Studies got me into his alma
mater with an admonition from the Admissions Office that they
were taking a chance because of my test scores but were frankly
dubious.

To hear them talk most of my new pals in the dormitory had
come at it from the other side. They settled for Rutgers after not
quite making; or making and being unable to afford, Harvard, Columbia, or Yale. While I was terrified of flunking out in my first
semester and going home in disgrace, they were arguing the merits of Albert Schweitzer and Harvard Medical School and debating
the relative stature of Chicago and Berkeley in Physics or English—institutions of whose existence I had previously been almost unaware. Having learned a bit more in academic life about
bluffing, I'm sure that most of the earnest discussions we held
deep into the night on Beauty, Art, Truth, Sex, and the Existence

The Higher Illiteracy

of God were entirely sophomoric. But to me they were effusions of the pure ether of reason, virtually the first indication I had ever really had that ideas did matter. To assimilate and understand a culture and its values, always with the consciousness of being an outsider determined not to be swallowed alive by the majority; to transform oneself and one's expectations without being changed—that we shared.

Ideas themselves, by God, that was the thing! One had neither to join nor fight, merely to become an intellectual. In an altogether serious way—and for once I do not mean to be glib about this—those Jewboys saved my life.

In very short order, moreover, lessons begun at the pool were continued. Just as Sandy Koufax was unquestionably the best pitcher in baseball history, and just as Elizabeth Taylor could lay claim to being the loveliest woman on earth (now that she had done the sensible thing), so were Marx, Freud, and Einstein the three great geniuses of the modern age—and all of them, of course, were Jews like Irwin Cantor, who never took more than five moves to beat me at chess when he really wanted to, having taught me just enough so that I could anticipate what he was doing to me. The only reason he played with me at all, I am sure, is that I puzzled him. Here I was tall, strong, and not bad looking. From one or two trips to the gym he knew that I was a decent athlete who had played at least creditably in high school competition. I probably did OK with the girls (little did he know); I was a *goy* in a Christian country. So what did I want with ideas? Ideas were for Jews. Better I should go out for beer and pizza with Dennis Murphy, Joe Helenowski, and Joe Gurassi—those misplaced louts—than kibitz the chess games, or talk about *Crime and Punishment*.

Neither Cantor nor any of the other Jewish friends I had at the time had much reservation about admitting, or sometimes insisting, and much more seriously than Greenberg, that Jews as a people were intellectually superior to the rest of us, and that the alleged superiority was, if not racial in origin, at least the product of a better genetic pool. My initial reaction to this idea was a kind of mild panic, because I knew I thought it was true, but had been trained by every respectable organ of public opinion since Joe the

Schmo that such invidious distinctions between races and cultures were by their nature evil. How in the name of all that was holy could *they* say *that?* My second reaction was suppressed anger and some resentment—because I began to suspect that no one, least of all the persons who made up the terms of the debate, truly believed in either cultural or racial equality, and to realize that I could not argue back against the idea of Jewish superiority because to do so would be beyond the bounds of civilized discourse as I had internalized them.

Our discussions of the subject were often, in fact, protracted games of "Catch a Gentile by the Toe," in which the object (unconscious most of the time) is to needle the half-despised *goy* into revealing his own presumed hatred, then to recoil in horror while he turns against himself in shame. As useful a survival mechanism as this must be it was not easy to cope with. One was not even supposed to notice, in those days, that there is sometimes such a thing as a "Jewish nose."

None of this I am sure is new to any thinking Jew, or to anyone, for that matter, who was raised around one of the larger Eastern cities, but it is rarely, if ever, discussed in print. Even to admit that you are troubled by such claims is suspect, the charge of anti-Semitism being difficult to evade and almost impossible to refute. Indeed the only way a non-Jew can entirely avoid it is by pretending not to notice at all. And what Jew who is not consumed with the alleged self-hatred will let you do that? Or one for that matter who is?

Perhaps nothing I have written or probably can write will convince some readers that I harbor no Nazi within, or explain what I mean by calling myself an "artificial Jewboy." I have neither knowledge of nor serious interest in Judaism—or in any religious doctrine for that matter. But then neither did most of the Jews I am talking about. What attracted and repelled me then was the restless, skeptical, categorizing intellect I came to associate with Jews. Yes, and the pride, the arrogance, and the moral superiority. I had to get out of the hole I was in somehow, and at the time and in the place I was educated literary Jewishness—a more complicated, subtle, and serious version of the games I am describing—was the prestige ticket.

Looking back, it is not at all difficult to see now that cultural metamorphosis came about. In the aftermath of the most unimaginably "inhuman" cataclysm in European history it was perhaps inevitable and certainly healthy that the Jews assume a position of special moral and intellectual authority in American life. For one thing it freed artists, writers, and thinkers to be as openly "Jewish" in their preoccupations as they cared to be without needing to be fearful or apologetic. At least publicly, anti-Semitism was viewed by almost every serious person in the United States as an unthinkable perversion. The extraordinary and continuing burst of creative and intellectual activity by American Jews and European immigrants reinforced this predisposition to see the Jews not as Superman but as Everyman. The Holocaust itself stood forth as the central historical event of our times: the suffering of European Jewry became the quintessential symbol for all that was mad in a maddened century. One could not look beyond or around it, and one could hardly call into question the credentials of anyone who wished to invoke its horrific shadow, even if one suspected at a level too deep for conscious articulation that the invocation was occasionally self-serving when used as a means of avoiding all criticism by persons no closer to the actual event than my father is to Belfast, and not so close as my grandfather, whose own parents fled it, was to deliberate starvation.

It was on the advice of friends in the dormitory that I first read *The Assistant,* a work which moved me at the time as very few books ever have, then or since. Most appealing to me as a young man almost wholly out of touch with himself and anything one could call a tradition, and I do not mean to be at all flippant about this, was the realization that one need not be Jewish to be a Jew. Witness the following exchange between shopkeeper Morris Bober and the repentant Italian thug Frank Alpine:

Nobody will tell that I am not Jewish because I put in my mouth once in a while, when my tongue is dry, a piece of ham. But they will tell me, and I will believe them, if I forget the law. This means to other people. Our life is hard enough. Why should we hurt somebody else? For everybody should be the best, not only for you or me. We ain't animals. This is why we need the law. This is what a Jew believes—

"I think other religions have those ideas too," Frank said. "But tell me why it is the Jews Suffer so damn much, Morris? It seems they like to suffer, don't they?"

"Do you like to suffer? They suffer because they are Jews."

Or, to reverse the near tautology that the novel creates by its end. "They are Jews because they suffer." My God how I wanted to suffer when I first read that book in 1961 or 1962. Not in any immediate or palpable way, of course, for while I hoped for a life of moral anguish and difficulty I expected no pain; novels like *The Assistant*, and the cultural climate that exalted them cultivated a sense of tragedy, of ambiguity, and of contradiction that was the only "mature" attitude that one could take toward life—life in those days being a more vivid but unforgivably random source of images from which to produce "art." The intensive emphasis upon the literature of high contemplation—if not of literary criticism itself, into the characteristic "human" act—was inextricably tied up with the idea of Jewishness. For those of us who were only imaginatively involved in an event which had transpired before we assumed consciousness, and in another land, after all, the disaster of the European Jews provided a kind of eschatological thrill. More than anything else it served to convince us that a life of passive virtue could have the tragic consequences we half-desired without having any more idea what we were talking about than so many children. Otherwise why not Hiroshima, Nagasaki, or even Dresden as totems?

I envied my new friends their ready made identity, to risk another cliche of the period, that they had, and for which I was obliged, heaven help me, to search. For a lost boy in an allegedly classless capitalist country in which the parameters of political debate were said to conform almost exactly to those of human possibility—for such a young man and such a country what figure could have been more appealing than one who had a historical identity whenever he wanted it, an identity moreover, that did not require belief or commitment (not in Cold War America anyway) and which might be claimed or denounced almost at will? In which ethnic and racial chauvinism of the mild sort I have described was not only permitted but looked upon favorably, at least in public.

I have learned remarkably little in the intervening years about the peculiar habits of mind and emotion that I have attempted to describe, except that I have read a good many more books and have grown skeptical in my dotage. Nor is there any point in discussing my personal dealings with those more formidable people I was to encounter later on. Not only are some of them public or semi-public figures whom I do not wish to embarrass for attitudes that some readers may conclude to be projections of my own, but as I have said, in Zarin and Cantor the pattern was laid. Throughout my remaining years at Rutgers and four more at the University of Virginia I never wavered in my private conviction that what I was getting was essentially a "Jewish" education. It was not just the big three, Sigmund, Karl, and Albert, but all the rest: Kazin, Trilling, Feidler, Howe, Rahv, Hook, Arendt, Fromm, Bellow, Mailer, Roth, et al. Truly it never occurred to me to think that there could be such an animal as a Catholic or an ex-Catholic intellectual. James Joyce, I suppose would have qualified, but he had after all, this thing about Jews himself. And who taught me Joyce? Why Robert Langbaum of course. In any case we are talking America here, and American delusions.

So I know exactly what Leslie Feidler means when he calls Ralph Ellison a "black Jew" and have no doubt that he is correct. Consider that unmatched set of affirmations in the Epilogue to *Invisible Man*, another novel I encountered at roughly the same time as *The Assistant* and which likewise bore the imperishable stamp of "art":

So it is now that I denounce and defend, or feel prepared to defend. I condemn and affirm, say no and say yes, yes and say no. I denounce because though implicated and partially responsible, I have been hurt to the point of abysmal pain, hurt to the point of invisibility. And I defend because in spite of all I love. In order to get some of it down I have to love . . . Too much of your life will be lost, its meaning lost, unless you approach it as much through love as through hate. So I approach it through division. So I denounce and I defend and I hate and I love.

Perhaps that makes me a little bit as human as my grandfather.

Denounce and defend what, one asks? Why literature itself, of course. Doubtless Ellison's rhetoric and its overwhelming acceptance at the time it was written was made easier by the lack of direct objects to all those high-sounding verbs. Who, after all, was there to be troubled by a dense and beautifully written novel of social injustice, moral blindness, and self-deception which proved literary intellectuals to have made the only possible choice? Ah, but to be human: to be above or outside the battle without proclaiming oneself indifferent. May I be pardoned for saying that for all its brilliance the novel is a period piece?—a contrivance not so bald as *The Assistant* perhaps, but mechanical and strained nonetheless.

Nor is this entirely to discount Ellison's achievement, for in the moribund cultural climate of the Cold War we were all made artificial Jewboys, and the bookish among us were prone to seek our coherence, poor things, through literature. One finishes one's books as one finishes them, and a writer can be pardoned a certain degree of esthetic enthusiasm for having done so. If *Invisible Man* now seems to lack the consolations of organic form, "imaginative wholeness," or whatever one chooses to call it, the fault may lie in the concept rather than in the novel. For when one writes honestly about a disintegrating personal culture one has relatively few choices about endings. The mere survival of a voice is no mean thing. Better that than the contrived and sentimental apotheoses of an Updike or a Malamud.

And then came the Vietnam years, the fragile intellectual and emotional compromises I have spoken of beginning to disintegrate on the great centrifuge of American life. During the worst of it (1969–72), I did a three year stretch as Assistant Professor of English at the University of Massachusetts in Amherst, a place my colleagues seemed to regard as a kind of academic heaven, but was very near to driving me mad. There the traditional righteousness of the New England gentry and the kind I have been describing combined to produce an atmosphere of guilt-ridden smugness the likes of which, I pray, I may never live with again. For many the Cambodian invasion of 1970 and the subsequent Kent State killings were the culmination, and very soon afterward the end, of a five year battle to preserve that sense of self-importance and passive virtue we had based our lives upon. We had gone so far in opposition to that hated but, for us, still imaginary war as to call off classes and demonstrate. We read statistics to each other through loudspeakers—trying to convince ourselves that Vietnam was a real place and that our own country was conducting an aerial pogrom as vile as that whose memory had formed us. More than anything else we wanted our rebellion taken seriously, because if it was not, then we were not, and then . . .

So when those shootings were announced we were for the briefest of moments confirmed, our world in order. They were coming after us at last as we had always known they would, those rednecks in the executive suites, those Fascist gentile hordes. For all of the prating about revolution that one heard we were so many Mitchel Greenberg's—and not Greenberg as he may have been but as I had imagined him to be. The whole idea, even by those who claimed to abjure the worship of books a good deal more unequivocally than I had done, was to insult, belittle, offend, and mock *them* into attacking *us,* so demonstrating our ethical superiority to the world—and to each other. I was back in that Rutgers dorm, except that by this time I had switched sides.

Only nobody was picking on us, not really. Unless we made deliberate pests of ourselves, no one, least of all our government, seemed to care what we did. Lies, cunning, and brutality more or less ended the war, while moral scrupulousness and literary intellectuals did less than nothing. And still they kept raising our salaries. Wasn't anyone going to punish us at all?

But I am representing myself as having been a good deal more comfortable with all that than I was at the time. For in spite of all the rage and anguish, office politics continued in the academic world as usual, with the Higher Politics temporarily substituted for the Higher Literature as the shibboleth by which one knew the chosen. The University of Massachusetts confused me to no end, because for a state university in which so many of the students were hirsute metamorphoses of my adolescent self, the faculty consisted in large part of older versions of my WASP high school classmates, my Jewish friends from the dorm, and my old professors. A tension hung in the air that was never discussed. I was as confused as were many of the students with the barely concealed assumption that one could not be who and what we were and be capable of thinking and acting coherently. As much as I had altered myself to fit the mold, a buried grain of rebelliousness

34

remained—a stubbornness that made me suspicious of the habit of equating what appeared to me to be unearned self-righteousness with virtue. Caught in the middle, I felt trapped and cheated, with exactly nowhere to go. I couldn't make myself—to use pop shorthand—into either Abbie Hoffmann or Norman Podhoretz (ever scanning the horizon for a classy Herman Wouk). So I tried to prove myself to people I did not respect by acting as if I had nothing to prove and becoming sullen when persons who had no reason to do so failed to take me at my own valuation of myself.

Into all this came Alexander Portnoy, pulling his pud. At first I found the novel simply and sheerly hilarious—the male adolescent mind, my own male adolescent mind anyway, revealed and parodied in all its permanent tumescence. Doubtless it helped that Portnoy's background was nearly identical to my own—give or take a few years. The Jewishness made not one bit of difference; had I Roth's talent and social perceptiveness, I felt, I could have written every word of it with certain minor changes of emphasis. Portnoy's story, up to the adult part of it anyway, was my own story, his guilt, isolation, resentment and confusion over the question of where he had come from and where he was going was so exactly parallel to mine that so small a difference as the exact nature of one's childhood beliefs made no real difference at all. So they said about the *goyim* at the Portnoy dinner table things as primitively tribal as we said about the Kikes—and apparently with a good deal more frequency and less ambivalence. So what? I knew that already. So what if it did help to free me from the guilt I felt for other people's crimes and the consequent reverence for all things Jewish, as if a Jew could do no serious wrong? Was that a bad thing? Wasn't it about time we got over all that and started taking one another seriously?

More important here was a real (if imaginary) Jewboy who was coming apart as I felt in danger of coming apart, who wanted some degree of continuity between his public and his private lives and with the ideas and values all of us claimed to revere so dearly; who wanted, in brief, to mature and prosper in contemporary America without surrendering either to the thugishness of the gentiles we imagined, or to the even more insidiously fashionable life of neurosis as value and staggering self-contradiction that seemed to me to be the essence of Amherst—and, I was sure, of Cambridge, New Haven, Ann Arbor, Berkeley and most of the way stations in between.

I do not, after all this, intend to overstate the impact of one novel, or even of a whole body of significant work. Nor is it my intention to defend Roth against his critics, either the Professional Jews or Irving Howe. Still it was disappointing to find the latter, a sophisticated critic with an unsparing eye for other people's sentimentalities, both defining the problem and missing his own point in his famous "Commentary" assault upon Roth's work:

> When we say . . . that a writer betrays a thin personal culture we mean, among other possibilities, that he comes at the end of a tradition which can no longer nourish his imagination, or that he has, through an act of fiat, chosen to tear himself away from that tradition . . . It is of course, a severe predicament for a writer to find himself in this situation; it forces him into self-consciousness, improvisation, and false starts.

Oh it does exactly that. Indeed it does. And not just in writing books either. But can he really imagine, this man of his own generation, that the Idea of Literature is going to get ours through too? Elsewhere Howe has spoken with feeling of "the difficulties of keeping alive a high civilization without a sustaining belief," to which there is but one response. What high civilization? In contemporary America? We are all too far from Europe now to preserve that sense of continuity intact. Or let us rather say we are unable to shut out the rest of it. The madness, the lies, the unimaginable daily assaults upon reason and sensibility that every day's newspapers bring us. For most of the last thirty years American literary intellectuals, like the secularized Jews I have spoken of, have been attempting to preserve the empty *forms* of a cultural tradition that has been progressively emptied of *content*. It is no wonder that our visions of coherence tend to be, when they are not strained and artificial, as "vulgar," to use the word Howe applied to the book, as Alexander Portnoy's:

> Incredible, but apparently true—there are people who feel in life the ease, the self-assurance, the simple and essential affiliation with what is going on, that I used to feel as the center fielder for the Seabees? Because it wasn't, you see, that one was the best center fielder imaginable, only that one knew exactly, and down to the smallest particular, how a center

fielder should conduct himself. And there are people like that walking the streets of the U.S. of A? I ask you, why can't I be out there in center-field! Oh to be center fielder—and nothing more.

One rather doubts that Howe ever wanted to be a big leaguer.

Beyond that there is very little more to report. Things never be-came that clear for me in Amherst, and my wife's and my own desire for coherence of the old-fashioned kind led us to wish, rather wistfully, that it could be had in the South, so we picked up and moved to Little Rock, where she had been raised as a part of a tiny Catholic minority. What Arkansas offered, I now see, was the 1950s all over again, this time 1,500 miles from home, where I could shed this truculence and discomfort of mine and get on with the business of affirmation. I could be the Camel Filter Man I aspired to be at Chatham High (tieless but disdainful of extremes), making my way ambiguously up the middle class ladder without seeming to want to—and where the possibilities of genuine social change were so remote that one could have one's moral superi-ority and live well too with a liberalism so tepid that it would qualify for the Ripon Society anywhere else. Arkansas is in a time-warp of ten to fifteen years in proportion, and is now in the midst of a regional version of Camelot, with Senator Dale Bump-ers and a new Governor named David Pryor sharing the title roles. But we screwed up, my wife and I. The farce is so trans-parent here, the swindles and brutalities so barefaced and callow, and the people who run things so generally incompetent or un-willing to cover up the mess they are making that I have been forced to be a different kind of Jewboy; whether artificial or real only a handful of people here know the difference—we are all Easterners to them.

So it is that I have finally begun to sort out the things that most bewildered me in that Rutgers dorm fourteen years ago. Litera-ture was a hell of a way to try to assimilate anyway, and I ought to have known better. Zarin and Cantor themselves, I am sure, would never have used the ideas for the protection and advan-tage they offered, but even if they believed them they wouldn't have expected the world to concur. Not for very long that is. Like them I am all sharp edges and suspicion now, restless, cynical, convinced that it is my duty to be a permanent member of the semi-disloyal opposition, touchy for signs of betrayal among my friends, and with the suspicion that one has to be an abrasive schmuck if one is to maintain one's integrity, and grown almost self-satisfied (and yes self-hating). I probably appear to be a moody, contentious egomaniac to most of the people I know. Whether sanely or madly I continue to believe that Jewboys artificial and real are the sand in the lubricated imagination of contemporary America and that which keeps it from dreaming visions of a simpler world than ever was or will be and trying to make it so with guns. So people like Irving Howe are correct in thinking that persons of my persuasion do not any longer believe in literature the way they do, but they are wrong in making us out to be cartoon figures and hypocrites, as I was uncharitable about those people in Amherst, and fools to think they can keep running that same old number. If they think we are going to let the idea of literacy die out they have not been paying attention. For the larger cultural despair that underlies my confusion, though, I have, like the proverbial Jew, no answers, only questions.

As for the next generation, I hope when I come to it I will be modest in my sense of what my experience has to offer them. Something definite ended back in there somewhere, probably when my family moved to the suburbs, although it has taken me over twenty years to figure it out. The very fact that ethnic and regional identity is now permissable in mass culture is the surest sign that it has become almost totally devoid of substance. For in spite of the fact that I am able to extemporize and abstract the question as no one else in my family ever has—no *because* I am able to do that, having been like so many others the first in its history to obtain a college education—a link with the past has been irretrievably lost. I am not to the past of my people as my father is. I am not even of my people in any real sense. If one of my own sons happens to read this essay fifteen years from now it will be as if written by a stranger. My oldest son Gavin, who is five, speaks with a pronounced Southern accent which he will probably lose when he gets a bit older and realizes the associations it has. He refers to "All in the Family," which he has seen a few times, as "The Man like Grandpa Show," based upon his perception that even a caricature like Archie Bunker has a certain basis in reality.

What stories of the clan I will tell them, I have no idea. Maneuvering the Dean into a bureaucratic sandwich where he was forced to allow my tenure recommendation to pass has not the drama of playing fullback with a dislocated shoulder. Writing is not fighting. Not in any way I can communicate to children anyway. So what images my boys will use to form themselves I have not yet at hand. They will have to reject something. But bookish old me? The farther I live from it the more I am conscious of the dominant shaping of an historic past, those places and the unknown heritage that lies inarticulate beneath my father's anger and his sadness and my mother's mute dread. But like ex-Jewboy Portnoy I can't be what I am not, and if one has difficulty in pretending it is not always easy.

In the meantime I must report that I have taken a renewed interest in *shicksas*. Not long ago I had in my office a young thing called, of all the alliterative banalities in the world, Wendy Wilson, one of those absolutely flawless Cybil Shepherd-Thereal McCoy types that tease your hope that there is somewhere in this world a life as simple and blissfully lovely as they are. The kind of girl, who when I was at Chatham High, could make me feel like a clot of dried mud by saying that she had plans to wash her hair for the next eleven Friday evenings, but how sweet you were to ask. Palms sweating, I am explaining dangling modifiers or somesuch, while my dangling immodifier is counseling lust, wanting to rest my hand on hers and tell her that all she need do is smile and forget the sick broodings of Conrad, Dostoyevsky, and Lyons and the world will be hers. But she has, I imagine, enough trouble getting people to take her seriously, looking as she does, and I am a good husband and father, like all us Jewboys, so I keep it to myself. Halfway through the discussion I notice her hands shaking and I begin to get the point. She is scared to death of me, but I suspect she is also intrigued. The metamorphosis is complete.

1975

39

Why I Live Where I Live

Why Little Rock? Most people who ask don't really want to know. "Why on earth?" or "Why, of all places?" is the way I'm usually asked. To such inquiries I've learned to give the shortest and least provocative of answers: my wife was raised here.

But moving to Arkansas wasn't her idea. Let's put it this way: due to the circumstances of my birth and upbringing, as they say in eighteenth-century novels, I needed to invent a place to live. Mine is a simple tale of dislocation, and very typical of my generation—the one born around World War II.

I was raised in New Jersey, a dense and very particular place to the sturdy Irish-Catholic peasant clan I come from, but an unplace, at best a place between places, to me. First Elizabeth, New Jersey, a decaying industrial port city; then, when I was on the edge of adolescence, my family joined the great postwar migration to Beaver Cleaver country, buying a large, four-apartment investment of a home in the only tacky neighborhood of a suburb fifteen or so miles inland. As far as our relatives in Elizabeth were concerned, it may as well have been Utah. We quit seeing them except on ceremonial occasions, which became fewer in number each year. We also quit going to church every Sunday. My father had to work and my mother couldn't drive. There went the faith of generations. Religious and ethnic bias, along with class envy, prevented my parents from making any effort at all in the suburb. So strong was their sense of who and what *they* were, it seems never to have occurred to them that their children's, in such circumstances, would fade. An orphan of ethnicity and place, I needed to invent a place to live.

It didn't have to be Arkansas, but that's how it worked out. I found its alleged backwardness appealing. Arkansas leads the nation in the production of chickens and rice; all the other numbers by which demographers and journalists purport to measure the quality of life are embarrassing. We sit at or near the bottom of the states in per capita income, literacy rate, quality of housing, teacher salaries, number of physicians, libraries and museums, and lead the rest in the incidence of venereal disease and unwed teenage mothers. We rank 51st in the payment of state and local taxes, yet the electorate clamors for cuts. You will hear liberals—we still have them—say "Thank God for Mississippi," on the grounds that our neighbor to the east totes up even lower in some categories than we do and has even worse image problems. But Mississippians reverse the compliment, I'm told, and call a plastic hose for stealing gasoline an "Arkansas credit card." A couple of years ago when a local women's group made some noise about Memphis and Little Rock running one-two on the statistical rape capital of the United States, a city director opined that we just have prettier girls than anywhere else. He has since been re-elected. Walter Cronkite never mentions Arkansas unless something awful or embarrassing has happened.

Arkansas is the smallest state west of the Mississippi in land area but comprises several distinct geographical regions—from the Ozark and Ouachita mountains, thickly-forested, sparsely populated and running with whitewater streams, to the cedar-filled bayous of the south and east, shallow, murky and inhabited by cottonmouth moccasins and alligators. Although it was a part of the Confederacy, only the plantation country near the Mississippi was fully settled at the time of the Civil War. The rest was—and, some would argue still is—a frontier. Certainly nobody ever talks about the wonderful antebellum days, and the very idea of an Arkansas aristocracy is preposterous. Indeed, until I just wrote the phrase, I'd never heard or read it. What you will hear is that a man "has enough money to burn a wet mule" or that a woman is "so ugly she'd make a freight train take a dirt road." My wife is a city girl in a place where the words "city" and "country" are used

41

to describe entities as different as the sun and the moon, but she has been known to refuse a second helping because she was "full as a tick."

The capital, business and financial center, rail and highway pivot, and only real city, Little Rock sits on the Arkansas River almost exactly in the middle of the state, just where, as if it had been arranged by committee, the hills meet the flatlands. For a variety of cultural and historical reasons, we have missed out on most of the great Sunbelt boom, and Little Rock remains as strongly flavored and provincial as it is possible for a contemporary American city to be, fancying itself the center of nothing more than the state of Arkansas. And that's a whole lot easier on the mind and spirit, I'm here to tell you, than being the imaginary hub of whatever metaphorical wheel you choose, whether it's the Free World, Art and Literature, or just Texas. In fact, living here is something like living in the capital of a remote and insignificant country. Arkansans are proud and touchy, resentful of condescending outsiders, yet bitterly self-critical. Just a little bit, in fact, like Irish Catholics. Yet provincialism confers a certain wisdom: most of us know that beyond a point achieved by almost everybody in North America, numbers have almost nothing at all to do with the sum of human happiness.

In Arkansas, anonymity is not one of your big problems. Not everybody knows everybody else, but it sometimes seems that way. Little Rock has, among other virtues, an excellent, locally owned newspaper, the *Arkansas Gazette.* We are not surprised to pick it up in the morning and read a story by someone we know about somebody else we know. For one who grew up around New York the effect is like inhabiting an endless Victorian novel. You can feel like a bit of an insider without having to work at it. The city has roughly 300,000 citizens and the state about two million, so it isn't exactly village life, but a reasonably gregarious person who has been here a few years rarely meets someone with whom he hasn't a few acquaintances in common. The gossip is fantastic.

Little Rock is big enough to have all but the most esoteric professions and jobs represented, but too small to permit tribalism. I commune at intervals with an obstetrician, several tennis pros, school teachers, a few varieties of lawyer, nurses, electricians, insurance salesmen, travel agents, a farm equipment salesman, an architect or two, several housewives, shopkeepers, a couple of basketball coaches, waitresses, cops, a toxicologist, an economist, public relations people, quite a few bureaucrats, at least one egg mogul, contractors, television and radio newspersons, restaurateurs, a judge, politicians . . . well, you get the picture. I could spend thousands of words detailing the familial and known or suspected sexual relationships among the above. Living in Arkansas, as a matter of fact, has spoiled my taste for the emptiness-and-sterility, grotesque-and-fools version of American culture served up by so many of our novelists. When you have a valued and trusted friend who works off tension by shooting baskets in his driveway while listening to cassette recordings of radio evangelists, you quit thinking categorically and lace up your sneakers.

Because gatherings of any size where one can be sure of meeting only persons of his own tribe and world-view are rare, civility tends to take precedence over outspokenness among all but the most far-gone adepts of what is now called the Moral Majority, which has been regnant here under one name or another since territorial days without effecting a visible dimunition of freelance sin. Little Rock may not strike you as Sin City, but when the state legislature hits town from such rustic venues as Oil Trough, Fifty-Six and Smackover, they tend to carry on like sailors landing in Singapore after six months at sea. When they are not passing resolutions in praise of Christianity, you understand.

Piety, moreover, only goes so far. Even heretics are admired if they have character and grit. My favorite example of this tendency was the general election of 1968, in which Arkansas elected liberal Republican Winthrop Rockefeller governor, re-elected iconoclastic Democrat J. William Fulbright to the Senate at the height of the Vietnam War, and gave George Wallace its presidential vote. The only clear pattern that emerges is that each was seen as his own man. It also helped that the latter two were from separate directions giving hell to Lyndon Baines Johnson, a prominent Texan of the era. We don't have much use for Texans here.

I love Little Rock too because the choices I've had to make are not so dramatic as they would be in New York, Washington, Los

Angeles, or Boston. Comfort costs a lot less; in buying some I
have not had to remove myself physically and, therefore, imaginatively from people who have less. My home is on a quiet street
of fifty-year-old two-story houses between the state capitol and
the University of Arkansas Medical Center. It is large and roomy,
permitting me to work at home even when my two noisy boys are
out of school. It costs $375 a month, taxes included. For a writer,
that means freedom. My wife can drive to her job in fewer than
five minutes. I can pedal my bike to the public tennis courts in ten
minutes. There are two stadiums in the same park, one where the
Razorback football team plays four or five times a year and the
other for the Arkansas Travelers, a Class AA farm club of the St.
Louis Cardinals. It's not the major leagues, but then neither are
the ticket prices and parking problems.

My boys attend public schools—black majority, incidentally—
to which they walk, as do all the other children in their classes.
Little Rock schools, having had a longer history of it than anywhere else in the South, are totally integrated all over, but here in
the middle of town, buses are not needed. The boys will attend
the famous Little Rock Central High School. Whether they stay or
leave they will grow up knowing where home is and what it is.
Right now they hang out at a local Boys' Club where two of Little
Rock's, and their, and my athletic heroes played ahead of them:
Brooks Robinson and Sidney Moncrief. Arkansas being Arkansas, they have something more than an imaginative relationship
with both. My father-in-law coached Brooks and the families were
close; when Moncrief played basketball for Arkansas (he's with
the Milwaukee Bucks now) I wrote something about him that he
liked, and he has been kind enough to remember my sons' names.

I love Little Rock because I can put a flatboat into the Arkansas
River inside the city limits and enjoy freshwater fishing that is the
equal of any in the United States, or into any of a dozen beautiful,
forest-ringed lakes within an hour's drive. I can load up four
beagles and go rabbit hunting with an old friend in soybean and
rice fields in the Delta flatlands little more than a half hour away,
or leave town to the west and be so far gone into the hills that
what few settlments one comes across seem frozen in time somewhere in the late 1940s. I even like the climate—tornadoes, floods,

and maddening heat waves notwithstanding. I'm not sure I could have survived here before air-conditioning any more than I'd have been able to stand the social climate back in the bad old days before segregation was laid to rest, but I do like the sense of living in a place where the urban-rural balance is tilted toward the country. The weather *means* something, you see. Right now, for example, I know they need rain out there a whole lot worse than I need to play tennis.

My work takes me away a lot. Maybe that's part of it too. But I get this funny feeling whenever I've been out of town for a while and find myself in an airplaine approaching Little Rock. I look out at the Delta or the Ozark hills, depending upon from which direction the flight is coming, and remember how strange it all seemed, what a *terra incognita* it was in 1966 when I first drove out here from the East to court my wife. Then, as the plane banks to approach the Little Rock airport, I am often reminded of those idealized American cities depicted patriotically in the Dick and Jane readers of my childhood. See, out there to the west are the hills and woods. A big, wide river comes cranking down the middle, and near the tall buildings downtown where Daddy works are the bridges where people cross the river. Look, there's the railroad yard and the airport! You can see factories, War Memorial Stadium, the hospitals and Central High. The houses are smaller on the other side of downtown from where you stay, because that's where the poorer people live. East of town the land is flat and there are lots of farms and the river goes down the middle to the Mississippi. Everything is just about the right size and you can see it all at once and wonder about why things are the way they are. It's not the center of the world, or even a very important place, as places go, but it's the center of my world, and it feels like home.

1983

The Higher Illiteracy

On the Prejudice Against Teaching College Students to Write

The idea of a "literacy crisis" fits so conveniently the current mood of cultural reaction that one inclines to doubt its validity. Contemporary students, we are told, display a growing inability to read and write the English language. College freshmen now read at what used to be considered the junior high school level; they write in fragments and cannot think at all. It is hard not to suspect hyperbole and to conclude that if we just wait a while this latest threat to civilized values, existing only in the metaphysical netherworld of the weekly newsmagazine feature, shall also pass.

But even those of us who would prefer to disregard the coming of a plague of semiliteracy must find the evidence persuasive. Consider, for example, the steady drop in the average national score on the verbal section of the Scholastic Aptitude Test; the fact that nearly half of the entering class at the University of California at Berkeley, a fairly selective school which takes only the top eighth of California high school graduates, failed placement exams and had to be enrolled in remedial composition courses; the news that applicants to journalism programs at Wisconsin, Minnesota, Texas, and North Carolina flunk basic spelling, punctuation, and usage tests at rates that vary between 30 and 50 percent; a survey by the Association of American Publishers showing that college freshmen *really do* read on what used to be considered a high-school freshman level.

"The great majority of American high-school pupils," wrote H. L. Mencken in 1926, "when they put their thoughts on paper, produce only a mass of confused and puerile nonsense. . . . They express themselves so clumsily that it is often quite impossible to understand them at all." Similar evaluations of the graceless muck churned out by the average student have been frequent ever since. The principal difference now, one might say, is that inarticulateness seems to be, in sociological terms, "upwardly mobile." No one expects very much more than gibberish from high school students these days; it is the colleges, the universities, and even the graduate schools that make the loudest moan. Bearing in mind the usual qualifications about the reliability and consistency of the SAT, the changing admissions standards, and other variables, it still appears that the language is in trouble.

Art For Art's Sake

One thing that is going on is business as usual in American higher education. Mencken, at least, was consistent. He blamed bad writing on bad thinking and bad thinking on faulty genes. Only a tiny minority of the human race, he thought, was fit to be educated. Of the rest, he said that "trying to teach them to think is as vain an enterprise as trying to teach a streptococcus the principles of Americanism." But although our schools, colleges, and universities are theoretically dedicated to the notion that Mencken was wrong, in practice they are agreeing with him. American students are not learning to write because nobody bothers to teach them how.

Teaching individual students to read, write, and think is surely not what the American university is about. Like many other bureaucracies our universities have become in large measure ingrown, so self-contained that most of their faculties believe, without ever pausing to think about it, that what is good for them is good for the culture at large. In English departments, where one would expect a concern for literacy to be located, the attitude of self-interest appears to be all but universal. Far from resisting the general dissolution, English professors as a group pay almost no attention at all to such mundane topics as literate writing. If they have the misfortune to get stuck in a school that forces them to teach that horror beyond contemplation, freshman composition, they teach it against their will.

The business of the American English department is not the teaching of literacy; it is the worship of literature. After eight years' experience as a student and seven more as a faculty member at five state universities, I am every day more astonished by the increasing distance between most English departments and the everyday concerns of the society that pays their bills. So accustomed have they become to thinking of themselves as the very vanguard, if not the salvation, of Western culture, that the average member of "The Profession," as it likes to call itself, believes that society exists to serve literary scholarship rather than the other way around. Consider the answer to the question "Why study English?" in a 1959 pamphlet distributed under the auspices of the Modern Language Association, the National Council of Teachers of English, and the American Studies Association, three groups which comprise virtually the entire academic literary Establishment:

> The literary part of our cultural heritage is rich in the past and alive in the present. Ignorance of it would leave one a barbarian, in the sense that he would have no real connection with the culture of the past which produced him, or with the deep and significant currents of feeling and thought in his own time.

With so lofty an ideal it is no wonder that the profession of teaching English has developed a rhetoric of transcendence very nearly resembling that of a priestly sect. Like all academics, English teachers have no objective standards for measuring books or each other. So it has been but a logical progression from an infatuation with the Joycean religion of art to the existence of an elaborate hierarchy that devotes most of its time to the intricacies of caste. The miseducation of the majority of American students thus confirms the academy in its monasticism. If the barbarians are at the walls, then the last thing the monk is about to do is take up his prayer book and reason with them. What he must do is see about protecting the holy texts.

This is particularly true in the higher reaches of the profession, in those universities with graduate programs. A survey in *College*

Composition and Communication (published in 1974 by the National Council of Teachers of English) showed that, among four-year state colleges with an enrollment of more than nine thousand, the percentage using regular full-time faculty members to teach freshman composition was 7 percent; for state schools of more than fourteen thousand students the figure was 4 percent. At least one, and frequently two, semesters of composition are generally required of nearly all entering freshmen in such institutions. Figures are less dramatic for other kinds of colleges because the survey does not provide a breakdown for private institutions. But, in general, if a university, public or private, has a graduate program in English, a freshman student will be very unlikely to be taught by a full-time member of the English department. Indeed, unless he or she becomes an English major or takes junior- or senior-level electives, which a sharply declining number are doing these days, the likelihood that the student will ever see a regular member of the English department inside a classroom is quite low. Remember, too, that this is the kind of school in which virtually all of the teachers at other colleges get their training and presumably form their professional values.

Before proceeding further, I should offer a modest disclaimer. What I am saying applies in varying degree to every academic discipline that I know anything about, particularly those in the humanities, arts, and social sciences. Only the metaphors of self-justification vary. "English" merely states them in their purest form. But the subject at hand is literacy, for which English departments presumably bear direct responsibility, and the profession has assumed the status of a small industry in this country. In 1970–71, the most recent academic year for which figures are available, more than 20 percent of all public secondary-school teachers and roughly 15 percent of all college faculty members were English teachers. Because of the composition requirement, the English department is usually far and away the largest academic unit on any given campus. (Quite a political factor when it comes to changing things from within, incidentally.) But in its failure, even its refusal, to concern itself with the fundamental needs of its students it is far from unique.

Exactly why persons will fight like proverbial Turks to be allowed to teach *Moby Dick* or *The Dunciad* for twenty consecutive semesters is beyond my power to conceive. The teachers who do so nevertheless count themselves among the company of the elect, with the result that they look with condescension upon the lowly teacher of basic writing skills. This attitude of disdain is communicated to the graduate students who teach most of the freshmen and to undergraduate English majors, who in turn carry it to the high schools, where it thrives. Except in those many school districts where they are given upward of one hundred fifty students at a time, high-school English teachers apparently have come to think of themselves as transmitters of the civilizing arts. They seldom stoop to lessons about complete sentences and coherent paragraphs. As things stand now, it is rare to find more than half-a-dozen college students out of a class of twenty-five who say that they were given regular instruction in writing in secondary school. (And that is as true, for those readers who still cherish regional prejudices, in Massachusetts as it is in Arkansas and Texas, the three states in which I have taught recently.)

The goal, the end, and ultimately the cause of all this is the practically universal demand made by American culture that every person "fulfill himself" at the "highest" level of activity that his calling offers. When it comes to the question of the relationship between what he *thinks* he is and what he *does*, the average literary academic can be as self-righteous as Henry David Thoreau. He expects, however, to be paid a good deal better, and by the rest of us. Far from being outside of, or even in opposition to, the consumer society, such a pedagogue is in fact its ideal end product, almost its archetype. For, besides sharing the customary intellectual and class biases of the trade (e.g., that driving, say, a Pontiac station wagon is evidence of vulgar materialism, while a Volvo station wagon, which costs more, is not), what the kind of academic I am talking about consumes is *himself*. He doesn't work, in the ordinary sense of the word. He has a career.

Most persons in a healthy society need to regard their work, at some level, as a *job*, a useful social task which they agree to perform for money. Most jobs are not "fulfilling" most of the time if one views them from the perspective of the nineteenth-century romantic artist, which, it seems, is the way many academics see their work. In living the life of the artist without any art (most do

50

not in fact do very much of the "research" they are given free time for), they are living one of the most personally and socially destructive forms of life known to middle-class man. The more perceptive students see such teachers less as dedicated practitioners of their disciplines than as persons whose good fortune it has been to convince the government or the trustees to underwrite their hobbies. And what students are learning from these teachers is that learning to write is simply not very important.

The Academic Elite

An example of what I mean can be examined in a controversy over the teaching of writing that took place at the University of Texas in the spring of 1975. Eighty-five percent of the freshman composition classes there, along with half of the sections of a required sophomore literature class, are taught by "teaching assistants." Together, the two courses make up 75 percent of the department's total enrollment, and 332 of its 452 classes. Yet, when it came time to cut the money, teaching assistants were getting $607,096 of a department salary budget of $2,237,450 and were being reimbursed at rates of $3,200 to $4,000 a year for half-time work. Half-time for them is two courses each semester (many carry a full-time course load as students). Full-time for a regular faculty member is three undergraduate courses. Yet the department voted down by a heavy margin a proposal that would have required all full-time faculty members to teach one section of freshman composition *every one-and-one-half years*. A report on the question written by a departmental committee stated:

> Not every English professor is suited to teaching freshman composition, just as not every English professor is suited to teaching linguistics. Doing a competent job in fact requires two skills: the ability to teach composition, and the ability to reach freshmen. Some of us have one skill but not the other; some of us have neither skill and openly acknowledge the fact.

The report goes on to say that students would be made unhappy and the life of the director of composition difficult by teachers who were forced to teach a course they disliked. Passing over the specious equation of teaching composition (which any literate person, with some training, ought to be able to do) with teaching a specialized body of knowledge, such as linguistics, one wonders about the logic of teachers who use incompetence and unwillingness to perform a task being paid for by public funds to justify their elevation to a "higher" level of activity.

Given the order of priorities in the academic world, the sort of persons who "acknowledge" so openly that they cannot reach freshmen are in fact boasting that they are incapable of descending to the freshman level. The answer to that claim, of course, is that an English professor who could not teach composition probably could not teach anything at all. I singled out the University of Texas because the squabbling of its English department produced a document giving facts and figures very difficult to come by most of the time. Both the figures cited and the results of such a vote would most likely be similar at any parallel institution anywhere in the United States.

The simple truth is that academic ethics today, like those of journalism, are very like those of the entertainment industry. Professors are paid and otherwise rewarded less for what they *do* as teachers than for *who they are*. Who they are is in turn decided almost entirely by "publications," of which the only judges deemed competent are other members of their particular specialty. The reader will recognize this is an aged issue that has been much discussed in the past, but the tired fact remains that the scarcity of jobs for college teachers has driven the frenzy for learned books, monographs, articles, bibliographies, and "scholarly editions" ever wider and deeper into the profession. The rebelliousness that characterized the academy during the Vietnam war years was, for the most part, directed against the society at large. Many of the junior faculty who let their scholarly publications slide while indulging in political and cultural protest were very unpleasantly surprised when they were denied tenure and let go. This was particularly true of persons who entered the profession in the latter half of the Sixties. When I took my first job as an assistant professor at the University of Massachusetts in 1969, for example, one demonstrated one's competence and goodwill to the English department by spending Sunday mornings on the

Amherst Town Common protesting the war. Besides politics, the only other important factor in making tenure decisions seemed to be duration; for all our collective fears of persecution, times were good in academia. Only an admitted Republican, or maybe a Jackson Democrat, should such an unlikely specimen have materialized, would have had any good reason to suspect that he would be denied a lifetime sinecure.

Then came the time of troubles. Enrollments dropped, money got tight, and administrations began to look very hard at departments in which 75 percent or more of the faculty was already tenured and no one had been "nonrenewed" within recent memory. Except for one man who wrote a book on Alexander Pope, everyone who hired on with a new Ph.D. in 1969 at the University of Massachusetts either has been fired or left on his own account. Things are pretty much the same everywhere else. Even marginal institutions of dubious repute which, as recently as five years ago, had difficulty hiring Ph.D.s now demand pedantry. Generally, a person teaching at such a place need not publish unless he gives the administration some other reason not to like him, but the fear is always there, and with it all the accompanying snobbery and posturing. For all the quibbling of the majority of literary scholars, one hears the word "brilliant," or the slightly more modest "first-rate," in the halls of an English department almost as often as variants of the verb "to hit" at a convention of football coaches.

If this behavior prevailed among Egyptologists at private institutions, it would be of no concern to the public. But what is at issue is the transmission of literacy and literary culture within our society. And while those skills and values appear to many observers to be going the way of sand painting, literary academia indulges itself even more than ever in hobbyhorse "research" of a kind that used to be done primarily by potty Church of England vicars when it was too rainy for croquet. In the nine years between 1964 and the most recently available Modern Language Association bibliography (now running two years behind, because of what one might call "the footnote explosion") the number of scholarly articles and books indexed in one category, "Twentieth-Century-American Literature," jumped from 778 to 1,986. In 1973 there were 457 publications on Shakespeare. Among the 133 items concerning Faulkner in the same year were two called "Community and the Country Store in "The Hamlet" and "A Word List of Southern Farm Terms from Faulkner's 'The Hamlet.'" One university press published a book on Irving Wallace.

The evidence suggests that this is only a fraction of the pedantry being produced. *American Literature,* one of the more prestigious journals, reports that it accepted only 50 out of 530 submissions in 1973. *College English* took 160 out of 800, and *Publications of the Modern Language Association,* a stuffy periodical which, as Edmund Wilson put it, "contains for the most part unreadable articles on literary problems and discoveries of very minute or no interest," printed 52 of 526 submissions. This is what professors are doing while accepting between $12,000 and $35,000 a year for eight or nine months of work and refusing to teach freshmen.

What is the point of all this stuff besides advancing the careers of the people who write it? Except for a veneer of truly fine and intellectually adventurous work, it is in the main devoted to two topics: the justification of its own existence and what Frederick Crews calls "hopeful guesses about the uplifting value of literature." Although literary critics, like historians, sometimes compete for the honorable designation of being "scientific," almost no one can agree that genuine progress has been made. In the sense of generating falsifiable hypotheses which may be tested against the evidence, ordinary scholarship is about as "scientific" as the weather predictions in the *Farmer's Almanac.* Frederick Crews makes a similar point in an essay called "Anaesthetic Criticism":

> The history of literary study is transparently a history of intellectual and political fashion, never more so than in recent formalism and neo-religious moralism. Critics have arrived at no agreement whatever about the meaning of beauty, the criteria of value, or even the grossest fact about books and authors, such as whether Shakespeare was or wasn't stoical, whether Milton was or wasn't of the Devil's party, whether Blake was crazy or visionary or both, whether *The Golden Bowl* is an example of self-transcendence or of colossal arrogance and evasion. Unless one had decided in advance to find criticism "coherent and progressive," he would be hard pressed to justify calling it an intellectual discipline at all.

What is even more remarkable to the average educated person is that academic criticism rarely concerns itself with deciding the relative importance of books and writers. As Crews points out, it is impolite to favor one theoretical approach or even one author over another. Why this is so is not hard to imagine when one considers that the stakes are often lifetime employment. Professor X is completing a study of, say, Hemingway, whom professor Y privately considers a ham-witted boasthard. But X will be voting on Y's promotion, and Y is himself engrossed in Faulkner, whom X thinks of as a dipsomaniacal obscurantist. The last one to say anything unpleasant is Z. He is doing a scholarly edition of the works of a long-forgotten poet whom all three recognize to be justifiably out of print.

An even sadder irony is that a reasonable case can be made for the proposition that pedantry and illiteracy are between them contributing as heavily as any other factors to the declining prestige of imaginative literature. Confronted as early as junior high school with the notion that reading fiction and poems is a moral exercise in the decoding of abstruse symbols and the unearthing of Deep Hidden Meanings, the majority of students these days either become fearful of literature, lest they miss too much, or grow disgusted and conclude that it is all worthless. I am often reminded in this connection of a friend who admitted to me once that when he read fiction, whether it was Bellow or Mailer or Graham Greene, it was generally for entertainment and pleasure. He was greatly relieved when I said that I thought most normal people did.

The role of the teaching assistant, who has most of the responsibility for writing courses at most large schools, is that of acolyte. That he is no longer an "assistant" at teaching the classes for which he is given sole responsibility is rarely remarked upon. Typically he has no training in teaching writing at all. How could he? Most English professors take only one course in the subject, when they are freshmen. That the terminology itself is every bit as dishonest and evasive as "protective reaction strikes" and "inoperative statements" is almost unmentioned. Nor does one hear much protest against the almost universal practice of setting up dummy "research" courses that do not exist and registering teaching assistants and other graduate students into them for the purpose of falsifying faculty teaching loads and generating more funds for salaries. No doubt many teaching assistants do an excellent job, but, if so, they do it almost purely by accident. Other departments commonly complain that the composition course they want their students to take is often turned into a literature class by teaching assistants.

My point in all this has not been to say that academic ethics are any lower than those of the surrounding community. As nearly as one can determine these kinds of things, they would seem to be about the same as those at Lockheed, Gulf, and the United States Congress, with the exception that academics rarely have direct opportunities for laying their hands on other people's cash. But for many years the American people have been sold the idea that quality education is their primary assurance that they and their children can get a fair shake in society. For the most part it has worked; higher education, especially the public variety, has served as well as anything else as an agency of class mobility. As the first person in my family to attend, much less to teach in, a college of any kind, I am not about to turn against education. But it seems to me that the Vietnam years exacerbated the already unfortunate tendency of many academics to see themselves as apart from and superior to the rest of American culture. With the costs of education rising so dramatically, and with performance standards dropping all around them, it is time for academics to cease pretending that criticism of *us* can only be couched in *their* (i.e. in anti-intellectual) terms. What we all share—Left and Right, businessman, plumber, artist—is an interest in seeing that persons paid out of public funds to perform a task that society wants done be held accountable for performing it. The swindling of the public interest should be seen as objectionable no matter what the motives of the swindlers.

Experience suggests that such abuses will never be altered from within the academy without a vast change in the society as a whole. "Academic freedom" has become so identified with self-interest and the profession so dominated by its hierarchical structure that many academics have come to believe that an English department deserves the unquestioning support of the state.

Most of the things that can be done by persons outside the universities entail self-evident dangers. No one who has watched members of the average state legislature in action can feel entirely at ease about recommending that they involve themselves in the internal affairs of universities, but there are things that can be done. Funding can be cut off for useless and superfluous "scholarly" publishing ventures; laws can be passed requiring that senior faculty teach a certain number of basic courses in all disciplines; funding formulas can be altered, particularly in overcrowded fields, so that it stops being so profitable for universities to exploit underqualified graduate students as teachers in order to fatten departmental budgets. Job categories can be written that will allow faculty members to identify themselves and be evaluated primarily as *teachers*. This would have three advantages: those who chose to be scholar-teachers would have to do the work and be evaluated on its worth or give up the free time; the costs of that research would be made visible and therefore manageable; and the reduction in hypocrisy might prevent many of the best young students from leaving graduate school as soon as they understand academic politics.

A final note: I have not mentioned those persons within academia who agree with what I have been saying. The controversy at Texas, I am told, was fierce, protracted, and acrimonious. There is a subdued minority within the universities that disagrees with what I have described as the prevailing ethos. It consists of people who feel trapped, often worried that their suspicions are a sign of an inability to make the grade as scholars. Quite correctly, they worry that if they announced or acted upon their convictions, they would soon find themselves unemployed. The "higher" one goes up the academic ladder, the more likely it becomes that an interest in teaching writing courses, particularly to freshmen, will be taken as a confession of intellectual inferiority.

As long as there are books there will be pedants, most of them arrogant, but teachers accepting public money should be required to do the job for which they are paid.

1976

Publishing the Backwoods Genius

The trouble, one hears with increasing frequency, is that nobody *reads* anymore. Not serious fiction, anyway, and certainly not good poetry. Even a very favorable review prominently placed in *The New York Times Book Review*, far and away the most important notice a book can get (most bookstores use it as a guide for ordering), will often fail to save a serious work from quick remaindering. And even that magazine, regardless of one's opinions of its editors and reviewers, cannot cover one quarter of the books published in a given week, and only a small fraction of those prominently enough to make much differene.

The real problem, writers themselves will tell you, is the publishing industry, with the emphasis upon "industry." Gone are the gentleman and lady editors of yore. In their place are corporate smoothies who flood the bookstores with cat horoscopes, treatises on curing acne through self-assertion, and how-to manuals for persons who want to have sex with poltergeists or invertebrate animals. No wonder Literature is dying.

But is it? It is true that the sales of original works of fiction constitute a smaller percentage of hardback book sales every year, that most paying markets for short fiction have disappeared, and that quality poetry usually loses money for its publishers. But most of us buy our fiction in paperback editions, and for perfectly understandable reasons. Why spend ten dollars on a clothbound novel that may have gotten respectfully mixed reviews when for two dollars you can read a paperback Faulkner, Hemingway, Dostoyevsky, Dickens, Kafka, Woolf, Camus, Austen, Twain or anybody else whose complete works have passed you by? Or for that matter a paperback Bellow, Roth, Greene, Powell, Nabokov, Lessing, Grass, or Malraux. And with a dozen or so exceptions, hardly any of them Americans and almost none since poetry became High Culture early in this century, real poets have never done anything but sell badly and lose money in the short run for their publishers.

Ordinarily generalizations so obvious as these would not need to be made. But the subject of this column is to be the "little magazines" and small presses, whose number is greater than all the barrooms in Jersey City and whose quality and points of view vary even more widely. On my desk as I write is a 1972 list of COSMEP (Council of Small Magazine Editors and Publishers) member publications with more than 350 entries, any number of which have no doubt ceased publication since then, having been replaced at least two to one by new ventures. Some like *Partisan Review, Triquarterly, Shenandoah,* or *The Hudson Review* have been around for quite a while and have relatively well-established reputations. One would think the number itself an encouraging sign of health in the current climate of pessimism regarding the literary arts.

Unfortunately many of those publications contribute to that pessimism by being dedicated at least implicitly to the conspiracy theory of literary eminence, that which holds that a novelist, say, like E. L. Doctorow, has grown recently rich and famous either because he hangs around the New York publishing great or because he has "sold out." Why right down the road in Boulder or Chapel Hill or Eugene is this guy who is better than Doctorow and Bellow combined, but he can't Make It in New York because . . . well usually because he isn't *commercial.* An energetic self-promoter named Richard Kostelanetz recently devoted an entire book called *The End of Intelligent Writing* to this theme, and in one of those nice literary ironies had it published by Sheed & Ward in New York and prominently (if not kindly) reviewed in all the major places. The funeral, should the incipient decline in the prestige of imaginative writing in American culture prove permanent, will be extraordinarily well publicized.

This is not to say that all in the literary world is as one would have it. Neither critical acclaim nor readers are distributed among writers in accordance with anybody's assessment of their achievements. There are many writers of considerable gifts who are all but unknown to the reading public. But the myth of the backwoods genius who will burst like a meteorite upon our bedazzled posterity is just that, a myth. If anything, one might successfully argue that the American publishing industry consumes the raw materials of literary talent so fast that our writers are damaged by premature notoriety before they can perish of neglect. Not that he is in any sense used up, but one can get an excellent short course in the ironies of early success by reading the essays in Philip Roth's *Reading Myself and Others*, published last year. Because of the kind of intensified scrutiny that large public success can bring, almost everybody had already assumed a position on Roth's work, so that when *My Life as a Man* was published in what, after all, was only its author's forty-first year, it was generally taken as just another Roth, rather than as what I think it was: Roth's finest book, combining his gift for barbed aphorism with the compassion and the kind of gravity that had informed his 1963 novel *Letting Go*, and made it perhaps the best novel of what one might call "domestic realism" of the decade.

But time, if my opinion is correct and posterity is fair, will take care of that. And nobody, least of all the man himself I imagine, expects you to have much pity for an author who has gotten the readers and the attention that all writers want, but most only dream about. My point is this: although I shall be reading and reviewing as widely in the small magazines and literary presses as I am able, the reader would be ill-advised to expect vast and fundamental surprises. While it would very much suit the vanity of any critic to believe that he could expect fairly regularly to bring to the public eye great undiscovered talents, like so many Hollywood starlets in the corner drugstore, experience shows that it is very unlikely to happen. Show me a fiction writer typing away in a cold and lonely attic, and I'll show you a writer who has either little talent and no discipline; or too much pride or too much masochism to take a couple of thousand dollars a month from a university in exchange for thirty twenty-hour weeks on campus each year; or one or both of the above plus a recent and ugly divorce. Poets, of course, are something else again, but a poet who expects to make his living at it is a fool. The romantic figure of the Joycean artist forsaking all for his work has little application in contemporary America; nor, received opinion in some Creative Writing circles notwithstanding, has the legend of the marvelous creator of the beautiful who cannot find a major publisher because his or her work is insufficiently salable. Besides reading and reviewing a good many books in the last few years for the *Arkansas Gazette,* *Harper's Bookletter,* and *The New York Times Book Review,* not to mention a number of little magazines, I have judged or read for a few literary prizes, the most noteworthy of which have been the National Endowment for the Arts Literary Grant Program and a literary fellowship sponsored by the Massachusetts Foundation for the Arts and Humanities. In all of that reading neither I nor any of my fellow judges, so far as I know, has ever encountered a single piece of imaginative writing that was neither in print nor about to be published that we thought should be. Needless to say there was a good deal in print about which the only remarkable thing was just that.

If my strictures seem unnecessarily harsh I offer as my only excuse the habit of hanging around universities, where there are any number of souls, not all of them students, who imagine that books are commonly rejected by publishing houses because they are too good. It is not at all a coincidence, then, that to glance down a list of mailing addresses of small magazines and presses is like looking at an academic travel guide: Iowa City, Tucson, Madison, Bowling Green, Gainesville, Princeton, Stillwater, Davis, Santa Cruz. But I do not wish to be misleading. If it is virtually impossible for a writer of any gifts at all to fail at publication, it is equally true that promotion, distribution, sales and readers are much harder to come by. An author who brings his work out in one of the high quality small magazines or presses is looking for two things: careful editing and production values and readers who are more particular and more responsive than the great lowing herd. If he chooses well he can have both; if not he will get neither.

The reader should not imagine that because a large number of small magazines and presses are located in college communities and often affiliated with universities that they are necessarily academic in tone. As one who is convinced that the influence of the American English department upon our national letters is near to being disastrous, I have no personal interest in boosting the careers of pedants. The average Ph.D. in English is a specialist. Unless he is in "Contemporary American" he has about as much interest in living and practicing writers as he has in Roller Derby. If he reads literary magazines at all they are those with scholarly overtones, and he reads them for the same reason that adolescents listen to Top Forty radio stations: to find out what it is permissible to like. If there is an actual fiction writer or poet on the premises he is generally regarded as both unsound and presumptuous by the majority of his colleagues. I wish that anybody who thinks the foregoing a bit strong had been with me to hear the chairman of the English department of one of our largest and richest state universities say that most persons in his charge "would have no use for the kind of writing done by a George Orwell or an Edmund Wilson." Subsequent time spent there convinced me he was right.

Even so the university provides many writers a fine and private place to work, combining decent salaries with ample free time. In spite of their official tone most places manage to retain a good number of persons who actually love books and are willing to risk making judgments of their own. Anyone who has tried to do so can tell you how hard it is to locate persons outside of the academic environment who have the knowledge, the time, and the inclination to do literary work at a rate that will allow a magazine to survive. Perhaps that is a shame, as Gore Vidal complains in his most recent essay in *New York Review,* but it is also a fact.

Enough of that. What I shall be trying to do in this space in future outings is to convey some sense of the breadth and the quality of work to be found in the literary magazines and independent small presses of America. Most of the time the best way to do that, it seems to me, will be to discuss the work of individual authors, even if it means speaking of material from several different sources at the same time. Nor do I think it would serve any useful purpose to confine myself strictly to writers whose work appears *only* in such magazines. Next month, for example, I should like to introduce readers to a novel called *Going After Cacciato* by Tim O'Brien, sections of which have appeared to date in *Ploughshares, The Denver Quarterly, The Massachusetts Review, Shenandoah,* and, of all things, *Redbook.* In 1973 O'Brien's Vietnam war memoir *If I Die in a Combat Zone* got numerous favorable reviews. To my mind his first novel, *Northern Lights,* published last year by Seymour Lawrence/Delacorte deserved far more attention than it got. O'Brien is one of those very gifted writers I mentioned earlier who, although he has had two books published by an unquestionably major New York publisher (Delacorte is a subsidiary of Dell) is not at all well known to the general reading public. I shall also be discussing a novella and seven short stories called *Separate Flights* by Andre Dubus, published by David R. Godine of Boston, parts of which first came out in *Sage,* the *Northwest Review, North American Review,* and *The New Yorker,* which hardly qualifies. That, it seems to me, is as good a way of surveying the field, and a far more amusing way too, as entering at random every little drugstore on the prairie, just hoping that Lana Turner will be sitting there in a tight cashmere sweater, typing away. Of course if I'm in there on business and happen to run into her, I hope I'll know what I'm seeing and be able to tell you.

1977

The Little Magazine:

Grow or Die

About three months ago I was asked to give a talk before the annual convention of the Associated Writing Programs, a group made up of creative writing teachers from colleges and universities across the country and the largest of its kind. The invitation came as a direct result of an article I had written for *Harper's* in which I had said some hard things against that amorphous, smothering academic entity, the English Department. The general thrust of that piece had been that our professional litterateurs in the academy had by and large metamorphosed into bureaucrats so preoccupied with their own prerogatives and self-replication that they were failing miserably at their three fundamental tasks: training students to be literate, preparing teachers, and seeing to the health of contemporary literary culture. Despite the fact that the majority of the fiction writers and poets who inhabit the academic world are only tenuously accepted there, and most of the ones I have known agreed with me either wholly or in part, I was in fact asked by the person responsible for inviting me to see if I could not enliven the proceedings by starting a fight among the members.

Now setting a convention of poets and fiction writers to feuding is about as difficult as arranging a pecking party in a henhouse: the hard thing is to get some light to penetrate the dust and feathers. As it has been my experience that most professional organizations with altruistic overtones prefer to keep the hortatory and the uplifting at a distance from the self-interested and the pecuniary, I decided that the proper place to generate controversy was at their juncture. I talked, in rough order, about jobs, money, students, and the literary culture in part spawned and nourished by creative writing teachers and their spiritual kin in the world outside the academy. My animadversions on the first three topics are of only passing interest to a general audience: what was, if anything, controversial about my remarks was my insistence that there exists an organic, if not a causal, relationship between a somewhat dishonest and benignly cynical attitude toward the academic world held by many writers and the somewhat dishonest and not so benign attitudes I had been encountering in so many of the "little magazines" and presses I had been reading in order to generate this column.

I said that it seemed to me both obvious and inevitable that an organization like the Associated Writing Programs would strive to become for creative writing teachers what the Modern Language Association or the American Historical Association are to their respective fields: job and prestige markets, the buddy system writ large and foundation-supported—the determiners of professional tone, style and prerogatives. You hire my protegé and I'll publish your poems. I read at your school's arts festival— you serve on the staff of my place's summer writer's conference. The Way of the World. And why after all should writers and teachers of writing not have as much contact as wallpaper manufacturers and merchants of deodorant? Not to mention specialists in seventeenth-century English non-Dramatic Literature?

What troubled me more, I said, since the waste and boondoggling in the academic world is so universal that only a genuine Puritan could continue to imagine the primary purpose of our schools to be education, was the Everyman an Artist But No Man Needs to Read syndrome encouraged by large and promiscuous enrollment in creative writing. Of course creative writing courses do not necessarily tend to turn everyone who takes one into an artist of the beautiful; by giving students experience in just how difficult, agonizing and joyously rare a commodity real creativity is, teachers hope to turn them into lovers of books. My experience, sadly, had been that the transfer was not being made. Apart from those blessed few who learned to read with the eager voracity of persons anxious to learn from, imitate and transcend their elders, most creative writing students I had observed spent too much time in far too close a community with their own presumed genius—as, I feared, did too many of their teachers. (I ought to add at this point that I cling to the old-fashioned notion that writing good fiction and poetry is a vastly more difficult and demanding thing than writing essays, articles and reviews, and that my own talents of invention and literary creation are nonexistent.)

The institutionalization of creative writing as a permanent, degree-granting part of the academy has brought with it a permanent faculty. Many of that faculty, as the MFA degree is now accepted as "terminal" for hiring and promotion purposes, are hothouse flowers like much of the rest of the faculty, i.e., persons who entered school in September of their 5th year and have never left it. Creative writing then becomes a "specialty" like many another. Rather than writing for altruism, recognition, and money like ordinary egomaniacs, academic writers and their spiritual kin write for grant- and tenure-bestowing committees. Welcome to the world of the "little magazine."

The discerning reader will have recognized much of the above, particularly the preceeding paragraph, as overly programmatic and tending in the direction of satire. Very well then, qualify it as you may. But before discounting entirely my assertion that there is a connection between the care and feeding of authors in the United States and the tone of petulance and animosity to be found in a great number of "little magazines," have a look at an essay in the Spring 1977 issue of *North American Review* by Stephen Minot called "Hey, Is Anyone Listening?" (Have a look, in fact, at the magazine as a whole, a well-edited, attractively printed and unfailingly *interesting* publication sold on many newsstands and in good bookstores.) Minot opens with some uncomfortable truths: he has never met a student or a colleague in a considerable academic career who has *ever* subscribed to or read a small magazine publishing fiction and poetry; in eighteen years of publishing in such magazines, every one of which is taken by his school's library and displayed in the periodical room, no one has *ever* volunteered to having read a single thing he has written; there is not a single newsstand or bookstore in his home city of Hartford which will sell a single literary quarterly on a regular basis.

He offers sobering statistics: a magazine called *Field: Contemporary Poetry and Poetics* got in 1975 10,500 poems submitted to it by 1,875 writers. *Field* has 520 subscribers. As Minot notes, that's better than 3 to 1 poets over poetry readers. Nor is that a freak. I have myself been present at a "writer's conference" and seen George Garrett wring a mass confession from a couple of hundred "poets" that *nobody in the room had purchased a single hardback volume of poems by one author for anything other than classroom use in a calendar year.* For those who would blame magazine and book publishers for neglecting the arts, Minot offers the confession that neither he nor anybody he knows subscribes to more than one literary magazine, if indeed they subscribe at all. And these are writers! That, I submit to you, is news, and tells more about the state of the little magazine and small press in this country than all of my own meanderings in and around the subject in this space for the last several months.

Minot tells of visiting a book fair in Cambridge, Massachusetts, and found that with several exceptions (among them *Ploughshares, Fiction International, Massachusetts Review* and *North American Review,* all of which impress me as excellent exceptions) "the great bulk of magazines there were so minor as to have no real following, no real public need for existing. Most were the private hobbies of their editors. Not one published work which cried out for national distribution. Yet most of these editors expected public aid in the form of grants. And some were very impatient."

Rather than summarize Minot's ideas about what ought to be done to remedy this situation, I shall further urge you to get hold of a copy of the article. In general he proposes that the foundations and specifically the National Endowment for the Arts stop supporting marginal and perennially moribund publications. Grow or die, he says to editors and publishers. There are too many of you for many of us to take you at all seriously.

Minot is in his strictures, I think, essentially correct. The habit that so many editor-hobbyists have fallen into of depending upon foundation support in order to survive has had at least three deleterious effects: to begin with they have grown paradoxically thin and lazy, as if public funding were a kind of digestible tapeworm capable of maintaining its host perpetually in a semi-moribund state. Minot records his own difficulties in trying to use little magazines in the classroom. One could not be bothered to box and send fifteen copies; another demanded prepayment after not replying to Minot's letter for a month, as if, he says, "the college would skip the country to save eighteen dollars." Secondly, famished prosperity encourages self-fulfilling prophecies about the assumed Philistinism of the audience. Traces of that attitude penetrate even Minot's argument, as when he observes that creative writing programs are "turning out more and more skilled literary craftsmen and craftswomen—an ever expanding tribe of basket weavers in a nation which at present prefers plastic." As he has earlier established that even writers themselves do not consume the magazines in which they publish, the equation of "creative writing" and "basket weaving" strikes me as doubly unfortunate, particularly since basket weaving is the sad equivalent of far too many courses and programs.

It is one thing to argue that Reggie Jackson is overrated and overpaid, another to claim that the world's best right fielder plays for Corpus Christi in the Gulf Coast League, or that the man with the best curve ball operates out of the bullpen for the Amarillo Gold Sox. I do not to mean to argue by that analogy that the creation of literature is a competitive activity, nor have I forgotten that Johnny Bench's eventual successor may at the moment be playing high school ball in Hurricane, Utah. But perhaps at the expense of seeming a bit prescriptive, it seems to me that the third harmful effect of depending upon foundation support for an editor, or for that matter for a writer, is a further weakening of the idea of writing as a public act, with a consequent advance in privatism and willful self-indulgence, or simple incomprehensibility, as manifested in the works of the Fiction Collective, recently discussed here. There is a large audience out there for seriously intended work and Minot is, in general, correct in saying that many editors, publishers, and even writers are not energetic enough in their attempts to entice it. On this score the activities of the Fiction Collective might very well be emulated and improved upon.

Having said all of this I should add that even those of us who profess to value serious writing are often astonishingly lazy in our way of going about it. Not to mention cheap. Just this weekend I personally blew twenty dollars in four hours of pizza, beer, a baby sitter, and the movie *The Deep*, an outlay made even more indulgent by the fact that I had read the novel for review and knew how the plot, which besides the eyeball massage was all the film had to offer, would end. That twenty dollars would have purchased one-year subscriptions to not only *North American Review* but to *Ploughshares* and the *Virginia Quarterly Review* as well, any one of which would have provided infinitely more pleasure and enlightenment even than a thirty-foot-high moving image of Jacqueline Bissett in a wet T-shirt. But then almost everybody I know spends more on liquor and/or cigarettes than they do on books. So right now, while you're thinking about it, why not grab your checkbook and subscribe to your favorite little magazine, or better still, to two. If you haven't a favorite, any of those mentioned above would be good for starters. Of course most people wouldn't do that once in ten years, but if they would, it could make quite a difference.

Oh yes, there was a fight at the convention of creative writers, and it was a good one. Many of the writer-teachers present did not agree with me at all, although more than I had imagined did, and a grand time was had arguing about it.

But that is enough of the vice and folly side of things for a while. Next outing I plan to take the high road by examining quality work from what may seem like unlikely places to some readers: a collection of fiction from *Redbook Magazine*, and a beautifully done limited edition of a translation of a novel, *Ourika*, called the first fictional attempt of a white writer to enter a black mind by translator John Fowles, and published in Austin, Texas.

1977

Good Fiction, Plain and Fancy

One of the pleasures of growing up middle class is the increasing freedom maturity seems to confer from the imperatives of the Large Philosophical Questions. Can God make a weight he can't lift? Could Joyce write a book he couldn't read? But a person following the profession of letters cannot hope to avoid such topics altogether, and I find that my last column, together with my reading for this month, have provoked just those sorts of questions one despairs of answering and hopes most to avoid. They are, in order: What is Fiction For? and How Much Is It Worth? Considering the first—I have no intention of answering it in anything but a negative sense—leads naturally into the second, or at least it does when one has for review a translated novella of sixty-four pages (introduction and epilogue included) that retails for ninety dollars the copy.

I have at hand letters from two magazine editors. One is from Anne Mollegen Smith, the fiction editor of *Redbook*, the other from Bruce Holsapple, who puts out a little magazine called *Contraband*. Each has a different reason for being annoyed with something I have written. Ms. Smith, in the course of commenting interestingly on the fiction of Tim O'Brien, which she has edited and published and I have reviewed here, wonders why I was so surprised that quality work had appeared in her magazine, as I had put it, "of all places." Mr. Holsapple accuses me of talking through my hat on the subject of little magazines, about which he thinks I know next to nothing. What makes their letters interesting from my point of view is the light each sheds on the other. For Ms. Smith is devoting her professional life to something Mr. Holsapple declares to be impossibility: locating and printing high quality short stories that are also "commercial."

Specifically Mr. Holsapple is offended by my remarks consequent to Stephen Minot's article in *North American Review* to the general effect that there are far too many small literary magazines, that most are of dubious or no quality, that hardly anyone, not even the people who submit stories and poems to them, ever reads them, and that the net effect upon American literary culture is harmful. In passing I had borrowed Minot's terminology to speak of persons editing magazines without readers as "hobbyists," and compared the achieving of public reputation as an author to gaining fame as a baseball player—both activities, it seems to me, requiring a combination of native gifts and acquired skills that makes them suitable for analogy. I said I thought it one thing to observe that recognition in either field tended to be somewhat arbitrary, but quite another to insist that the best practitioners are all unknowns. To this Holsapple replied:

> Your comparison of an exceptional poet to a professional baseball player is stupid; and literature is not a sport or a hobby . . . It is insulting that you don't see the necessities we face. Your idea of a national forum, or publication, for our best writers is obsolete. Publishers who can command national attention today, with the exception of presses like Capra, Black Sparrow and City Lights, also have no relations to literature. . . . What small press does, with the aid of grants lately, is to put publication into the hands of writers, and to sustain a literature there is no popular audience for. It is an obligation. . . . The world is obviously enriched by the literary arts. It can afford to pay attention. If your idea of growing up means to commercialize, I suggest you take another dive into *The Deep.*

Now there is a good deal to be said in response to this letter, but as I have said much of it before, I should like to concentrate upon two aspects, both of them relative to the recent publication of Ms. Smith's mass-market anthology, *Redbook's Famous Fiction,* now available in the vicinity of the checkout counter at supermarkets all over the country.

Obviously literature is not a sport. But my dictionary defines a "hobby" as: "occupation, activity, or interest . . . engaged in primarily for pleasure; a pastime." Clearly that is not all it is; most of us who are passionate about it prefer our bookishness to have greater consequence in the scheme of things than "stamp collecting or gardening," the activities given in the dictionary as specific examples of hobbies and omitted by my tactical ellipsis.

But matters have not always been so: an eighteenth or nineteenth century novelist could, paradoxically enough, characterize someone as a bit of a trifler by including among his or her qualities a fondness for novel reading. As a popular art form, prose fiction has been subject to attack from aristocrats and would-be noblemen of taste, in which number Mr. Holsapple no doubt includes himself. Nor has the desire on the part of a literary man to improve himself socially or financially ever served as a deterrent to such assaults on the public taste. Particularly in America one gains the respect of a substantial proportion of the middle-class book buyers by means of lampooning its entertainments. How else can one explain the career of Gore Vidal, author of *Myra Breckenridge* and disdainer of the best-selling novel? My point, a simple one, is this: unless the habit of reading imaginative writing begins in pleasure, it ends nowhere. Probably the most damaging thing about the way books are talked about in American classrooms for example, is that so many teachers are convinced that the love of books begins in moral duty and ends with the ferreting out of maxims for the general improvement of mankind.

Editor Smith's concerns are less exalted. In selecting fiction to appear in *Redbook* she must try to find work that will attract an audience of young women 18 to 34 to buy the magazine, thus raising its circulation among this target group, and justifying the higher advertising rates, which in the long run help to turn higher profits for the Redbook Publishing Company, and for the conglomerate which owns it. To entice a young woman into choosing *Redbook* over *Good Housekeeping* or, heaven protect us, *People,* Smith must offer her something she wants by way of entertainment. According to contemporary theory, then, and most surely by editor Holsapple's lights, such priorities can result in the publication of little more than vapid trifles. Right? Wrong. In fact, and almost without exception, the stories and novellas contained in *Redbook's Famous Fiction* are good, well-crafted pieces of work. If there is not a work of rare genius among the twenty-eight stories included—although more than a few show considerable skill and promise—neither is there any lumpish, pretentious hack work of the sort that one encounters all too often in publications ostensibly dedicated to higher aims and a more sophisticated audience. The market system, one is tempted to observe, seems at first glance to work at least as well as the buddy system.

To be sure there is a certain delimitation of subject matter, and in general the narrative strategies employed may be described as conventional. Fully fifteen of the titles, by my count, are devoted to young women in and out of love and marriage. Nor is the view given of those subjects uniformly cheerful and uplifting. Some, like Lynda Schor's "I'm Really Dead," or Rosellen Brown's "How to Win," could be described as harrowing. The latter, which deals with the mother of a hyperactive child, touches chords too often unheard in much contemporary fiction. Exactly how so many educated Americans have come to feel that the sane and ordinary concerns of their private lives are not worth the examining is a topic far too ambitious for a book review, but one which an open-minded reading of *Redbook's Famous Fiction*, which assumes the opposite, is likely to provoke.

Not all of the stories are so commonplace, however. "The Beautiful View" by Louise Blecher Rose was voted their favorite story of 1973 by *Redbook's* readers and was a finalist in the 1974 National Magazine Award for Fiction. It deals with a fat, neurotic woman whose "normal, happily married" best friend may or may not be dying from cancer. Nita Regnier's novella "An Opening of Doors" concerns the return to affective life of a young Frenchwoman who survives the death camp at Ravensbruck. Tim O'Brien's story is about Vietnam and is not uplifting. Byrd Baylor's "A Faint Glow under the Ashes" attempts to illuminate the life of a Papago Indian family on welfare in an Arizona city. The houses of Mexicans or Yaqui Indians, one learns, are surrounded by flowers and ferns: "Only Papago Indians grow out of a bare dirt yard. Maybe a clump of corn around by the back door. But almost never these masses of leaves and flowers. More often you'll see a little heap of pretty rocks, blue copper ore or ancient grinding stones—*manos* and *metates* from the reservation. Here a yard may be raked or swept for special days. A Papago admires an area swept flat and hard." Such small discoveries constitute the pleasures of fiction for ordinary readers. Without ordinary readers and such "ordinary" fiction as *Redbook* customarily publishes, moreover, truly extraordinary writers have neither a tradition to work within or against, nor readers to support them. Neither do I wish to seem a defender of mediocrity. The general standard of *Redbook*'s anthology is well above that of what a novelist friend of mine calls "the divine Irvings" and their aesthetic brethren who make seasonal runs at the best-seller lists. Probably there are subjects and kinds of writing that Ms. Smith will not touch: in that *Redbook* is like every other magazine, big and little. But what she does take is commendable. In the contributor's notes Rosellen Brown, herself no stranger to little magazines, tells about a friend and neighbor who happened upon her *Redbook* story in the doctor's office, read it because the drawing accompanying it reminded her of her own little boy, and cried, all without realizing until several months later that she knew the author: "her response was the essence, for me, of what I hope for when I write: to make friends of strangers and strangers of friends, by saying for them some of the things they will never get to say." If this is commercialism, and it is, Holsapple and his like-minded colleagues would do well to sit down and try to say exactly what special values inhere to *their* literature that the rest of us should feel obliged to pay for it with our taxes.

For a bibliophile, rare book dealer and part-time publisher like W. Thomas Taylor of Austin, Texas, the last twenty years have brought about an increasingly paradoxical and sad situation. For at the same time that the High-Church criticism centered in university English departments sought to sanctify literature, the huge growth of those same institutions, together with the "paperback revolution" has not only brought cheap editions of classic works within the economic range of Everykid but has also succeeded in making books into cheap utilitarian objects. The printing and collecting of fine editions is now seen as vaguely shameful, much as a taste for pornography used to be. Wallace Stevens said that "Poetry/ Exceeding music must take the place/ Of empty heaven and its hymns," as clear a statement of the contemporary credo as one is likely to find. If you want a copy of the hymnal you can buy it for a couple of dollars, but if you read it more than twice the pages are likely to fall out and you will have to get another. Nor are trade hardback editions well enough made to last very long without deterioration. The art of bookmaking, or trade if you prefer, is one of those that is passing out of existence. To the extent that it survives at all is mainly a phenomenon of the small press.

Mr. Taylor is a man who knows his own mind. Several years ago, while an undergraduate at the University of Texas, he grew so disgusted with a pedant's autopsy of Gerard Manley Hopkins that he left the classroom, walked directly to the Registrar's office, and withdrew formally, and, he says, forever, from Higher Education. In the course of pursuing the rare book dealership he subsequently established, Taylor came to know John Fowles, whose work he greatly admires, and who is also an antiquarian book lover of sorts. In the epilogue to *Ourika*, the novella Fowles has translated from the French and Taylor has published, Fowles laments the disappearance from Britain and America of the second-hand bookshop, the sort of place where treasures might lie promiscuously next to trash, establishments rapidly losing ground to the collectivized efficiency of the omnivorous research libraries of universities.

It was in such a bookshop that Fowles first stumbled upon *Ourika*, first published in Paris in 1824, and designated by him as the first known attempt by a white writer to enter a black mind. His immediate conviction, Fowles says, was that he had stumbled upon a minor classic, a feeling that has grown in him over the years, to the point that he felt he ought to do a translation. The difficulty with a work of such length, however, is obvious: Fowles wanted to do more with the novella than bury it in a magazine or anthology, as its qualities are subtle enough to be lost in such a format. But it is too short and too specialized in appeal to make a trade book. The format that he and Taylor have settled upon, a Morocco bound large page (approximately 7 1/2 × 10 inches) edition on handmade paper, is a handsome one, and seems exactly appropriate to the kind of book *Ourika* is. Five hundred copies were printed at the Bird & Bull Press, bound by Gray Parrot at

Hancock Maine and signed by Fowles. The retail price per copy, as I have indicated above, is ninety dollars.

To produce five hundred copies, Taylor says, has cost him twenty thousand dollars, not counting his own and his secretary's time. Rapid calculation shows that his markup is about 100 percent over cost, compared to the publishing industry's usual 500 percent. "The truth is," he continues "that it has become very difficult to make a profit on a handmade book, and most producers and publishers of such books don't do it for a profit. Some are subsidized by universities, some by the National Endowment for the Arts, and some by other businesses, my bookselling business for example. But a woman who would think nothing of spending fifty dollars on a pair of shoes would think it ludicrous to spend the same on a fine book, although the shoes will last a year, the book five-hundred years. A man might spend one hundred dollars on a meal for friends, but not on a book. I think this is the last generation that will see a really good book produced." This is an irony I have discussed earlier in relation to the general public's refusal to support literary magazines.

Is *Ourika* itself intrinsically worth the loving care its publisher and translator have given it? A difficult question, and one not likely to be answered to the satisfaction of prospective buyers. Like it or not, most persons who will spring that much for a book they have not read will be collectors either of fine books or of John Fowles. Either that or they won't be persons at all but libraries. That is the reason I have put off for so long discussing *Ourika* as fiction. Never having myself worn a pair of fifty dollar shoes or paid one hundred dollars for a meal, perhaps I should be disqualified in any case.

The novella is the creation of Claire de Durfort, Duchess of Duras, born in 1779, survivor of the Revolution and passionate friend to Chateaubriand in what Fowles calls "one of those physically unconsummated but intellectually passionate liaisons for which their race has such a special genius." The idea of writing about a black Senegalese who is raised and educated in the aristocratic society of her time almost as a kind of house pet seems to have occurred to the Duchess, according to Fowles, as her way of dealing with her jealousy and loneliness at the great man's ab-

76

sence and infidelity. "I am certain," Fowles writes, "one reason Claire was able to enter a black mind was that she saw in that situation a symbolic correlative of whatever in her own psychology and beliefs had always prevented her from entering into a full relationship with Chateaubriand."

The tale is framed by a young doctor, who tells of visiting a dying nun in the Faubourge Saint-Jacques. The nun is black and shows "every sign of having suffered from prolonged and acute melancholia," now transformed to happiness by religious faith, she tells him. On succeeding visits the doctor befriends the woman, who agrees to tell her life story, which makes up the bulk of the text. It seems that she was taken from Senegal as a baby and placed into the household of Mme. de B., who educates her almost as she would a child of her own. "Her fondness for me," she says, "the kind of life I was leading, everything prolonged my mistaken view of existence and made my blindness natural." But the idyll, as one might expect, is short-lived. One afternoon she accidentally overhears a conversation about her between her mistress and a "certain marquise, a bleakly practical lady with an incisive mind, and frank to the point of dryness." When the marquise asks after Ourika's future, the girl hears her mistress confess that "I see the poor girl alone, always alone in the world." She realizes the extent of her plight even as the marquise denounces "evils that arise from deliberately upsetting the natural order of things. Ourika has flouted her natural destiny. She has entered society without its permission. It will have its revenge."

The marquise is correct, as Ourika not only falls into the bleakest kind of romantic despair but complicates her predicament by conceiving a hopeless passion for Mme. de B.'s son, who remains both oblivious and brotherly. "I needed what I loved and it had never crossed my mind that what I loved did not need me in return." Ourika falls into mingled resentment and self-hatred: "There is something humiliating in not knowing how to tolerate the inevitable." She dresses in veils and removes her mirrors in an attempt to render herself invisible. After the object of her devotion marries she finds religion, enters the convent and dies ostensibly happy, a fictive contrivance as unconvincing and ultimately irrelevant to the story's thrust as it must have been to its creator.

As Fowles comments in his convincingly thoughtful epilogue: "Ourika is a striking case of a fictional character mutinying against the writer. . . . The love of freedom, of justice, keeps seeping from behind the mask of reaction. The political 'common sense' is trumped by a much deeper human pity." Fowles sees in this self-contradiction a triumph for the ideas of the French Revolution, the Romantic Movement, and "the novel form, whose only true function, beyond amusement, must always be to create a greater sense of personal freedom in both writer and reader."

Blindness and invisibility, self-hatred and muffled rage, a character inwardly divided against herself and the society that has caused the division, all of that within less than twelve thousand often epigrammatic words from what Fowles calls "the heart of the unlikely woman who dared to think black in the whitest of all white worlds." Who is to say what such a thing is worth? At the very least we ought to be grateful to Fowles and Taylor for bringing it to our attention and lavishing such care upon its production. All the rest is bookkeeping.

Report on the Fiction Collective

The appetite for recognition, like the hunger for love and approval, is never satisfied. There isn't enough recognition in the world to satisfy even one cultivated appetite.

—George Garrett on writers and fame

Anything worth doing is worth doing badly.

—Anonymous

On the surface of things it is at least curious. Here we are devoting substantial chunks of the national treasure to something called higher education. Probably there are more literature professors proudly brandishing their "terminal" degrees than there were students of the subject forty or fifty years ago. Although the percentage of English majors is down somewhat from what it was when I was in college in the early 1960s, probably only Chicken Little would make much of the fact. Back then, nobody worried much about making a living. Guns, butter, fellowship, and draft exemptions were all a part of the wartime economy. Teaching and other jobs were plentiful for college graduates, even in the liberal arts; within the American culture the prestige of imaginative literature was probably at an all-time high. To hear some people talk more recently, though, you might think it is now at an all-time low.

Part of the problem, we are told, is the publishing industry itself. Big business and the multinationals are taking over and flooding the bookstores with commercial sludge. Unless a novel has a Nazi assassination plot, a group grope, and two flying saucers somewhere in the first chapter, it doesn't stand a chance. Even so, according to Ronald Sukenick, a founding member of an organization called the Fiction Collective, "at the same time that publishing has been starving out serious fiction, the genre has experienced a resurgence of vitality and inventiveness." The group's answer has been to establish "not a publishing house, but a 'not-for-profit' cooperative conduit for quality fiction, the first of its kind in this country, in which writers make all business decisions and do all editorial and copy work."

Since its founding in 1974, the Fiction Collective has published more than twenty titles, for each of which the author has put up $3,000 or more of his or her own money to cover production expenses. Books are accepted or rejected by a vote of the membership, consisting of previously published writers. Copy-editing chores are shared.

Exactly what Sukenick meant by "not-for-profit" was unclear in the 1974 "Guest Word" column in the *New York Times Book Review* announcing the formulation of the enterprise. The article also stipulated that each author "splits profits evenly with the Collective and gets 60 percent of its share of other rights." During its existence, the Fiction Collective has been variously supported by grants from the National Endowment for the Arts, a state agency; Brooklyn College, a public institution; and an organization called the Teachers and Writers Collaborative. Brooklyn College also helps out with office space, postage, and other small favors. That may be the key to the "not-for-profit" designation, since most public universities have regulations forbidding their faculty (which most members of the Collective are) from using their facilities for private gain. But that may be a quibble. More important to notice is what the group's members do not mean when they complain of being neglected and all but censored by something they call "The Establishment." They do not mean the governmental or educational establishments.

Almost everybody who knows and cares anything about serious fiction knows a few horror stories about agents, editors, and publishers. Having a book published, it seems, can often be an excruciating ordeal. Without promotion and distribution no book can succeed in attracting an audience in the short run; then corporate computers dictate remaindering or shredding long before word of mouth can create a demand for work that may have escaped early notoriety. There are also the tales about fine novels and short story collections which are never accepted at all by commercial houses. I confess to being of two minds about those. On the one hand, I have served as a reader in several literary competitions, including the National Endowment for the Arts Creative Writing Fellowships, and have never read—nor have I spoken to another judge who has read—unpublished fiction that we thought should be printed. I have read a great deal of "serious" fiction that I thought a waste of ink, and I have more than once directed friendly challenges to writers' groups to produce examples of such injustice, so I could promote them in a column on little magazines and small presses that I used to do for the *Nation*. I never got any takers. On the other hand, everyone knows that *Catch-22, From Here to Eternity*, and any number of other artistically respectable and commercially successful books were initially rejected by scores of publishers before finally being accepted, so perhaps it is best to temper one's skepticism.

In any case, most literary people are predisposed to accept arguments against both free enterprise culture and the vulgar herd—perhaps too easily. Almost everybody reading this magazine [TriQuarterly] shares a common disdain for the average novel on the best-seller list. So when the Fiction Collective announces that it is selecting, printing, and distributing the "books of its peers on the basis of literary merit, free of the implicit commercial standards of the book business," and hopes by so doing "to open a path toward the maturity of the American novel," we ought to be interested. We ought also to be suspicious. For the Fiction Collective has done no such thing. Nor, from the evidence at hand, does it appear likely ever to be anything but what it is: a well-publicized, tax-supported vanity press. How and why the enterprise has failed, moreover, can tell us a good deal more about what is happening to the idea of serious fiction in our time than success could ever have done.

The fact that almost all of the Fiction Collective's organizers and authors are academics who teach creative writing is symptomatic. The institutionalization of creative writing as a permanent, degree-granting part of the academy has brought with it a permanent faculty. Since the M.F.A. degree is now considered sufficiently respectable so that one possessing it may gain tenure, many of that faculty are hothouse flowers like much of the rest of the faculty, i.e. persons who entered school in September of their fifth year and have never left it. Creative writing has become a specialty and, as such, is in a fair way to developing a kind of world view to protect itself from hostile scrutiny by outsiders. The components of that world view are not, thankfully, so widely shared by author-teachers as the following list may seem to imply, but I think it worthwhile, for the sake of clarity, to have them all in one place:

The Need to "Publish"

Academic employment confers substantial benefits upon the young or would-be author, primary among them a decent salary and lots of free time. To keep getting them, he must compile a bibliography like any other assistant professor's. The result of the consequent frenzy is the same in literary magazines as it has been in scholarly journals for some time: an explosion of unread mediocrity. An article by Stephen Minot in the Spring 1977 issue of *North American Review* offers some exemplary statistics. In 1975 a magazine called *Field: Contemporary Poetry and Poetics* had 10,500 poems submitted to it by 1,875 authors, FIELD has 520 subscribers. Nor is that a freak. I have myself been present at a "writer's conference" and seen George Garrett wring a mass confession from a couple of hundred "poets" that *nobody in the room had purchased a single hardback volume of poems by one author for anything other than classroom use in a calendar year.* Minot reports, moreover, that in a considerable academic career he has never met a student or colleague who has either subscribed to a small magazine publishing poetry and fiction, or ever received one comment on work of his own published in such a magazine—not even when his college's library subscribed to and displayed the magazines printing his work. When it comes to fiction, there is no way that the centralized American literary marketplace can merchandise more than a fraction of what all those teachers and their students are writing, even if the work were of high quality generally, which most of it is not. An author can have a list of credits several pages long without being certain that anybody but editors has read his or her work. While the large number of outlets can in part be seen as an index of the health of our literary culture, for all their value in sustaining writers' hopes and accommodating their energies, too often they contribute to the every-man-an-artist-but-no-man-needs-to-read syndrome encouraged by large and promiscuous enrollment in creative writing courses.

Status Frenzy

As a hierarchical bureaucracy, the American university rivals the Kremlin. Even if poets and fiction writers are employed everywhere in academe, they are only tenuously accepted there by the resident scholar-critics and are often regarded as presumptuous hacks. For some reason, the writing of unread criticism is considered an honorable pastime, while writing poems and stories is like mocking the gods of Parnassus. Literature professors themselves rarely trifle with contemporary work unless that happens to be their specialty. In many years of hanging around English departments I never heard the honorific adjective "brilliant" applied to a writer of fiction, although it is used quite freely otherwise. Mention to the average scholar that you have spent the weekend curled up reading Tom McGuane, Don DeLillo, or Lisa Alther and your reward will be a numb stare, as if you had confessed a passion for "Charlie's Angels" or professional wrestling, and a "From the reviews I shouldn't have thought . . ." If, that is, he has even read the reviews. Most Ph.D.s know and care less about contemporary fiction and poetry than your old man, and are fearful of being caught going ape over something posterity judges to be second-rate. Of course, most work is bound to be second-rate by the standard the ages have set—as, at best, is most criticism. A writer who may begin with ambition, humility, and what Hemingway called a "good shit detector" often learns to suppress or conceal the two latter qualities in order to survive. Self-deprecation and modesty are the worst possible traits one can have in a generally humorless world where everybody has got the knives out. Hence organizations like the Fiction Collective and the Associated Writing Programs may be seen as essentially self-protective, like the Modern Language Association or the American Historical Association: job and prestige markets, the buddy system writ large, would-be determiners of professional tone, style, and prerogatives. You hire my protegé and I'll publish your poems. I will read at your school's arts festival; you will serve on the staff of my place's summer writer's conference. The way of the world. Of course such groups are partly altruistic, and certainly necessary for maintaining the individual writer's dignity in an otherwise inimical climate, but that should not blind anybody to their primary function.

Academic Values

Professors are interested in books that teach well, and that justify by their complexity the professorial mission. Not for nothing do Faulkner's *The Sound and the Fury* and *Absalom, Absalom!* sell hundreds of thousands of copies each year in campus bookstores, while the more accessible of his works are rarely required. That the average undergraduate at most American colleges and universities can scarcely grasp even the surface meaning of Joyce's works is precisely the reason so many of them are asked to read *A Portrait of the Artist as a Young Man* in their freshman composition classes. According to the English department, a novel is above all an encoded narrative, the understanding of which depends largely upon a system of hidden symbols requiring explication by a professional. Since the discovery of The Novel, there have been two main purposes for reading fiction in the academy: moral improvement and the demonstration of intellectual refinement. Such motives as pleasure and curiosity are rated quite low. Thus the most highly regarded sort of fiction is self-referential or "experimental" in nature. Anything traditional or too easily understood makes an academic fiction writer vulnerable to charges that he is a literal-minded simpleton or a shameless panderer to mass tastes. Once upon a time, part of fiction's appeal was in its bringing to a broad middle-class audience parts of the world—geographical, socio-logical, or what have you—remote from that audience's ordinary experience. But it is little recognized in the English department any more that a legitimate reason for reading a novel may very well be that one would like the vicarious experience of being a British policeman in Burma, sailing up the Congo in a flat-bottomed steamer, taking part in a abortive revolution in Shanghai, or smuggling cocaine from Colombia. For a writer to do actual "research" on a book, the way Harold Robbins and Irving Wallace do, is seen as a concession to the vulgarity of subject matter, which sophisticated novels no longer have.

Isolation

All these tendencies taken together only serve to magnify a fact of academic life so familiar that one who even brings it up is showing bad taste and can be accused of anti-intellectualism. One reason why classroom-oriented authors write the sort of claustrophobic, subjective, and willfully incomprehensible books they write is that they don't know enough about what goes on in the outside world to do anything else.

I wish that readers who think the foregoing a bit strong could have overheard a luncheon conversation I had a couple of years ago with several former colleagues just before departing on a magazine assignment to write about the Texas Prison Rodeo—an annual function put on in Huntsville by the Corrections Department, with volunteer inmates, in order to raise money for the system's recreation and education fund. None of those present had ever done more than drive across Texas, and none had ever been inside a prison or so much as seen a live rodeo. Nevertheless, neither had they, to a (wo)man, very much difficulty in converting the nouns *Texas, prison,* and *rodeo* into abstract symbols, joining the symbols together and presenting me with the "meaning" of the experience I had not yet had in quite a neat package. Over the discussion hung the question that none knew me well enough at the time to ask: why would I give up tenure to do such tiresome, and tiring, things? As it was, the story took me almost two months and several drafts to write, and was perhaps not one of my best. Suffice it to say that the symbolic meanings offered by my well-intentioned academic friends were useful mainly in providing straw men to attack in the first draft, delaying for a time my getting anywhere near the real story. I should recommend as therapy to anybody suffering from hardening of the categories, or a sense of wonder atrophied by communing too long with adolescents and their mentors, a week or ten days interviewing inmates, guards, and wardens at their friendly neighborhood state pen. If that fails to cure the malady, it is probably terminal.

Now then. After all the above I must confess to never having been able to read any novel published by the Fiction Collective from beginning to end, although I have not tried all of them. As an example of why not I offer the following passage from *Althea*, by J. M. Alonso, who is also an editor of the *New Boston Review*. Generically speaking, the book is academic-sexual, the tale of "a wretched and paralyzed graduate student who never finished his thesis." The man's name is Muldoon, and as he is an Irish Catholic by birth and upbringing, naturally he despises and fears women, although like the man in the joke he can't seem to get along without them either. We come upon him in front of Harvard's Widener library, where he has been left by a fellow student who has gone inside to use the men's room. Ordinarily he avoids the place because he is afraid of meeting his faculty adviser.

So there I was, unknowingly positioned . . . in a most humiliating position before the Widener God, with my back turned, my face averted, practically cowering and reduced to cursing Ben (who, incidentally, was a pervert) for leaving me there.

Though not daring to look at the living temple directly, I could feel the Widener God's life behind me with all its massive silent vibrations of obscene mental electricity. Sparking from books to minds and back again. All contained in the shadows of the stacks within the infinite creases, in the darkness deep beyond the Cyclopic, glassed mouth behind me, with that low, dark square mouth.

So, to protect myself, to undeify the living temple, I tried thinking of the Widener God as just one more Harvard corporation-owned factory, meshing stacks and stacks of minds with rows and rows of books. After all, professors author books which themselves author professors, and the Widener factory God was in the business of producing both, which were sometimes barely distinguishable entities. Come to think of it, I knew many books that were far more perceptibly human, both in their affects and contents, than many a professor who had turned through his life's work into a walking thesis with hat and shoes.

Where to begin? With a "Cyclopic" mouth, whatever that is, which in the same sentence is also "square"? With the barbarism of "author" used as a transitive verb not once but twice, the second time with "books" as an implied subject? With "undeify"? With "affects" used for "effects"? Or for something; the clause makes little sense either way. Alonso is equally apt at the coinage of adverbs. In other passages, *Althea* is a novel in which characters are "uncommentingly patient," and stand "homosapiently erect" while "looking Biblically up at the sky." Almost any selection of similar length from anywhere in the novel will yield such howlers. And this man is an editor! The daily newspaper, not to mention Harold and Irving, is better written.

Even more characteristic of the Fiction Collective's (pardon me) collective practices are the many paeans and asides Alonso's first-person narrator delivers to what he calls the "Unseen Mysterious Forces"—the UMFs for short. Essential to what the group calls "The New Fiction" is a sort of juvenile self-consciousness which demands that the author prate constantly about what he is doing, has done, or is about to do with his story—like a child learning to ride his bicycle with no hands. In Alonso's case the UMFs stand alternately for the wonders of the unconscious, for chance, and for coincidence. Every turn in *Althea*'s turgid plot must be explained as one or the other, or perhaps some mixture of all three.

A large part of the Fiction Collective's case against commercial publishers in fact rests upon its alleged hostility to, or incomprehension of, what is "new," or "innovative," or "experimental." In the organization's lexicon all of those words are good ones, as "traditional" and "commercial" are bad. Now, in America no one ever uses "new," as in the "new, improved lemon-scented Chevrolet Malibu," unless he is trying to sell us something. The word has virtually inescapable intimations of cant, never more than when it is being applied to ideas or attitudes, as in "new morality," "New South," or here in "The New Fiction." Were the Collectivists as a group not obsessed with irony about everything on earth except their own "voices" (another cant term), they might have spared us some of their claims to originality. In fact there is nothing even remotely novel in the fictive practices of the group, and a good deal that is so tiresomely conventional in the contemporary fashion as to verge at times on self-parody. The best single place to verify the charge is in *Statements 2*, the Fiction Collective's most recent anthology. At the risk of seeming reductive, I should like to list, with representative examples from that book and a couple of others published by the group, the three main discoveries about prose fiction that the Collective and many of its academic allies seem to regard as daring:

1. Stories calling themselves "fiction" are not true. They are made up.

From Russell Banks' "By Way of an Introduction to the Novel, This or Any":

You know, it occurs to me that I really needn't bother with all this. Certainly not at this point. Perhaps later in the narrative such descriptions will be of significance, but here, now, I'm merely attempting to explain how I, Russell Banks, came to write a novel with a hero whose "real life" prototype is my friend, my own "hero," as a matter of fact. . . . I had reached a point in my relation to him where almost anything could happen and where whatever did happen would be believable to me. . . . In other words, the man had become sufficiently real to me that I could, and therefore should, write a novel about him—even if that "reality" were nothing more than a projection extruded by my unconscious life, even if it were no more than imaginary.

More UMFs! One would think that Durrell's *Alexandria Quartet*, among forty or fifty others, had done this kind of thing to death.

2. Since stories are made up, it follows that the traditional beginnings, middles, and ends of retrograde, old-fashioned fiction are somewhat arbitrary and not to be confused with genuine necessity. Any story could have been told differently. The narrator, by entering his story as a "voice," demonstrates his advanced sensibility by pointing this out as often as possible.

The following passage is from Raymond Federman's Fiction Collective novel, *Take It or Leave It*, described on the back cover as a book in which "the narrator involves his listeners in digressive arguments about politics, sex, America, literature, laughter, death, and the telling of the story itself. Consequently as the story progresses it also deviates from its course and eventually cancels itself [whatever that means] as the voices in the fiction multiply . . . [and] makes a shamble of traditional fiction and conventional modes of writing, and does so with effrontery and laughter."

Why, when, where, how, why me, why then, who, and then, in which direction? How the hell do I know! . . . Dammit! If you guys keep talking all the time/And at the same time/We'll never get it straight! We'll never get there! Do you think it's easy to tell a story? Any story? Hey! Particularly when it's not your story—A second hand story! Anywhere? To retell a story which was already told from the start in a rather dubious manner. Do you think it's easy to set it up so that it looks coherent? Or even readable? Not to mention credible? I tell you it's not easy.

Fearless innovator Federman also refuses to number the pages of his bulky text, and speaks of a "battle against the linearity of syntax," which he wages with the dazzling new weapon of creative typography.

3. Words and languages themselves are also made up, and may have a purely noumenal existence. It is this supposition that makes it impossible for any "real" writer to use the word "real," or any other that might imply metaphysical earnestness without the ironical quotation marks. Hence the flatulence of a writer like Federman indicates neither incompetence or self-indulgent, lazy thinking and writing but extreme sophistication. At its furthest reaches, this skepticism about language compels the writer to demonstrate constantly that language is a kind of trap-door through which all must fall. He does this through a kind of linguistic play (see Huizinga and other authorities on the seriousness of play) known as a "pun" or "play on words."

From B. H. Friedman's "P———: A Case History," a tale in which a horny middle-aged man has a case of priapism, or permanent erection, which turns out to be a symptom of terminal leukemia: "As he finishes dressing he wonders if he should call the office and tell them—what?—that something has come up. He smiles. That is just the sort of vague explanation his secretary gives. In his case it's precise, too precise." And later, "but the analogy won't stand up (another joke, another smile)," and again "he tells the nurse that this is an emergency. She says she will fit him in. P——— smiles. The world is filled with cruel jokes."

Not to mention juvenile ones. In Peter Spielberg's "The Hermetic Whore," about a government project to cheer up the elderly by encouraging masturbation that ends up so popularizing the practice that intercourse goes out of fashion and the birthrate plummets, there are more. Spielberg tells the one about

The crazy scientist who killed and cremated all the cats he could get hold of. Yes, cats. You know: kittens. Meow, Meow! He sifted their ashes into empty coffee cans, or maybe it was baby-food jars, and tried to sell them to the hard-up dudes on 42nd street.

"Psst! Want a piece of the best stuff in town?" He would buttonhole a likely customer.

"Sure. Where is she? How much?"

"Right here in the jar. Five dollars a spoonful. Just add some hot water. My invention—instant pussy. . . .

And so a one-liner copied from twenty-five-cent vending machines in half the gas station men's rooms in America becomes a whole routine.

In *Take It or Leave It* Federman explains why his narrator has decided to travel across America by car (a daring new plot):

To penetrate you (all the way to the west coast) because (up to now) I must admit I hadn't gone very far—very deep. Mostly stayed on the margin. Yes, dealing mostly in the cuntfrontation. But now it was really going to be an enormous penistration. I couldn't wait to get going. America here I come!

When he is not altering the shape of literary perception Raymond Federman is a professor of comparative literature.

Not all of *Statements 2* or of the Collective's novels are so bald as the passages quoted. But I chose each of the writers above not only because his work was illustrative of what seems to me to be the Fiction Collective's guiding principles and general tone but also because he has a book in print with the organization and is therefore a member of its editorial board. The sexual obsessiveness of the last three is equally characteristic, as if a group of academically employed solipsists has no other subject matter available to it. Spielberg's "The Hermetic Whore" contains a carefully enumerated list of ways for men to masturbate, which seems just about right. Any of the three could easily make a living writing to the *Penthouse* Forum if they could forgo the puns for a while. But that would be commercial. It would not be art.

I find it puzzling that writers of genuine talent like Jonathan Baumbach, Russell Banks, and Ronald Sukenick seem content with the self-imitation of easy effects that their work in *Statements 2* shows. Reading too much of it is like watching a basketball game in which the players have gotten so cool that they have agreed true devotion to the sport requires that all shots be missed and the ball double-dribbled on purpose. I find it depressing to imagine the Fiction Collective version of contemporary literary "reality" becoming the currency of seminar tables all over the country—a gloom that is partially lifted by my knowledge of how little attention the most promising young writers will pay in the long run to any teachers. I emerge from my reading tempted to paraphrase Flannery O'Connor's remark on the effect of the American university on the national literature: if the publishing industry is stifling writers, it isn't yet stifling enough of them.

We have more mediocre fiction writers, poets, and critics than we need. What we lack is readers. Most of the Fiction Collective's members would do themselves and the rest of us a favor by knocking off the boasting and the bitching for a while and getting back to the classroom to train some.

1978

Harper's Bizarre

There comes a time for simplicities. Permit me one: I love America. Could not imagine, really, living anyplace else for the balance of my life. I love driving across Texas, country music, American women, certain Jewish novelists, a number of American poets, the NCAA basketball tournament, hunting rabbits in cotton fields without needing to ask formal permission or pay anybody, New York, Boston, Little Rock, Austin, the Arkansas Razorbacks, and the way the east wind smells before it rains. There is a paper mill downriver from where I live and when we can smell it here we know we're in for a downpour; when the wind goes back to the west they can smell the damn thing in Pine Bluff and I can be glad I don't live there. In certain moods I feel like a warm-hearted H. L. Mencken and confess a secret thanks for the Arkansas legislature, and if that don't make me a patriot, good buddy, then I don't know what one is. When Linda Ronstadt sang the national anthem before the fourth game of the 1977 World Series in her blue-jeans and Dodger warm-up jacket with her hair pinned up on her neck I had shivers for six innings.

Having made so bizarre and shocking a series of confessions, I owe the reader a detailed explanation. Time was, and not so long ago either, that I would have kept a passion shared by half the adult males in America, more than half the adolescent ones, and celebrated on the cover of *People* magazine, to myself. Perhaps even successfully repressed it. But I have been accused in a prominent place of harboring anti-American sentiments, of "flirting," as it were, "with guilt and tyranny." It is enough to make me wish that Farah Fawcett-Majors did something for me other than making me self-conscious about the coffee stains on my teeth. Then I could confess that too. How better to prove my dedication to Truth, Justice, and the American Way?

If you are subtle enough to grasp the connection between warmblooded mannequin and the glories of our democracy then you had better skip the article by Eric Larsen in the December *Harper's* in which he charges the lot of us "liberal" literary critics with a skulking admiration for truncheons and jackboots. All writers love attention, of course, so while I'm at it I can admit that I did not at all mind being placed among a masochistic elect that includes: John Leonard, Roger Rosenblatt, John Gardner, Saul Bellow, Elizabeth Hardwick, E. L. Doctorow, and Hilton Kramer. If one is headed for even a metaphorical dungeon, how comforting to know there will be lively conversation.

Larsen's central thesis is that by demonstrating impatience with the doom and neurosis school of contemporary American novelists, and by displaying simultaneously a deep respect for those Soviet and Latin American authors who have made their lives and works into symbols of anti-totalitarianism in their own countries, we liberals have shown that we harbor secretly a romantic preference for extreme situations that has weakened our cultural resolve against dictatorship. You may wish to read that sentence again. Long as it is, I think it useful to have it all in one place. Exactly how the lot of us came to be "liberal critics," I am not entirely certain. Evidently the term means something to Larsen. In a rambling preamble he identifies liberalism with "a sense of guilt," that essence which over the last fifteen years, as the world knows, "was observed to rise up a number of times from the recreation room in the suburban basement and come out the front door onto the lawn."

The loading of terms is characteristic; everybody hates the suburbs, or is supposed to, anyway. At the expense of two more confessions, then, let it be known that this liberal critic lives in the city, and that his fifty-year-old home here in Kirkpatrick Sale's hedonistic Sunbelt (where we have at this writing enjoyed six inches of rain and a steady thirty-seven degrees during the past seventy-two hours) has no basement at all. As for that free-floating omnivorous undergraduate guilt Larsen speaks of, which I agree has been one of the prime constituents of a liberal arts education in this country for many years (and about which I shall have more to say anon), I was personally cured of it long ago.

Larsen's argument is, on its face, as he admits, at least curious: it would seem that critics objecting to alienation and nihilism as the inevitable themes of "serious" American fiction would come, in his words, "more commonly from the direction of social and political conservatism than from the side of liberalism." This paradox he evades by asserting that in backing away from worshipful praise of the works of such novelists as: "Cheever, Joan Didion, Joseph Heller, Kurt Vonnegut, Francine Gray, John Updike, Renata Adler, Jerzy Kosinski and so on and on and on" (the list is borrowed from John Leonard) we liberals have revealed nothing less than our own "disenchantment and mortification . . . (our) cultural self-loathing." It happens that I have no opinion at all regarding several of the above worthies; but if thinking of Vonnegut as a sharp-edged Art Buchwald and harboring large reservations about Heller, Updike and Kosinski qualifies me, perhaps it is time I sought counseling. Since I have never written about three of the above at all, and about Updike just once several years ago in an obscure academic quarterly, Larsen is decidedly clever to have found me out.

But lest I be suspected of responding too personally to an attack that includes me only parenthetically, I should add that with the exception of Leonard, who was after all with his characteristic style of overstatement only writing a newspaper column anyway, Larsen does not bother to establish in his argument that any of the rest of us have ever written anything much about *any* of the above. In fact, the only member of the group who is quoted by Larsen in reference to any of his own implied culture heroes (whom he never names) is Elizabeth Hardwick, who actually wrote favorably about Pynchon in an article praising Solzhenitsyn, but speculated that the formal and philosophical differences between the two authors might have everything to do with the nature of the societies that produced them.

As for the rest of us, we have sinned against the light by arguing, at least implicitly, "that the brand of deeply negative high seriousness we find in our art is essentially a fraud." How, without demonstrating what that high seriousness consists of or even attempting to tell us who displays it and in which passages of what books it may be contemplated, does Larsen hope to convince readers he knows what he is talking about? Now I must urge you to peruse the piece yourselves. For I haven't the vaguest notion.

What the man has done is to assemble a list of generalizations made by each of us in the course of book reviews concerning authors not on Leonard's list (and in Bellow's case from his Nobel Prize acceptance speech), then performed the trick of applying them in series as if they did refer to those authors. By so doing he comes up with a list of adjectives, some of which, it is true, were employed by their authors in the course of general and sweeping denunciations of the current scene, but others of which were quite specifically intended. This method then provides occasion for a rhetorical question considerably larger in scope and more pointed in application than any of us could ever have had in mind. To wit: "Is anyone, come to think of it, indeed really prepared to follow happily along and call these and other of our best-known writers mediocre, peripheral, inadequate, unrepresentative, solipsistic, stupid, terrible, self-pitying, whining, liars?" Well I'm not, but then I never did. Of course that is not the same thing as accepting the individual views of those authors concerning things American as graven in stone, or as saying their works are unassailable either.

I *do* think that writing a serious novel is incomparably more difficult than writing occasional criticism, and I truly believe, false modesty aside, that every last person on John Leonard's list of doomsayers is my superior as a person of letters. But I do not believe, therefore, that it is the duty of critics or ordinary readers to prostrate themselves before the golden calf of "artistic vision," or whatever Larsen would call it, when I think the result would be to share in a literate form of mass delusion.

Two more examples of Larsen's reasoning should suffice. Liberal guilt, he says, eventually turns into envy: "life under the tyrannies, for literary purposes at least, and very likely for moral purposes as well, actually comes to be seen as superior to life in freedom—more immediate and stimulating, more heroic, more unquestionably and intensely productive of *real* truth." Doubtless there is *something* in what he says. Probably there is not a soul in America so void of romanticism that he or she has never daydreamed of throwing Molotov cocktails (nice irony) under Russian tanks in the streets of Prague or Budapest. It was after all *The New York Review of Books,* whose readership is almost entirely academic, which printed the famous cover some years ago detailing how to make them. The presumed target was then our own wicked military establishment, but the emotion was nevertheless a similar one. Democratic institutions in a post–industrial bureaucratic state can become rather a bore when one has been raised on endless cowboy movies and spy thrillers. I have myself given up watching the evening network news entirely: in 1968 CBS could have replaced Walter Cronkite with Chicken Little and the population would have gone along; today it often seems our whole system of government has evolved into the world's largest and dullest faculty senate meeting. But romance fades and most literati make do with their usual pastimes of adultery and psychoanalysis. Even so, I have heard more than one wistful cuckold observe of late that he wished it were one hundred years ago and he could resolve his troubles with a gun. Of course many people here in Arkansas still do, but rarely among the Updike-reading set.

Observe, though, the heavy-handedness with which Larsen pounds Hilton Kramer. He quotes from an article of Kramer's praising Russian dissidents: "In the West, the success of our political system, despite its well-publicized troubles, has given our writers the freedom to be trivial, cavalier, and myopic, even about the politics that guarantees this choice—and this is a freedom that a great many of them have exercised to the fullest." What we literary patriots ought to notice in Kramer's statement, Larsen says, "is the subtlety of tone that castigates our writers for the offense of being free." He continues in a similar vein to accuse Kramer of "romantic envy." Of course anyone with what used to be a high school junior's command of English syntax can see that Kramer is in fact criticizing triviality, myopia, and cavalier attitudes, but a deep reader of Larsen's zeal is not to be put off from the pursuit of truth by mere grammar.

The use made of my own work would be less obvious to most of his audience, the majority of which will not have read the article he has quoted. We liberal critics are said to object to the fictive pessimism we complain of because our novelists "have not earned the *right* to it." Accordingly, our secret contention is that "Americans are cut off from life itself," an opinion Larsen finds corroborated in one of my previous essays in this space: "Writing in *The Nation* this spring, Gene Lyons described the numerous volumes published by the *presumably lively and experimental* Fiction Collective as, by and large, the self-indulgent work of 'academically employed solipsists'" (my italics). Now any writer has a right to be annoyed when a carefully reasoned, or at the very least, detailed argument of his is swept aside as if it had never been made, but the tone of special pleading here deserves further scrutiny. Why indeed should one *presume* the works of the Fiction Collective to be anything at all without having examined them? As it happens, my own review had dedicated considerable space to that organization's promotional rhetoric, in which the word "experimental" is unfailingly used as an evaluative rather than a descriptive term, in a more or less self-conscious attempt to disarm potential critics.

Anybody who complains, as I did for a few thousand words, that "there is nothing even remotely novel in the fictive practices of the group, and a good deal that is so tiresomely conventional in the contemporary fashion as to verge at times on self-parody," may be dismissed as an out-of-date crank. The body of my essay was devoted to showing why, with extensive quotations from the works themselves, I believed the collectivists to be misguided in their claims to originality, since everything they call "experimental" and "innovative" and "new" is in fact old. For Larsen to have lifted three highly prejudicial words from the end of that essay, and to have implied by using them that I intended a description of Americans in general when he knows perfectly well I did not, is more than slipshod. It is dishonest.

Beyond the fact that it appeared in *Harper's,* which is usually one of the best edited of our general circulation magazines, even so transcendentally silly a bit of Dumbthink as Larsen's article would not ordinarily deserve elaborate refutation. But the man is

onto something important, and the logical backbends he per-
forms to account for all us liberals sounding like conservatives is
symptomatic of the confusion many bookishly inclined people
feel today about our national literature. Ironically enough, one of
the most perceptive articles I have read in many years about the
subject appeared one month before Larsen's piece in the November *Harper's:* Joseph Epstein's "A Conspiracy of Silence." I urge
everyone with an interest in the subject to take the trouble of
reading it.

It is Epstein's contention that most persons in America today
who would describe themselves as serious about imaginative
literature are products of a special kind of education, a kind of
loose attitudinal indoctrination that has made them receptive
only to certain kinds of very negative messages about the country
they live in and the culture they inhabit. He summarizes this attitude with the term "adversary culture," and claims that

> Adversary culture is not so much experienced as it is learned. In liter-
> ary studies in American universities, the way for it has been smoothly
> prepared. The modernist writers have become entrenched in the curricu-
> lum. Eliot, Joyce, Pound, Beckett—these became the great literary fig-
> ures. As they were taught, their views—The jig is up, the game is over;
> in short, the "Wasteland" outlook—became not merely prominent but
> dominant. That these views were taught in wildly oversimplified form is
> not beside but part of the point. . . . Over the same period American
> literature cast off its former status as a dependency of English literature to
> become a full-blown subject of its own. But it was a subject taught with a
> special twist, for American literature, in the classroom, became a litera-
> ture chiefly of alienation. . . .
> The battle [was] against business, the small town, the middle class,
> then (though assuredly not now) the academy—against everything, in
> short, that used to travel under the banner of American Philistia. But
> that banner has since been lowered; Philistia long ago ran up the white
> flag. . . . The adversary culture now bids fair to become the mainstream
> culture.

I hope no one concludes from my use of the word "indoctrination" that either Epstein or I is talking about a plot. But I think it is
true that American culture is growing more rather than less tribalized by the year, by which terminology I mean to imply that its

internal divisions are increasingly superstitious in nature rather than political, more governed by irrational prejudices about the humane values and intentions of members of other tribes, more a product of emotion than of self-interest. In a democracy such a process can only lead to muddle and confusion; in our national literature, I would argue, it has led to a kind of crisis in the relationship between author and audience. But hardly of the sort Larsen is talking about.

1978

The Famous
Bread Loaf Writers' School

Bookchat in the Vermont Woods

Along with literally hundreds of new, academically sponsored "little magazines" and the decision by many university presses to publish original poems, short stories, and novels, the creative-writing boom—the only growth area these days in the humanities—has led to the great expansion of writers' conferences. The May, 1979, edition of *The Writer* magazine listed 137 held in June, July, and August of that year alone. Twenty-two were convened in California, among them "Women's Voices: A Creative Writing Workshop" at Santa Cruz, "Children's Literature and the Human Dimension" at Davis, "The Black Writers' Workshop" at Los Angeles, and the "Forest Home School of Christian Writing" at Forest Falls. New Yorkers could choose among twenty conferences; Texas had four; and there were three writers' conferences each in Connecticut, Maine, Virginia, Kentucky, Minnesota, Arkansas, Indiana, Utah, North Carolina, and Massachusetts. Colorado had seven; Michigan five; Nebraska, New Hampshire, and New Mexico two each; Kansas, Iowa, Tennessee, and New Jersey one apiece. The Second Annual Crossroads Writers' Conference convened last September in the Canal Zone, at just about the time the zone became Panamanian property.

In promoting writers' conferences, as in saving souls, celebrities are the big draw. What Oral Roberts and Billy Graham are to the ambitious evangelist, John Gardner, Irving, and Updike are to the conference director. Messrs. Irving and Gardner put in appearances this summer at Bennington in July and Bread Loaf in

August; Mr. Updike showed up at the Eastern Writers' Conference at Salem State in Massachusetts. E. L. Doctorow was at St. Lawrence; Joseph Heller, Irwin Shaw, Betty Friedan, Edward Albee, and Peter Maas testified at Hofstra; and Bernard Malamud, Grace Paley, Seymour Krim, John Leonard, John Ashbery, Charles Simic, and W. D. Snodgrass were all at Bennington with Messrs. Gardner and Irving (giving that gathering a heavy lead in the celebrity sweepstakes). But there are too few celebrities to go around. Novelists and poets who earn little or nothing from the sale of their work can nevertheless make the 40 percent bracket by teaching and hitting the reading and conference circuit. Just a few years of this business, one realizes, and almost every respectable author who rides the circuit will know all of the others. If one is impressed by the derivative nature of much of our national literature and by the relentless overpraising of bad and mediocre books as if they were effusions of pure genius, only half the answer is to be found in the economics of corporate publishing. For the rest one must inquire at camp meetings like Bread Loaf, which is both the oldest and best-known of them all.

The Bread Loaf Writers' Conference began in 1926, during perhaps the most fruitful period ever in American letters. Among the books published in 1926 alone were Dos Passos' *Manhattan Transfer*, Dreiser's *An American Tragedy*, Fitzgerald's *The Great Gatsby*, Sherwood Anderson's *Dark Laughter*, and volumes of poetry by Pound, Eliot, and MacLeish. The 1926 Pulitzer Prize for fiction went to Sinclair Lewis for *Arrowsmith;* he refused it. Langston Hughes, busing tables in Washington, D.C., was unable to get into the segregated theater where Vachel Lindsay was reading, and so he left three of his own poems beside Lindsay's plate as a tribute. Lindsay began his performance by reading them, and reporters greeted Hughes in the hotel kitchen the next morning.

In 1926, first novels by Hemingway (*The Sun Also Rises)* and Faulkner (*Soldier's Pay*) were published, and outside the United States books by D. H. Lawrence, Ford Madox Ford, Aldous Huxley, Kipling, Kafka, Yeats, Isaac Babel, Freud, Gide, Nabokov, T. E. Lawrence, and I. A. Richards. Sean O'Casey's *The Plough and the Stars* provoked a riot in Dublin.

Neither in the United States nor anywhere else was it possible to earn an undergraduate or a graduate degree in creative writing. Hemingway did not attend college at all; Faulkner lasted a few months as a "special student" at the University of Mississippi before dropping out.

Sponsored by Middlebury College on its Bread Loaf campus (consisting of a former inn, several guest houses, and outbuildings sixteen miles from Middlebury, Vermont, in the Green Mountain National Forest), the Writers' Conference did not in 1926, and does not now, offer academic credit. Many other conferences do, including Bread Loaf's downstate rival at Bennington College, where graduate credit may be earned toward the Master of Fine Arts, accepted as the terminal degree for the purposes of becoming a tenured faculty member. Its first brochure stressed "professional criticism that should result in marketable writing"; the 1979 edition emphasizes "writing as a skill (a crafty art), and writing as trade or profession," a construction whose cuteness may betray an intent to compromise between the worlds of commerce and art. In his history of the conference's first thirty years, former director Theodore Morrison says flatly that writing cannot be taught, although as a skill it can surely be learned. Instruction, he holds, may be as wasted on people of great talent as it is useless to people with none at all. "Talents of a middle order, from humble to truly distinguished," he says, "may well profit."

Through the Depression and the war years, Bread Loaf sometimes had to struggle to find enough students to survive, gaining eminence gradually, and chiefly, Mr. Morrison makes clear, through the continued association of Robert Frost. Others associated with the conference over the years—Bernard DeVoto, John Fischer (both former *Harper's* editors), Louis Untermeyer, William Sloane, John Farrar, George P. Elliott, and John Ciardi—have all been men of letters in the fullest sense: poet, novelist, essayist, critic, anthologist, editor, publisher, columnist, short-story writer, translator, historian, and teacher.

But not all literary talents are nourished by two weeks of "book-chat" in the Vermont woods; a list of people who visited just once is as revealing as would be a list of writers who never came. Sinclair Lewis and James T. Farrell—whose death in Chicago during this year's conference was scarcely mentioned—got famously and obstreperously drunk on brief visits. W. H. Auden, Saul Bellow, William Carlos Williams, and Richard Wright also did not see fit to return. As early as 1930, however, Bread Loaf was already attracting sufficient notice for Frost to write Untermeyer complaining: "I am left out of the Two Week Manuscript Sales Fair." At present, Bread Loaf rests on its reputation as the most serious and selective of all the writers' conferences held in the United States. Last August it drew as staff members John Gardner, Gail Godwin, John Irving, Donald Justice, David Madden, Howard Nemerov, Tim O'Brien, Robert Pack, Linda Pastan, Stanley Plumly, Lore Segal, Nancy Willard, Geoffrey Wolff, and Stanley Bates to tutor more than two hundred writers and aspiring writers. For two weeks, television and radio were outlawed, and newspapers were eschewed in favor of forty-three fiction and poetry readings, scheduled (and more impromptu) workshop sessions, student-teacher conferences, and endless talk.

Instruction at Bread Loaf has always been more practical than abstract. These days, the bias of the staff, in keeping with the participation of John Gardner, is Aristotelian, according to conference director Robert Pack, and deliberate: toward narrative forms possessed of a beginning, middle, and end, in poetry as well as in fiction. "Plot," poet Stanley Plumly told his students, "is what is so damned important for establishing the poem's ability to be believed." Mr. Plumly spoke as one heartily sick, as well he might be, of what Brendan Galvin in *Ploughshares* recently called "angst by blueprint . . . , the Mumbling Poem (that) substitutes odd imagery for direct statement, and a maundering tone for real feeling, and . . . patronizes the reader by *Telling* him how to feel rather than *Showing* him coherent particulars and letting him judge for himself."

Fiction-writing classes at Bread Loaf are devoted to matters of technique: characterization, point of view, plot, and openings. The first paragraphs of a fictive work, John Irving told one workshop on beginnings, compose a promise by the author that he has a *story* to tell, a promise he or she must be prepared from the outset to keep. "It is hard if not impossible," Irving allowed, "to begin a story without knowing the end. If you don't know where you are going, you cannot begin with any authority—unless you are good at faking authority, which in the long run you have to be able to do as well. The best beginning is the one that makes you want to go on and which has no evidence of a single incompetency. That's the best reason to stop reading—an incompetency." Editors overwhelmed with manuscripts, he said, citing a remark by former *Esquire* fiction editor Gordon Lish, are looking for a reason not to go on reading. When they find one they quit.

All the classes I attended but one were like that: solid, practical advice. Even the limits of craftsmanship were discussed with unusual candor. After spending an hour and a half delineating and giving examples of every means of characterization he could think of, Tim O'Brien scratched his head and confessed ruefully: "If I tried to think of all this stuff while I was writing, I'd never get anything done." I had been warned by a novelist friend that "The more stars, the less serious the conference." Bread Loaf's "stars," however, have been attending for years; they are paid only $1,500 for two weeks' work and take their pedagogical responsibilities seriously. Here is no "Famous Writers' School" such as Jessica Mitford exposed.

Yet Bread Loaf is a school taught by famous writers, and suffers for that both in the workshops and at ease. For example, in one class Geoffrey Wolff told his charges, by way of accounting for problems in an amateurish student story, that first-person narration was almost always to be avoided. Perhaps he meant to say that the first-person mode often leads the beginner into autobiography, pointless digression, or both. In any event, the class received this information solemnly, although a young man sitting next to me joined me in quietly writing a list of American novels one would use by way of refuting Mr. Wolff's contention: *Moby Dick, Huckleberry Finn, Lolita, Invisible Man, All the King's Men, The Great Gatsby, A Farewell to Arms. . . .* It was when the class sat on its collective hands that I began to conceive serious doubts.

Many of the staff members and assistants were grumbling privately about the level of talent and sophistication among the paying guests. Perhaps those other 136 conferences last summer had thinned the talent pool. Could it be that Mr. Wolff's auditors had not read enough books to dispute him? Not likely. A roomful of junior English majors would be prepared to cite at least *Huckle-*

berry Finn. No, the silence of Mr. Wolff's class was a matter not of ignorance but of politesse. At Bread Loaf, public disagreement of any kind was rare. The idealism of both teachers and taught was matched by an inert reverence that I have witnessed before only in the most socially prominent churches. Mr. Wolff was not taken to task, because at Bread Loaf simply *Being a Writer*—that is, having one's name on the spine of a book or in a byline—is mana. *What* one writes is at best secondary. In the holy penumbra of authorship, even the most common-place matters are mystified or ignored: who reviews whom, for example.

Art is by definition ethical, so anything goes in its appreciation. When book reviews are assigned to friends and colleagues of the author, the result is a form of consumer fraud that not only deceives the public but also cheats young authors with no taste for or access to the circuit.

Geoffrey Wolff's name was known to me before I arrived at Bread Loaf chiefly as a book reviewer for *Newsweek, Esquire,* and the *Washington Post.* For years, in short, his occupation has been the making and unmaking of literary reputations. The naive might wonder whether it is entirely appropriate for a critic to appear at such a gathering. But Wolff also writes novels, although I have not read any of them. I knew they had not been successful with reviewers or readers. I also knew he had just this summer published a biography of his father, *The Duke of Deception,* and that it had been prominently and kindly reviewed on the cover of the *New York Times Book Review* just prior to the convening of this year's conference. The reviewer was John Irving, a Bread Loaf colleague of Mr. Wolff's for several years. The lead review in the *New York Times Book Review* is not unimpressive; because of the low state of reviewing for many years in most of the country, it has assumed outsize visibility and authority everywhere. Most bookstores use the *Book Review* as a guide for ordering. The decision about what goes up front belongs to the editors; reviewers know roughly how important the editors think the book is by how long a piece they are asked for. It is simply the way of the world that a member in good standing of publishing circles such as Mr. Wolff will receive consideration from editors, as an unknown first novelist writing from Minot, North Dakota, will not: considerations of merit aside, I think most would say he has earned it. But the *Lead* review, written by a friend who had not only known him for years but had heard portions of the book read aloud at Bread Loaf, and who, moreover, was about to spend two weeks with him face to face there?

I have no reason to doubt that Mr. Irving's review was sincere, but nonetheless, I was mildly shocked by this nexus of interests, the most egregious example I had noticed since Kurt Vonnegut's review of his friend Joseph Heller's *Something Happened* occupied the same space. On my first day at Bread Loaf I made the mistake of mentioning my misgivings to the editor of a quarterly published in a location quite as far off the map as my home in Arkansas. "I suppose John thinks Geoffrey hasn't had enough commercial success," she sniffed as coolly as a Newport dowager whose formal dinner has been invaded by a cousin of the butler.

Not that I shouldn't have grown accustomed to it by then. As a journalist, my only experience comparable to Bread Loaf was in a small Texas town whose sons had shamed their elders by organizing a strike against their high-school football coach, who had led the team just the year before to a state championship. The reception accorded me as an outsider who had come to observe and take notes was very like my reception at Bread Loaf. Representing *Harper's*, in whose pages some hard things have been said recently about contemporary literature, I was all but frisked for my hatchet.

"If I were paying for this myself," one young woman told me early in the week, "I'd have left the second day. Bread Loaf has nothing to do with writing or with life. It has to do with drinking, sex, and hustling for influence."

Inasmuch as all professional conventions, whether of wildcat oilmen in Dallas or of *Litterateurs* in a mountain fastness, have much to do with these sins, I tried without success on later occasions to draw her out about why she thought she wasn't learning anything. Apparently she had concluded that it was best she keep mum and avoid my company. Later in the week, a woman with whom I had enjoyed a pleasant conversation about children and her husband's book demanded from a mutual friend to know whether I could be "trusted."

Trusted with what? I wondered at the time, but when I recalled the awed silence of Mr. Wolff's class, I understood. What the lady wished me to do was to become, in the conference argot, "a Bread Loafer," which is to say, a member of the club. The club is exclusive; members, furthermore, must be reliable not to notice the contradictions in the charter. In the immortal dualism first made prominent by George Babbit, a member of the club is a Booster, not a Knocker.

Sinclair Lewis' novel satirizes the American provinces of fifty years past; clearly the quality-literature business has nothing whatever to do with double-knit suits, joy buzzers, or adhesive-backed labels that read: "Hi! I'm John Irving, *Novelist* (Bread Loaf Group, Inc.)." Neither has it very often to do with the grosser forms of chicanery and self-deception familiar in, say, politics or commercial banking. But it does have to do with the care and feeding of serious writers in this country and with the propagation and dissemination of attitudes and opinions among consumers of their work. Like many another summer camp, Bread Loaf operates on the buddy system; because the camp activity is art, however, nobody is supposed to notice the teamwork.

Gone are the days when the dust jacket of a first novel summarized the author's history like this: "Bob Quinn has been a bartender, a professional gambler, a district attorney, a short-order cook, and a concert pianist." Now the dust jacket will say: "Robert Quinn is the recipient of fellowships from the Guggenheim and Rockefeller Foundations and the National Endowment for the Arts. The holder of an MFA in Creative Writing from the University of Massachusetts, he has taught at Ohio State, the Iowa Writers' Workshop, Columbia University, Amherst College, and Stanford. His short stories have appeared in *Kenyon Review, Sewanee Review,* and numerous other periodicals." The literary artist, in short, has signed on with the bureaucracy, and has a health and life insurance package quite as good as anybody else's.

I don't begrudge his security, for that matter. But what the Booster is not supposed to notice or inquire about is that in signing the contract, the author has made choices—about how he will live, what he will do, and the audience he seeks—almost as important as a decision to write in Spanish or French.

How delimiting this choice can be I did not entirely realize until I talked at Bread Loaf with the wife of a poet who had recently accepted a teaching position at a large public university known for its football. Acquaintances, she said, were muttering that he had "sold out." As his previous career had been not unlike that of the imaginary first novelist above, it took me several minutes to realize that what she meant was that his salary was high and the institution unfashionable. Whatever would those acquaintances say, I wonder, to an insurance executive like Wallace Stevens, a physician like William Carlos Williams, or a bank teller like the young T. S. Eliot, not to mention a Poe, Melville, or Thoreau? It is either a cheap irony or a significant one that while poets in much of the world are jailed because their governments fear them, in America they earn large salaries but are read, if at all, only by their fellows.

Bread Loaf has a formal hierarchy not unlike that of academe or the Great Chain of Being. Occupying the unofficial point of the pyramid are those staff members held most in awe by the customers. This year it was occupied by Messrs. Gardner and Irving, and, just below, O'Brien and Wolff. Mr. Irving had a best seller, Mr. Gardner a considerable academic following as well as a recent cover of the *New York Times Magazine* in connection with his assaults on everyone but Tolstoy, Mr. O'Brien a surprise National Book Award (he had been a staff assistant until 1978), and Mr. Wolff the recent front-page review. None appeared quite comfortable in the role of guru except possibly Mr. Gardner, who admittedly cultivates a vatic air.

Just off that eminence stand the rest of the staff. I did hear it said that Howard Nemerov was the *real* hero of Bread Loaf, but it was a flat assertion by a person who meant that by rights he should be. As nobody cared to differ in class with a *writer*, so nobody I heard talked about books written by staffers except in the most oblique and general ways.

Just below the staff in the Bread Loaf hierarchy are the staff assistants, less well-known and generally younger writers of promise—assistant professors of a kind. Then come the teaching assistants, or Fellows, who are nominated by the publishers of their first books, their agents, or other literary professionals. [Fellowships to Bread Loaf are underwritten by CBS Educational Publishing (parent company to Holt, Rinehart and Winston, which published Frost), by Houghton Mifflin, and by Time, Inc.] Below them and officially excluded from Treman Cottage—the scene of after-hours conviviality as well as lunchtime Bloody Marys—come the waiters and waitresses, who labor in exchange for conference scholarships. The base of the pyramid is composed of Contributors, who may submit manuscripts to the staff, and of Auditors, who may not. The rest, including myself, attend as Guests and have Treman Cottage privileges. Living quarters are similarly arranged so that Bread Loafers commune primarily with others of their station. This arrangement is as venerable as the conference itself, and a perennial disappointment to the more innocent contributors and auditors, many of whom imagine that their $450 or so will buy them intimacy with the staff. I am told that it was former director John Ciardi's defense of the hierarchy—staffers, staff assistants, and Fellows used to have tables set aside in the dining room, where all participants take their meals, and Treman Cottage was firmly off limits to paying guests—that was a factor in his replacement during the egalitarian early Seventies. Somewhat paradoxically, the Middlebury College trustees are also said to have been disturbed by Mr. Ciardi's indifference to individual manners, aside from the rules concerning who consorts with whom. As elsewhere, Bread Loaf became rather wanton in the late Sixties.

I think I would have preferred the old days. Now that *Being a Writer* is sacrosanct, the question of who ranks where in the hierarchy is suffused with a furtiveness that quite prevents honest discussion not only of how, in the simplest practical sense, a writer manages his business affairs, but of what one writes *about*. For example, David R. Godine, representing the publishing industry, told an assembly not to bother about finding a literary agent. Fellow Sanford Smoller objected, and sensibly so. Like selling your house without a realtor or playing the stock market without a broker, setting up to make a living writing books without an agent is something only the shrewd can afford. In the debate that followed, Mr. Smoller was made to feel like someone who has come to the Harvard Club in a leisure suit.

As for substance, I realized I was not alone in my bewilderment when I talked with staff assistant Larry Heinemann, a Chicagoan whose first novel, *Close Quarters,* is one of the most scarifying and detailed first-person accounts of Vietnam yet published. "What I keep hearing here is that you begin a book with a critical idea. That's not how it is, not for me anyway. The way I write, you begin with a story, a strong story. For me it's the Vietnam war—it won't go away . . . just won't go away." Reading Larry Heinemann, listening to him read, talking to him, you know right away that if his books do not meet with success it will not be for an excess of abstraction or a want of feeling.

What was most dispiriting about Bread Loaf was finally just that: its passionlessness. One found in place of passion an abundance of anxiety, the anxiety of people worried about where they fit and whether they are clever enough on their feet to engage their betters in conversation without embarrassment. I am told that in private—and among equals—very intense friendships, love affairs, entire cycles of human relationships are there compressed into a space of days. But I saw little of that. I find I must deal in negatives. There were no blacks, no Hispanics, or members of other visible minorities at Bread Loaf. I heard no earnest arguments about anything that matters other than books—very little discussion of the world beyond the horizon. And as for the literary concerns, the authors whose work did not merit discussion—whose names, indeed, hardly passed anybody's lips in all that "bookchat"—were: William Styron, Philip Roth, Saul Bellow, John Barth, Graham Greene, Anthony Powell, Thomas Pynchon, Patrick White, Walker Percy, E. L. Doctorow, Joyce Carol Oates, Joan Didion, Jerzy Kosinski, Bernard Malamud, Mary Gordon, Paul Theroux, Mary McCarthy, Norman Mailer, Richard Yates, James Baldwin. . . . Why go on? At Bread Loaf, the universe of accomplished writers is small indeed. Mention of Newton Thornburg, Richard Rhodes, Mark Smith, Charles Portis, Don DeLillo, Ella Leffland, Frederick Buechner, of any author notches below Very Famous, inspired no interest in most. I found that odd; most practicing writers I know read a lot. I wondered how many of the contributors, auditors, waiters, and waitresses on hand were getting any real idea of how difficult it is to earn anything like one's keep writing fiction these days (it is almost impossible to do so writing poetry) or of how many talented people cannot make a go of it.

When it came his turn to give a reading late the second week of the affair, Michael Angellela, a young nonfiction writer, took note of his genteel audience and hesitated to read the chapter he had chosen from his forthcoming book, *Trail of Blood*. *Trail of Blood* is the story of Albert Fish, a psychopathic murderer in the early part of this century, and of his capture by an obsessed New York detective. The chapter Mr. Angellela was persuaded by friends to read described Fish's capture and confession in words partly taken direct from a police deposition describing the madman leading officers to the body of a little girl. It was strong stuff. Not so strong as the pawnbroker's murder in *Crime and Punishment*, perhaps, no more graphic than the murders in the opening chapters of *Native Son*, no worse than the raid on the farmhouse in *In Cold Blood*, certainly no more upsetting, to come right to the point, than various of the mutilations and grotesque deaths in *The World According to Garp*, but strong.

As Mr. Angellela read, the discomfort in the room grew. One or two people got up and left, then more. After a time, staffer Gail Godwin walked out, signaling a more general exodus. Mr. Angellela was understandably upset, particularly later on when he heard that the word *sellout* had been bruited about, and that some of those who left had said they simply had to "make a statement." Mr. Angellela had his defenders after the fact, conference director Robert Pack among them. "I think it's far superior to Capote's book," he told me, having read the galleys prior to making Angellela a Fellow. "Capote somewhat romanticized those killers of his. The shock of *Trail of Blood* comes from the world—from reality. If anything the book is understated." The only people who would talk to me about why they left said they had been inadequately warned, or that Mr. Angellela had read with a dismayingly sinister glee. Most refused comment.

Larry Heinemann, however, had plenty to say. "The ones who left," he said, "are people who are never going to write anything worth a nickel. They want a certain kind of nice little story, something to go to bed on. Michael said, 'This is the psychopath against

111

which all others are measured.' What did they expect, a story about a puppy dog? Then there are the ones who walked out because they found something inside themselves that they can't handle. The kind who are really fascinated by the carnage of something like *The Deer Hunter.*

"They come here to learn to be writers, and what they want is a formula, and that's what a conference like this pretends it can give them. But there is no formula. You have to start with a passionate idea. Darwin had only one idea. But it was powerful."

I cannot here settle an argument over the merits of a book not, as I write, available. It is an argument that in any event was not pursued beyond the theatrical moment, though it should have been. But in the word *sellout* was hidden the whole complex of questions about subject matter, audience, method, and, yes, money that every aspect of Bread Loaf seems organized at once to exploit and to keep hidden.

Postscript

Harper's got a score or more of angry letters from Bread Loaf boosters, many shrill and personal—a confirmation of what I'd observed in the Green Mountains, I thought. But a couple did give me pause. My account of the reception accorded Geoffrey Wolff's novels had been dead wrong. In general, Wolff's reviewers had been well-pleased, and rightly so, I concluded after reading his witty first-person novel *Inklings.* It is about a creative-writing teacher who can't write his novel. The luxuriantly embittered professor goes to a literary conference, and here is what he finds:

> The air was sour, polluted by the complaints of ambitious people suffering from ulcers and disappointed appetites. They were spoiled children, bright kids, most of them, whiz-bangs at twelfth-grade English, people who would tell you an hour after you met them that they had scored perfect marks on their college board verbals, and many of them had. Most of them had announced themselves as writers before their second college year: writing seemed like a good idea, clean work for a bright spoiled kid. To go into business for yourself, keep easy hours, make quick killings with the movie folk, score with literate groupies—what could be nicer, more suitable? . . .

On what evidence did they base their claims for such a sweet bookish life to come? Intuition mostly and the invincible certitude that what bright spoiled kids want bright spoiled kids had better damned well be given. Hard evidence too: creative writing A and creative writing B. I had taught both; I had seen the future and there it was . . . ex-students who knew they were good because their fellow students had told them so, log rollers who had casually read one another's stories every week and criticized them as though they were consequential works: I like it, it's interesting, there are some interesting things in it, it didn't bore me, I wonder if that's how you spell "tragic," otherwise it's perfect, pretty interesting.

And now later . . . hungry, spoiled, bitter mummers and mountebanks parted up in their modish caps and bells, mixing their metaphors, wondering what had gone wrong, wondering who was screwing them, why they were always locked out of the interesting wing of the house, the wing they heard all the rumors about.

1980

The Other Carters

Five years ago, when Hodding Carter was dying, the city of Green-ville got its first McDonald's hamburger stand. Until then the company had considered the Mississippi Delta too poor and un-promising a place to invest. But only last year the owner of the McDonald's franchise for the area, a handsome young Oregon na-tive who is active in local Republican Party affairs, bought Feli-ciana, the home Carter had built for his wife and sons in a cypress grove south of town. As ancestral homes go in the Mississippi Delta, Feliciana was hardly venerable; built in 1947, it had served just one family for something less than a generation. Yet the mark that the Carters and The Delta Democrat Times—the newspaper that they have owned and edited there since 1936—have left on Greenville and on Mississippi generally is as indelible as it is in-calculable; many people see the sale of the house as the sad sym-bol of the end of an era.

No doubt many of the Americans who have become familiar with Hodding Carter's son, Hodding 3d, for the first time this year in his role as spokesman for the State Department—the offi-cial title is Assistant Secretary of State for Public Affairs—imagine him to be a relative of the President. In fact, he and Jimmy Carter are no kin. If a debt of gratitude is owed by either man, for that matter, it is the President who is the long-term beneficiary. It was the Hodding Carters of the South, father and son, who made a politician like Jimmy Carter possible in both a metaphorical and a practical sense. By their integrity and persistence they helped liberate the South from its own worst impulses—and from a politics of futile posturing which had alienated it from the rest of the country.

As a newspaper editor, as a civil rights advocate, as an organizer of the Mississippi Loyalist (i.e., integrated) Democrats and as a pragmatic analyst of the new order of Southern politics that began with the 1965 Voting Rights Act, Hodding Carter 3d may fairly be said to have been looking for a Presidential candidate answering Jimmy Carter's description for some time before the man himself came forward. As both a Southern chauvinist and a calculator of the odds, he knew a winner when he saw one.

For liberal Southerners, Hodding Carter 3d's decision to join the Jimmy Carter campaign staff was symbolically as important as the endorsement by Andrew Young—whose curious pronouncements the Mississippian is now obliged to interpret to the world. Since Reconstruction, white Southerners with liberal views on race have grown accustomed either to compromising their principles or consoling each other in honorable defeat. By training, inclination and inheritance, this other Carter, now only forty-two, is unsuited for both roles. He is also very ambitious.

So they are partly right in Greenville when they say that the sale of Feliciana means the end of an era; but as one era ends another begins.

Big Hodding—or simply "Big" as he is still called around town—is dead. Big was courageous, mercurial, shrewd, often sentimental, sometimes violent, a writer of prodigious output, an editor who won the Pulitzer Prize in 1946 and whose newspaper, some say, probably deserved two or three more in the contentious and ugly quarter-century that followed. His passing in April 1972 of a stroke was like the passing of a natural force in his community. The day of his death was like the day the Army Corps of Engineers dammed the Mississippi River above Greenville, a small port city between Memphis and Natchez, transforming the main channel, which used to run past the levee at the foot of Main Street, into a lake that opened into the river some miles downstream. The city's life would be calmer perhaps, but less vivid.

Little Hodding, as Hodding 3d is also known, has packed and gone off to Washington. People in Greenville half expect that he will never be back. Those inclined to gossip, which is the only thing about his hometown that Hodding Carter 3d says he does not miss, say that his pending divorce from Peggy, his wife of 21 years, makes him awfully like a man who is cutting all the traces. And while even his enemies are proud to see Mississippi providing the nation with an Assistant Secretary of State for Public Affairs—with any public figure, in fact, who is not an athlete, blues singer, demagogue or novelist—they cannot help but feel a small twinge of loss at the prospect. They wonder whether Hodding's younger brother, Philip, who has returned after an absence of twenty years to assume the editor's job at *The Delta Democrat-Times,* can feel a genuine commitment after all this time to the newspaper and the place, or whether he and his mother and brother will now sell out to a chain and leave Greenville diminished by just a little bit more.

"Something went out of Greenville forever when Feliciana was sold," says Ben Wasson. Wasson was a contemporary and friend of William Faulkner's—he helped trim the unpublishable manuscript that became Faulkner's first novel, "Sartoris," to an acceptable length. Under Big Hodding he edited, and still edits, the only weekly book page in a Mississippi newspaper. Dr. Matthew Page, a black physician who had been helped by Big in his student days and who later became a close friend, says that if he had known the place was for sale he would have tried to raise the money to buy it.

But "New South" symbols come cheap and often in Mississippi as elsewhere these days, and it is best not to make too much of the house alone. Mike and Nancy Retzer, the McDonald's people, are charming and self-deprecating about the question, and are respected here for having kept up the tradition of the place, which has always been to house and entertain visitors, particularly international ones, who are passing through town. Back in 1972, just after Big's death, it was one of several homes in Greenville that took in a group of young Russian Communist Party members who had been invited to Greenville by Hodding 3d on a State Department-sponsored tour. The Russians later voted Greenville their favorite American city. Earlier this year, the Retzers turned over their new house to opera singer George Johnson, the son of the Carter family's cook, Phalange Word, because he had long wanted to be married there. "Everybody expected me to put up Ronald McDonald where the Pulitzer Prize used to hang," Mike Retzer says with a laugh, showing off the study where Big worked as if by way of demonstrating that he has done no such thing.

The civil rights war of the 1960's, which made Mississippi perhaps the most uniformly disliked of American states, ended with an abruptness that startled everyone. The time is not so long past when Big was considered "the most hated white man in Mississippi," to use Leroy Percy's term, and was so treated: obscene letters, telephoned death threats, hangings in effigy, attempted economic boycotts against the newspaper, burning crosses and all. Percy is a planter and businessman who is the nephew of William Alexander Percy, author of *Lanterns on the Levee*, a pessimistic and beautifully written elegy to what he thought were the vanishing virtues of the agrarian South. Leroy's older brother is Walker Percy, the National Book Award-winning novelist whose most recent book is *Lancelot*. They were raised together with a third brother in their cousin's house, and Leroy especially was a friend of Big's. "The Greenville public schools," he says "are now 72 percent black, [Greenville's overall population is 52 percent black] and the two segregated academies seem to have gotten all the students they are going to get. If you had told me—or Big—in 1954 that this would happen, we would have said you were crazy." Indeed, after his Pulitzer Prize for editorials advocating racial tolerance, Big, who was regarded at the time as a wildly controversial speaker—Senator Theodore G. Bilbo of Mississippi announced in a campaign speech in 1946 that "no self-respecting Southern white man would accept a prize given by a bunch of nigger-loving, Yankeefied communists for editorials advocating the mongrelization of the race"—told an audience at the state university in Oxford that "I consider any program which would end the segregation of races in the south as unrealistic and dangerous to the hope of progress in race relations." Whether those were exactly his private convictions at the time is almost impossible to say. One thing Big never forgot, according to his son Philip, is that "we were putting out a paper in a Mississippi Delta town and Dad had no intention of being a broke martyr. He never wanted to give his enemies that much satisfaction. But there were several occasions on which he risked everything."

The story of Greenville and the Hodding Carters in the forty-one years since they started their paper there is an old-fashioned American one. It is a story about a man and his wife who came to a new town in the depths of the Depression with almost nothing in their pockets and almost nothing to their credit except talent, education, idealism, and introductions to the right people. The husband was ambitious and high-principled almost to a fault; the wife was beautiful, charming, some say even more intelligent and steady than her husband, with the will, as one Greenville native put it, "of a cast-iron butterfly." They began a newspaper and turned it into one of the best small dailies in the South, if not the country. They had many close and dear friends and had three fine sons, two of whom have lived to value, uphold and, each in his own way, honor his father's name. The third son died tragically in the middle of a time of public tragedies that seemed to conspire toward the end almost to break the father's heart. But in the end their ideas did seem to be prevailing and their paper had turned into a secure financial success as well. "My father died a prophet honored in his own country," Philip Carter says. "By preaching the virtues of place and treating its indigenous evils as aberrations, he did more than anyone else to make it so. In one sense what I'm saying may seem to reduce his life to Chamber of Commerce truisms, but he really did live the most gloriously productive life anyone in his generation could have lived. How many people can say they lived to help mold and change a place and make it just as good as anyplace else? That's all he fought for. That's what his life meant."

Many people say that Greenville and Washington County, of which it is a part, have always been different. Certainly it is the most *written about* community in the state, with the possible exception of Faulkner's Oxford. Greenville's reputation as a cultural center has long extended beyond Mississippi's borders, and Greenvillians boast a seasonal schedule of operas and symphonies that would make a much larger city proud. Not only W. A. Percy and his nephew Walker, who lives now in Covington, Louisiana, come from Greenville, but also David Cohn, a successful freelance writer and author of a fine book about the region called

Where I Was Born and Raised. Shelby Foote, the novelist and Civil War historian, is from Greenville and once worked on *The Delta Democrat-Times,* as is Josephine Haxton, a novelist who writes under the pen name of Ellen Douglas and whose *Apostles of Light* was nominated for the National Book Award in 1973. The Ku Klux Klan never got a foothold in Washington County, thanks in part to the efforts of W. A. Percy's father, LeRoy, and the immediate area never has known the mob violence common to many parts of Mississippi. Most blacks are prone to remind one that when the subject is the Mississippi Delta—the flat, crescent-shaped, almost incredibly fertile area of bottomland that David Cohn said "begins in the lobby of the Peabody Hotel in Memphis and ends on Catfish Row in Vicksburg" and which he characterized in 1935 as "cotton-intoxicated, Negro-obsessed, fearing the wrath of God and the Mississippi River"—one is talking about differences of small degree, of style, as it were, more than substance.

Big's immediate roots were elsewhere, in Tangipahoa Parish, Louisiana, fifty miles north of New Orleans. His own father, from whom he seems to have derived much of his quick-tempered nature and sense of fair play, had inherited some land there without acquiring, like so many other Southern gentlemen of his day, much of a knack for capitalism. Family legend holds that much of Big's drive for success was due to the fact that his father was bankrupt, or nearly so, in the year of his birth, which was 1907.

But Big's father was a local patriot, too, apparently to the detriment of his private affairs, a founder of what is now Southeast Louisiana University in Hammond and a member of its board until removed by Huey Long. Four years after his son had emigrated to Greenville, in fact, Will Carter won a seat in the Louisiana Legislature and there, at the age of sixty-one, distinguished himself and made the son proud by punching a pro–Long colleague flat in a brawl on the House floor.

It was, in fact, a combination of David Cohn and Will Percy pulling and Huey Long and his minions pushing that eventually brought Hodding and Betty to Greenville. Fired from his job with the Associated Press in Jackson, Mississippi, for "insubordination," Hodding first went back to Hammond, Louisiana, with his young wife and their life savings of $367—and founded the *Hammond Daily Courier.* This was in 1932. Their collaboration was to prove lifelong. Betty Carter was a Werlein of New Orleans—the music company that her family owned there used to advertise itself as "the original publishers of 'Dixie'"—and was educated at Sophie Newcomb. Probably no one but her will ever know the extent to which her activities as researcher and amateur editor of her husband's work made her more a co-author than anything else, nor how many editorials she wrote in Big's absence over the years, but the number must have been considerable. Not long after progressing past the stage where he and Betty reported local news, wrote editorials, sold—or more often traded for—advertising, and used an upstairs radio for a wire service, Big felt that he had to take on the Long machine.

The issues for the Carters were quite simple, much simpler than they have been for recent scholars and biographers of the Kingfish: Regardless of the highways and bridges, hospitals and free schoolbooks, what Longism threatened was the end of representative democracy. In his mostly autobiographical book, *Where Main Street Meets the River,* Big wrote that Long "spoke for objectives that we, the young men and women of Louisiana, had dreamed of in our dreaming days; but his voice was the voice of the soul's destroyer, and, for some of us, the price he asked and got was far too high for anything he could offer." Then in his mid twenties, Carter wrote editorials urging "shotgun government" to prevent the stealing of ballot boxes by Long cronies, an approach he later regretted. He joined the "Square Deal Association," a paramilitary organization that held armed drills and rallies of defiance, on one occasion burning Long in effigy. In 1934, on the floor of the United States Senate, Long accused the Square Dealers of plotting to kill him, a charge that was surely excessive, although, as Big wrote subsequent to the event, there were any number of men in the group who would have been happy to see the Kingfish dead, and he himself was not saddened by the event. Betty Carter remembers the afternoon in 1935 when Long was shot: "We had been upstairs listening to the radio for the news bulletins when we heard Walter Winchell say that Huey Long had been shot in the State Capitol by a man in a white suit. Almost immediately the phone rang, and it was Hodding's mother looking for his father. I said, 'He's here with us, now hang up, I've got to find Hodding.' For it was summer, and at that time any man in Louisiana might have been wearing a white suit."

But before Long died his puppet regime in Baton Rouge had passed a law requiring that all printing of public notices—tax lists, county proceedings, sheriff's auctions, etc.—be done only in newspapers approved by a State Printing Board appointed by the Governor. The Carters' paper among some other Louisiana dailies was not approved. During the Depression public notices, paid for in cash, were often the lifeblood of small newspapers. The Carters sold out and moved to Greenville. From that point forward, things in the city would never be quite the same.

Greenville already had a newspaper, *The Democrat-Times*, but the editor did not believe that a newspaper should hurt anybody's feelings and ran the operation accordingly. The names of white citizens convicted of misdemeanors, for example, were not printed. The Carter's newspaper, *The Delta Star*, published such information routinely; it survived its first major test by printing the name of a prominent local man arrested for drunken driving, despite the intercession of his relatives and friends. In a town of twelve thousand as Greenville was then, that was real news. The newspaper made some enemies, but everybody began to read it. Will Percy and David Cohn understood that over an extended period the thoroughness and honesty of a newspaper's reporting can make a difference to a small city, and it was that understanding that led them to persuade some of their friends, not all of whom would agree with Hodding Carter's editorial positions, to invest in the new venture. The old *Democrat-Times* responded to the challenge by falsely inflating its circulation figures in order to keep its advertising; at one point in the battle Carter and a notary public sat in a rented room across from the rival's offices counting aloud as copies came off the press, then filed an affidavit testifying to the true figures. Shortly afterward, *The Democrat-Times* capitulated and sold out to Carter and his backers; *The Delta Democrat-Times* was born.

In the years that followed, Hodding Carter became as fierce a local patriot as ever willed himself to love a town. Partly he followed his own father's example, and partly that of Will Percy, an enigmatic, melancholy, and stoical kind of romantic who seems to have strongly affected everyone who ever came into significant contact with him. Fearing the worst from the modern age, and having seen some of it in the Argonne in the First World War, Percy had retired to Greenville to run the family plantation at Trail Lake as if he were the benevolent lord of a feudal demesne. Big often quoted with approval Percy's injunction that "our mission is to live as men of good will in Greenville, Mississippi, because it is the sum total of all the Greenville's in our country that will make the kind of nation that we want or don't want." Given his combative and shrewd nature, moreover, there is no doubt that Big took delight in loving Mississippi more as the rest of the country loved it less. He was fond of listing, for Yankees who thought that the life of a dissenter against orthodoxy in the South must be one of unrelieved and bitter solitude, the civic and social organizations to which he belonged. When the Mississippi Legislature resolved in 1955 by a vote of eighty-nine to nineteen that he was a traitor and a scurrilous liar for criticizing the white citizens council, he was chairman of the Rotary Club's Ladies' Night, a counselor to the Boy Scouts, a Cub Scout den father, a director of the Chamber of Commerce, a member of the Board of Visitors of Tulane University, president of the Mississippi Historical Society, and a rector of St. James Episcopal Church. He gave frequent speeches on all manner of historic and contemporary topics to everything from the Mississippi Bankers Association to fifth-grade biology classes and served as master of ceremonies for horse shows, high school newspaper conventions, and Delta debutante balls. He hunted deer and ducks and turkeys in the bayous and on the islands of the nearby Mississippi and Arkansas Rivers, and was never so proud as when a suspicious game warden, who from what he had heard expected Hodding Carter to have a hammer and sickle secretly tattooed over his heart, admitted to him after a morning spent huddled together in a duck blind that "there can't be much wrong with a fellow that likes to hunt."

As *The Delta Democrat-Times* crusaded for reform at home, so Hodding Carter in books and magazine articles sought to make the state comprehensible to the nation. Altruism, it happened, made a nice fit with opportunity, and Big made the best of it. By the end of his career he had published close to twenty books, (among them such titles as *Southern Legacy, First Person Rural,* and *The Angry Scar*). His magazine articles numbered in the hundreds, and were published in every sort of periodical. While he made no claim to literary genius, he had a quick, lively, and lucid style, reminiscent, at its best, of a benign and slightly less intellectual Mencken. For those who do not remember it, a characteristic example of Big's direct approach may be seen in his answer to the Mississippi legislature when it designated him a slanderer of his state. He ran it as a front-page editorial in capital letters:

BY A VOTE OF 89 TO 19, THE MISSISSIPPI HOUSE OF REPRESENTATIVES HAS RESOLUTED THE EDITOR OF THIS NEWSPAPER INTO A LIAR BECAUSE OF AN ARTICLE I WROTE. . . . IF THIS CHARGE WERE TRUE IT WOULD MAKE ME WELL QUALIFIED TO SERVE WITH THAT BODY. IT IS NOT TRUE. SO, TO EVEN THINGS UP, I HEREWITH RESOLVE BY A VOTE OF 1 TO 0 THAT THERE ARE 89 LIARS IN THE STATE LEGISLATURE BEGINNING WITH SPEAKER SILLERS AND WORK-ING WAY ON DOWN TO REP. ECK WINDHAM OF PRENTISS, A POLITICAL LOON WHOSE NAME IS FITTINGLY MADE UP OF THE WORDS "WIND" AND "HAM." . . .

I AM HOPEFUL THAT THIS FEVER, LIKE THE KU KLUXISM WHICH ROSE FROM THE SAME KIND OF INFECTION, WILL RUN ITS COURSE BEFORE TOO LONG A TIME. MEANWHILE, THOSE 89 CHARACTER MOBBERS CAN GO TO HELL, COL-LECTIVELY OR SINGLY, AND WAIT THERE UNTIL I BACK DOWN. THEY NEEDN'T PLAN ON RETURNING.

But putting out a first-rate newspaper in Mississippi through the fifties and sixties involved much more than sticking one's colorful neck out from time to time. As an editorial writer, Big was what Dr. Matthew Page calls "the conscience of Mississippi" and its gadfly as well. The real uniqueness of *The Delta Democrat-Times*, though, lay as often on the front page as in its editorial columns. The collusion of the state's journalists in helping foster and maintain the racial status quo is well known. Crimes and acts of terrorism by whites against blacks, particularly by white law offi-cers, were simply not reported. Crimes that gained national atten-tion, like church bombings and killings of civil-rights workers, were often subject to fantastic distortions. The most ludicrous and well-known example was the *Jackson Clarion-Ledger's* five-column headline on the day Byron de la Beckwith was arrested by the F.B.I. in June 1963 for the sniper killing of Medgar Evers:

"CALIFORNIAN IS CHARGED WITH MURDER OF EVERS." In fact de la Beckwith had been born in California, had moved to the Delta city of Greenwood at the age of 3 and had lived there ever since.

In Greenville things were different. Hodding Carter's reporters covered the courthouse, the police station, and the community with accuracy and impartiality. If Carter may sometimes have seemed a bit behind the times by Northern liberal standards, he had always been a fundamentalist where the Bill of Rights was concerned, and recognized no color line in the administration of justice. Bern Keating, a close friend of Big's and himself a success-ful travel writer and photographer, says, "You have to remember that this was Mississippi and the way things were. But one thing that was different about Greenville, and this was mostly Big's doing, was that you couldn't just go out and beat up on some black you didn't like, or put a shot through his house. Because if you did and you got caught, it would be in the paper. In effect, Big said, 'You constables and deputies can't just go out and shoot a nigger on Saturday night—goddam it. You can't do that. There's no open season on 'em.' For that he won the Pulitzer."

Big's love of Greenville and the Delta, what amounted to his unabashed boosterism, was sometimes lost on his segregationist enemies. Like Will Percy, he foresaw many of the changes that the mechanization of agriculture would have on the area, and as a businessman and local patriot he lamented the out-migration that he feared would take away the best, most industrious, and tal-ented citizens of both races. But unlike Percy, he neither feared nor regretted change. If he saw danger, he also saw possibility. Indeed if there must be a "New South," and if it is to be mean-ingfully distinguished from the Old, a scholar could do worse than to study the passage of intellectual leadership in the city of Greenville from Percy to Carter. Where Percy defended share-cropping as "one of the best systems ever devised to give security and a chance for profit to the simple and the unskilled" (although with the admitted drawback that it was often greedily admin-istered), Carter recognized that it was doomed as an institution, that in order to survive and retain their virtues cities like Green-ville would have to attract industry, and, further, that industry, capital, and a mixed economy would bring inevitable change.

Such subtleties escaped the nightriding and cross-burning set and their spiritual kin in the Mississippi Legislature, which during the troubles made denouncing Hodding Carter by resolution almost as much a ritual part of the session as voting dry and drinking bootleg liquor. What most of them did not know was how badly it hurt Big to make enemies. He took all criticism personally, and often went to extraordinary lengths to maintain friendships with persons he disagreed with. Physically, however, he was fearless to the point of foolhardiness. Dr. Page, who was himself a leader in the civil-rights struggles of the 1960's and came in for his share of threats, remembers Big as what he calls "a true river person," alluding to the free but violent subculture that existed up and down the Mississippi even in slavery times. "Big had his Hemingway side. He was very volatile, a tough customer who would fight anything that moved. He loved to take up dares. He was a fighter, a drinker, a lover. You name it, and that was Big." Even in the middle and late sixties, by which time he was legally blind from the combination of an Army injury in one eye and a detached retina in the other, and when Hodding 3d was for all intents and purposes running the newspaper and writing the editorials, there were nights when the family could hardly get through dinner without a telephoned death threat. Philip Carter remembers evenings when the phone would ring and "somebody would say 'Carter, you'll never hear the one that gets you. We're going to shoot you in the back.' Dad would take the receiver and shout as loud as he could, 'Kiss my ass, you country son of a bitch. You'll have to get in line to shoot.' He thought that would really gall 'em—being called country." He was rarely without a pistol and kept loaded rifles and shotguns stashed around the house. He and his sons spent more than one night concealed in the brush near the entrance to their drive in anticipation of assaults that fortunately never came. Mayor Burnley recalls that when, as police chief, he had occasion to visit the Carter house in times of danger, he was always frightened more of Big than of his threateners. He would telephone ahead before going up the drive. "There was enormous tension in the house I grew up in," Philip says, "between a feeling for this community that almost amounted to a civil religion of place and the anticipation of violence. 50 percent of that violence was in Dad himself and 50 percent was real." During the worst part of the troubles, Greenville had a kind of vigilante posse of white and black men who patrolled secretly during times of stress to be sure nothing happened to the Carters, Dr. Page, or any of the other persons in town prominently connected with the civil-rights movement. Several persons expressed the opinion that in towns like Meridian or Philadelphia, Mississippi, Big could never have survived.

Guns never brought anything but misery into Big's life, although he never did learn to live without them. Philip Carter accidentally fired a .30–.30 rifle slug through his foot while on a deer-hunting trip to the Mississippi River island in 1959, and if Hodding 3d, just back from the Marine Corps, had not been in condition to carry him a half-mile through the woods to a Jeep, he might easily have died. But it was the death of his youngest son, Tommy, at age nineteen, in 1964, of a self-inflicted pistol wound while drinking with a girlfriend and playing Russian roulette in New Orleans, that came as close to crushing Big's spirit and will as anything ever did. Lifelong friends say he was never quite the same. Bern Keating says he will never forget when Big was led into the room in his house where friends had gathered after hearing the news: "He had just that day come back from Detroit, where they had operated on his good eye to try to save it. There were bandages over both eyes. Someone whispered, 'Oh, God, King Lear.' It was the saddest thing I have ever seen—tragic." The worst thing Big could have done to his eye was cry. At the funeral he wept.

Toward the end, Big was less and less himself. He drank more than he should have. Periods of the old lucidity and vigor alternated in the last few years with moodiness and dark mutterings. It is symptomatic of this period that his family does not know whether an anecdote he told that illustrates his character is true or not.

In June 1968, Big flew to California to give a talk on behalf of Robert Kennedy's effort in the Presidential primary there. The idea was to demonstrate Kennedy's appeal to persons from all sections. He used to tell audiences that he knew Kennedy was a "ruthless S.O.B."; that was why he was for him. Big had stopped off in Denver after giving his speech. He was on an airplane between Denver and home when word came of Kennedy's assassination. A stranger in a seat behind him made a remark to the effect that two Kennedys were now out of the way and someone should get the third. Sixty-eight years old and legally blind, Big came out of his seat, hauled the stranger to his feet and pummeled him to the floor. The co-pilot of the plane, upon hearing the cause of the brawl, told the stranger he deserved it. That is how Big told the story.

If Hodding Carter 3d ever felt stifled by the pressure of being the eldest son and namesake of his famous father, his public career has never shown it. A close family friend characterizes father and son this way: "Little Hodding is much more capable of compromise than Big was. Big could never have been a politician. Hodding is extremely intelligent, probably even more intelligent than his father. He is equally hard-driving. If you wanted to be unkind you could use the word ruthless. And he is at least as dedicated—no, I'll go flat out and say even more committed to civil and human rights. Of course, it's not as hard now as it was, so maybe he doesn't deserve the same acclaim, but he is probably even more effective at knowing how to bring about what he wants."

In 1951, when he was enrolled at Exeter, a prep school in New Hampshire, Hodding 3d asked his parents if he could come home to finish his junior and senior years at Greenville High School, on the grounds that, as he would probably have to leave Mississippi to make a living, he wanted to finish school there. He did come home, and after winning his class presidency, playing on the basketball and tennis teams, and becoming valedictorian, he went off to Princeton, where he graduated summa cum laude. In 1957 he and his wife decided to come back to Mississippi for a short time. "We felt," he says, "that we owed it to Dad and the paper to go back there and give it one year." He was tempted to go to Washington in 1960 when John Kennedy became President and try making a career, but decided to stay. After that, the civil-rights struggle began in earnest, and he never again thought about leaving until he considered it won.

That seventeen-year battle, he thinks, may have been the last of its kind that his generation, and perhaps the country itself, will ever see. "Those of us who stayed on in Mississippi and in other places in the South were always contemptuous of short-term soldiers. The conflict was elemental in a sense—maybe the last one we will see in the United States in which the lines were clear, and the enemy would stand up and identify himself openly. Now the question is less dramatic for a Southerner—it's what do you want to do for the next few years? We—the South—are on the plateau the rest of the nation wanted us to get to. On the surface, at least, our racial problems are solved. Now we find out that the whole nation stinks as far as that's concerned and that the underlying problems—the vast disparity of wealth between black and white, of opportunity—are not solved. But some of us, at least, are freed to a certain extent now. There are other things to do, and it comes down to a question of what's best for you to do as an individual."

Some in Greenville maintain that what Hodding Carter 3d really wants to do, and perhaps should do, is run for public office. They recall that in 1972 when he was actually—if quixotically—nominated for the Vice Presidency in Miami Beach (he withdrew before the balloting) he seemed for a time interested in more than just the honor. Certainly he has the politician's gifts. Witty and verbally articulate Hodding Carter has the rare ability to seem—perhaps in fact to be—spontaneous and entirely at ease, even self-deprecating, without saying anything at all that he does not intend to say or that will look bad in the morning newspaper. Like Jimmy Carter, he has the genteel Southerner's preference for avoiding both open conflict and the appearance of effort. He is also said to be a considerable flirt. He might have been born for his job as State Department spokesman, so naturally does he fit it. Others say that Mississippi has still not come far enough, and may not in his lifetime come to the point where anybody named Hodding Carter could win an election there. Carter himself is noncommittal about his personal future. He insists that his job in the current Administration is exactly the one he wanted, and while noting that, historically speaking, State Department spokesmen have not lasted above a couple of years in the job declines to speculate about what might be.

Reporters who cover the State Department regularly give Carter high marks for his handling of a difficult job—difficult both in execution and in its limitations. A man in his position can have a good deal to do with how an Administration policy is perceived without, however, having had much to do with its creation. As a former journalist himself he has not been surprised or nettled by the antagonistic undertone present in Washington news conferences as one of the legacies of Watergate. "If there weren't an adversary relationship between the Government and the press, I'd wonder what was wrong with the press." Credited by reporters with having assimilated an enormous amount of material very quickly, he detects a bit of regional chauvinism in the praise. "There is an inherent and ridiculous assumption up here that there is no way to be intellectually informed or involved unless you live in the East. I didn't write seventeen years of editorials for nothing."

Carter is said to enjoy excellent rapport with Secretary of State Cyrus Vance, with whose policies he describes himself as "very comfortable." He says he would rather resign than begin systematic lying. To date, no one has been able to accuse him of talking through his hat on that score. Tact and an ability to align himself with the moving edge of compromise have marked Hodding Carter's career throughout.

In the early sixties, Carter's opinions on the race question were very close to his father's—opinions he later had a good deal to do with changing. He describes himself as having been "a moderate segregationist moving toward becoming a moderate integrationist." Indeed, in 1963, just a week after the killing of Medgar Evers, *The Delta Democrat-Times* was editorially dubious about the wisdom of the provisions in the civil-rights bill of that year covering lunch counters and other private small businesses. "Just how can the Federal Government claim such powers?" the paper asked. To do so was "extending the interstate-commerce theory to a ridiculous degree, while depriving the individual of his historic right to do business with whom he chooses." But the rioting and, more than that, the shameful behavior of Mississippi's Gov. Ross Barnett over the enrollment of James Meredith at the University of Mississippi in 1962 began to convince Hodding 3d that "gradual," where the state and much of the South were concerned, in effect meant "never." By 1964, the year of the Freedom Summer, the

Goldwater delegates he observed while covering the Republican convention as a journalist, and particularly the Southern ones, "scared the hell out of me." In the following year he began his political career by becoming active in the Mississippi Young Democrats as part of a biracial group which took control of the organization. The Voting Rights Act of 1965, by effectively promising the franchise to millions of previously excluded black citizens in the South, had the potential, he understood, of changing the whole political ballgame. In 1968, he became a co-founder, along with Aaron Henry, a druggist from Clarksdale who was president of the state N.A.A.C.P., and Charles Evers, of the Mississippi Loyalist Democrats. The Loyalists, an odd amalgam patched together of Fannie Lou Hamer's Freedom Democrats (the black group that had so discomfited L.B.J. at the 1964 Democratic convention in Atlantic City), elements of the N.A.A.C.P., the National Council of Churches Delta Ministry, other civil-rights organizations, and a group of white liberals led by Hodding Carter 3d, were seated at the 1968 convention after a contentious struggle with the regulars of the Mississippi delegation, who could not, as a group, find it in their hearts to pledge support to the Democratic nominee. As co-chairman with Charles Evers and spokesman for the delegation, Hodding Carter made a good impression. But George Wallace carried Mississippi in 1968.

By the 1972 Democratic convention, Hodding Carter had put in three years on the party's committee on reforming the rules, and was made chairman of the Credentials Committee. He went to Miami Beach to nominate former Gov. Terry Sanford of North Carolina, then president of Duke University, one of a number of liberal Southerners who hoped that the convention would deadlock and turn to Sanford as a compromise. By then, he was chairman of the Loyalist delegation. He delivered a prime-time nominating speech for Sanford and had his name placed in nomination for Vice President. This time, Richard Nixon carried Mississippi with 78.2 percent of the vote, his largest margin among the 49 states he won.

In 1971, Philip Carter wrote a series of articles on the South for The Washington Post in which he suggested that a countertactic that the Democrats could use against the then much-discussed

"Southern Strategy" Kevin Phillips had invented for Richard Nixon was to invent one of their own. Quite early in the 1976 Presidential campaign, Jimmy, of the Georgia Carters, paid a visit to Greenville. Hodding, who once again favored the candidacy of Terry Sanford, believed he had seen the right man come in the door. When Sanford withdrew in January of 1976, Hodding switched to the Georgian, and joined the staff in the summer of that year. In November an odd-seeming, carefully nurtured majority of blacks and white Wallaceites carried Mississippi for Jimmy Carter by the barest of margins, with 49.6 percent of the vote— the first Democratic Presidential candidate since Adlai Stevenson in 1956 to do that. The solid South was intact once more.

Not everybody in Greenville is unanimously charmed with the success of the hometown boy. Besides predictable dissatisfaction on the right, there are voices from Hodding Carter's left. One of those is Owen Brooks of the Delta Ministry, a native of Boston who came to Mississippi during the Freedom Summer of 1964. Brooks believes that the current ascendancy of white Southern liberals disguises the fact that the races are still divided in Mississippi virtually everywhere but in the public schools and the shopping centers, and that "the kinds of changes we began struggling for ten or fifteen years ago have still not happened. In retrospect, certain individuals with national ambitions were able to get a lot of mileage out of the moral authority of the Freedom Democrats. After 1968 there was no real effort to organize the party at the grass roots. I like Hodding, but I have seen white liberals like him before. Hodding has always prided himself on his ability to talk to what he would call both sides. They will bargain for you, operators like Hodding. They will bargain for you without asking. When Hodding and Andy Young were down here for Fannie Lou Hamer's funeral, they had their arms around each other's shoulders and were crying.* 'We in the South wouldn't be where we are without her,' they said. Some of us say, 'We wish you weren't.'"

To a certain extent Carter understands and agrees with what

*Mrs. Hamer was a black sharecropper's daughter from the Delta town of Ruleville and the founder of the Mississippi Freedom Democratic Party. Many considered her the spiritual leader of the movement for black equality in the state. She died in March 1977.

Brooks says. He is uncomfortable in the role of "liberal white crusader," he says, but thinks some persons who now attack him as a power broker are being disingenuous about how the politics of the Loyalist Democrats—or, for that matter, any politics at all—actually work. "We had to make a symbolic statement in 1968 that we wanted an integrated party. After Kennedy was shot that year I didn't care one way or the other who got the nomination. All I cared about was getting seated. But those deals were all brokered, so to speak. At least a quarter of the battles I fought were with the left. We were arguing about image, and what it came down to was so many seats for the Freedom Democrats, so many for the N.A.A.C.P., so many for the Loyalists, and so on. This year at the Mississippi state convention it worked out almost exactly to 50–50 white and black and there were no deals at all. It was politicking, honest and open. I think a lot of our opposition is morally corrupt, too, but as I understand the democratic system you've just got to get in there and fight it out for votes."

Indeed, it is easy to see that like many other wars, the civil-rights struggle of the sixties was a rear-guard action against an economic and social system that was, for all intents and purposes, already gone; the beginning of a new one was still evolving and only partly understood. Neither Will Percy nor the elder Hodding Carter ever quite anticipated that the agriculture and industry they saw as antithetical to one another could, by 1977, be seen as practically indistinguishable from a sociological point of view. Sharecropping is virtually extinct. The isolated tin-roofed shacks that were as much a part of the Mississippi Delta as the August heat are being bulldozed to make room for crops. There never were very many small farms in the Delta to begin with, but the economics of the last decade that has driven overhead up 122 percent for the local planters, while prices have risen only 6 percent, has resulted in forcing small landholders to sell out or lease their land and work in town. Even cotton is no longer king. The number 1 cash crop in Mississippi in 1976 was soybeans. Rice farming is growing rapidly. Mobile homes and housing developments are extending into the fields around the larger Delta towns as the smaller ones slowly die. The highways are newly panoplied with businesses catering to an emerging class of industrial and semiskilled agricultural workers who until very recently never had money to spend on anything but the basics. Not just Mike Retzer's McDonald's, but a seemingly endless variety of franchised chicken, hamburger, and ice cream outlets, motels whose lounges are replacing the old roadside honky-tonks, shopping-center department-store chains, Datsun and Honda dealers, muffler shops, bowling alleys, all-night Konvenience Marts and vendors of mobile homes, all compete for the integrated dollar. Mississippi is still fiftieth among the states in per capita income, but the figure is now $4,529 against a national average of $6,399; in 1950, it was $755 against $1,496. Mississippi still has poverty, of course, and so long as the United States' economy is structured as it is, Mississippi, like New York, always will. But Mississippi is losing some of its distinctiveness, and provides less fuel for indignation every year to the Long Island Expressway School of Moral Outrage.

But what about the future of the Carters and their newspaper? A recent column published in *The Ocean Springs* [Mississippi] *Record* was entitled "Hodding Goes to Washington—DDT Goes to Pot?" According to Wayne Weidie, the author, *The Delta Democrat-Times* was suffering a deterioration in quality and foundering staff morale in the absence of Hodding 3d and the departure of a talented managing editor. When the article was written in January, however, it was assumed that Philip Carter, himself a talented journalist with a writing style quite reminiscent of his father's, would have nothing to do with the paper. Philip has been, since 1972, the editor and publisher of *The New Orleans Courier*, which he characterizes as a "vaguely alternative weekly, whose main kinship with the counter-culture is that it has never made any money." Even now that Philip is editing *The Delta Democrat-Times* and commuting to New Orleans every week to get out his paper there, Greenville gossips speculate that he is trying to talk his mother into selling the newspaper to finance his other ventures. While he admits that selling the paper has been discussed, that kind of talk makes him angry. While the figures that have been mentioned are tempting, all of the Carters know that the end of the newspaper would, in a way, be an end of their continuing emotional relationship with Big—and in a symbolic way perhaps the death of the family. None of them is ready for that. Betty

Carter is as active in the civic and community life of Greenville as she has always been, and continues to keep an office at the newspaper. Hodding 3d says he has too deep an emotional relationship with Greenville ever to call it quits. His brother Philip says that "one of the happiest discoveries of my life is finding that I can live in my own hometown. It's like resolving one's adolescent crises at thirty-seven. The place has a kind of vividness for me that only New Orleans can match."

Philip says he finds the newspaper a challenge of a kind he had nearly forgotten: "In New Orleans we are one of many newspapers and, being small, function as what you might call a 'reflexively impassioned advocate,' involved, but at a distance. In many respects that kind of journalism, which is very fashionable, is also very simple. Nobody expects objectivity or completeness. Here, people expect me to be fair and as complete as I can possibly be. I can't arrive at an editorial decision glibly—whichever way I go on a subject, say, like the proposed expansion of the hospital, I'm going to alienate friends. It sharpens the wit. We have too much of a tendency these days to slight the primacy of local issues and local personalities. If the republic is going to work at all, its going to work at this level."

Which is just about, when one gets to thinking about it, where the story began.

1977

Post Script

The Delta-Democrat-Times was sold in 1980 to Freedom Newspapers of Santa Ana, California.

Inside the Volcano

The Mexican Revolution Is Always Possible

Next morning, we came to a broad causeway and continued our march toward Iztapalapa. And when we saw all those cities and villages built in the water, and other great towns on dry land, and that straight and level causeway leading to Mexico, we were astounded. These great towns and cues and buildings rising from the water, all made of stone, seemed like an enchanted vision from the tale of Amadis. Indeed, some of our soldiers asked whether it was not all a dream. . . .

And when we entered the city of Iztapalapa, the sight of the palaces in which they lodged us! They were very spacious and well-built, of magnificent stone, cedar wood, and the wood of other sweet-smelling trees, with great rooms and courts, which were a wonderful sight, and all covered with awnings of woven cotton.

When we had taken a good look at all this, we went to the orchard and garden, which was a marvelous place both to see and walk in. I was never tired of noticing the diversity of trees and the various scents given off by each, and the paths choked with roses and other flowers, and the many local fruit-trees and rose bushes, and the pond of fresh water. . . . Then there were birds of many breeds and varieties which came to the pond. I say again that I stood looking at it, and thought that no land like it would ever be discovered in the whole world. . . . But today all that I then saw is overthrown and destroyed; nothing is left standing.

I have already described the manner of their sacrifices. They strike open the wretched Indian's chest with flint knives and hastily tear out the palpitating heart which, with the blood, they present to their idols in whose name they have performed the sacrifice. Then they cut off the arms, thighs, and head, eating the arms and thighs

135

at their ceremonial banquets. The head they hang up on a beam, and the body of the sacrificed man is not eaten but given to the beasts of prey. They also had many vipers in this accursed house, and poisonous snakes with something that sounds like a bell in their tails. . . . They were fed on the bodies of sacrificed Indians and the flesh of the dogs that they bred. We know for certain, too, that when they drove us out of Mexico and killed over eight hundred and fifty of our soldiers, they fed those beasts and snakes on their bodies for many days, as I shall relate in due course.

—Bernal Diaz del Castillo, *True History of the Conquest of New Spain*, 1632

There is no frontier anywhere in the world quite like it. It is as if Algeria were to border directly upon the South of France, or West Germany upon Zaire. To enter Mexico overland from the United States is to travel, in a matter of a few miles, the vast distance between those who have and those who have not, to be stunned into recognizing what most Americans, in our enormous self-absorption, forget: the first couple of thousand dollars make the greatest difference; virtually all of us live closer to the Rockefellers than we do to the overwhelming majority of the world's people.

In our literature the journey south has always seemed a descent into the infernal region of the human spirit, the zone of torpor, lust, rage, and barbarism. Norman Mailer, in his Hemingway period, speaks of the bullfight, which measures "the great distance a man can go from the worst in himself to the best." The Mexico Mailer saw appears in the works and often in the lives of the writers who have gone there and written about it: Katherine Anne Porter; Tennessee Williams; B. Traven; Jack Kerouac; Wright Morris; Hart Crane, who drowned himself by jumping off the ship bringing him home from Veracruz; and Ambrose Bierce, who vanished forever during the revolution of 1913, leaving in his wake a letter to his niece: "To be a Gringo in Mexico—ah, that is euthanasia!"

By and large the English have seen it the same way. Writers as diverse as Malcolm Lowry, D. H. Lawrence, and Graham Greene have found in Mexico their own visions of hell. Lawrence, who went in search of Quetzalcoatl, the feathered snake of regeneration, was moved to observe to his friend Witter Bynner, "It's all of one piece . . . what the Aztecs did, what Cortes did, and what Diaz did—the wholesale, endless cruelty. . . . The heart has been cut out of the land. That's why hearts had to be cut out of its people. It goes on and on and always will go on. It's a land of death." The protagonist of Lowry's *Under the Volcano* is murdered by Mexican police; his corpse is thrown into a barranca with that of a dead dog. Graham Greene in the 1930s feigned an interest in the Mayan ruins at Palenque in the jungles of Chiapas, in order to be allowed passage through the state of Tabasco. After riding two days on muleback to reach Palenque, he was moved to observe, "It seemed to me that this wasn't a country to live in at all, with the heat and the desolation; it was a country to die in and leave only ruins behind. . . . One was looking at the future as well as the past."

State of Crisis

Like all borders between very different cultures, the one between the United States and Mexico seems a kind of mirror, returning to the earnest gazer on the other side a reversed simulacrum of himself. Most Anglo-American writers have gone to Mexico in flight from the industrial middle class, from what Greene has more than once called "the empty, sinless, graceless, chromium world." Seeking heaven or hell, they have tended, in a country of economic extremes, to find it.

The traveler from the North plays out the scenes of his moral romance in a landscape conveniently dramatic, on a stage furnished with bandits, starving peasants, and rumors of revolution. Geographical distance in this regard is not so important as imaginative distance. But Mexico is, at least in the schematic sense, a Western country. Not only does it share two thousand miles of frontier with an overdeveloped nation it calls "el coloso," but it is filled with American investment and "el know-how." It is almost impossible to overstate the impact of things American upon the everyday life and imagination of the Mexican people. Sixty-three percent of Mexico's exports, 57 percent of her imports are to or from the United States. American banks have lent Mexico the greater part of her foreign indebtednes of twenty-five billion dollars, the highest such debt in the world. A huge proportion, perhaps more than 80 percent of the patents, are held by American firms.

Mexicans drive American cars when they can afford them, although they are made in Mexico and cost much more than they do here. When they cannot afford them they drive Volkswagens and Datsuns, also made there. Along with the rest of the world they drink Pepsi and Coca-Cola, eat hamburgers, and yearn for Kentucky Fried Chicken. They watch "Bonanza" and "Perry Mason," and they kill each other with American guns bought from the proceeds of smuggling heroin and marijuana into the United States. As economic imperialist and solitary hope, as protector and threat, the United States is regarded by Mexicans with a strength of emotion that surprises us, since we think of Mexico hardly at all, and then more often than not as a melodrama.

As diligent readers of the newspapers and newsmagazines know, Mexico is in a state of crisis, that most popular and indigenous of North American art forms. Her economy is a shambles, the so-called Mexican miracle of rapid growth during the Sixties having given way to an inflation rate in excess of 30 percent and a labor force of fewer than 17 million in a country of 63 million. Matters are complicated by a population growth of 3.7 percent, at which rate Mexico's population will double in twenty years. The Mexico City newsmagazine *Proceso*, quoting government figures, predicts that 1,195,000 Mexican youths will reach the employment age each year between last year and 1982. If things go as well as expected there will be jobs for about 300,000 of them at a time.

Agriculture, which employs just under half of Mexico's workers, is in disarray. In recent years the country has had to import food—despite its supplying roughly 60 percent of the winter vegetables consumed in the United States. The Secretaria del Trabajo (Labor Department) estimates that of 8 million persons employed in farming, 5.6 million earn less than 300 pesos a month (roughly $15). In the southern state of Oaxaca, Mexican government statistics show that 74 percent of the population exist on a family income of less than 200 pesos ($10) a month, 87 percent live in dwellings of one or two rooms, only 25 percent have electricity (fewer than that running water), and fully 87 percent cannot afford to buy milk, eggs, or meat. They live on beans (prices up 300 percent since 1975) and cornmeal tortillas (up 400 percent in the same period). A recent study in Oaxaca showed a 50 percent increase between 1972 and 1977 in the rate of illiteracy among persons of school age and older. Of Oaxaca's 2.5 million citizens, more than 812,000 are unable to read and write. Not only is the government incapable of building schools sufficient for the population, but many children must work at menial tasks, or are kept at home simply because they lack shoes, or clothes, or, because of their diet, the mental capacity with which to attend.

Similar conditions exist all over the country. Mexico has no form of unemployment insurance or public welfare. Mexico City, which offers the best begging and often the only hope of employment, however illusory, currently has 10 to 14 million inhabitants, and is growing at a rate that will double its size in six years, so that it will soon be far and away the largest city in the world. At the moment it is said to have almost a half-million whores.

During the presidency of Luis Echeverria, which ended last December after six years of mostly empty promises, there was much debate within the country and in other interested quarters as to whether Mexico did indeed, as Echeverria insisted, belong in the Third World. Like the argument about whether a good boxer can beat a good wrestler, such a question may seem more one of pride and point of view than anything else, and as such purely symbolic. *Purely* perhaps, but *merely* never.

Mexico is a capitalist country that has for decades invoked the shade of Emiliano Zapata in its election campaigns and employed left-wing muralists to adorn its public buildings with government-approved socialist surrealism borrowed from Orozco and Diego Rivera. The dominant, and, for all practical purposes, the only political organization calls itself the Partido Revolucionario Institucional (Revolutionary Institutional Party, or PRI). Here more than in most other countries the art of maintaining power requires the careful manipulation of dangerous symbols. The barest knowledge of Mexican social history suggests that most of its population enjoys objective material conditions as good as or better than ever before. If it were possible for persons on the ground to console themselves with the buzzard's-eye view, which has always given the best perspective on Mexican history, one might simply observe that Mexican medical care and sanitation improved sufficiently in the second third of the twentieth century so that the infant mortality rate fell from almost 100 per 1,000 live births to half that, and that for forty years there were no civil wars or large-scale rebellions.

This is the line pretty much taken by the boosters. In order to hew to that line, however, one has to ignore almost everything that cannot be expressed by numbers. For all of its closeness to the United States, and despite the more than fifty million Americans who cross the border each year (although fewer than two million venture deeper than twenty-five miles, and most of those to sterilized tourist sanctuaries), Mexico remains more foreign than Europe. It is not just that we are rich and they poor, as Octavio Paz says, nor even that our "legacy is Democracy, Capitalism, and the Industrial Revolution" while Mexico's is "the Counter-reformation, Monopoly, and Feudalism." There is nothing in the Mexican past, whether Hispanic or Amerindian, to inspire the cultural optimism upon which our society and economic system rest (as does classical Marxism). The ideas of progress and of the almost infinite malleability of nature and history simply do not exist. Paz writes in *The Labyrinth of Solitude:* "Man is alone everywhere. But the solitude of the Mexican, under the great stone night of the high plateau that is still inhabited by insatiable gods, is very different from that of the North American, who wanders in an abstract world of machines, fellow citizens, and moral precepts."

The Mexicans want what we have got, and if getting what we have involves the destruction of everything that makes them what they are, then with the other half of themselves they are ready for exactly that. Hence there is tension in the air, an almost palpable feeling of inward conflict that cannot help but take outward forms, and which expresses itself everywhere, from the way the people dress to their politics and the stories they tell.

Ciudad Juarez

The border itself is not so immediately dramatic as the traveler seeking vivid contrasts might wish. El Paso, Texas, tapers off culturally and economically into Juarez, Chihuahua, and one sees very few Anglos on Stanton Street in the last mile-and-a-half before the bridge. Between the dying hotels, the street is lined with vendors of cheap and used clothing, furniture, kerosene heaters, and previously owned hand-wringer washing machines. The peso devaluation late last year had the effect of doubling prices for the Mexicans who normally cross over to the American side to shop. Only the sellers of television sets and other small appliances seem to be prospering in the general decline. Although their products are still cheaper than the Mexican counterparts, and though it is in theory illegal to import them, they are subject only to small tariffs in the form of bribes to Mexican border guards.

Petty bribery, known colloquially as "la mordida," or "the bite," is Mexico's way of paying its civil service. One cause of what seems to Americans the excessive pride of office and officiousness displayed by Mexicans in uniforms and behind desks is not only that such a job is a badge of middle-class status in a country where that really means something, but also it is every man his own tax collector, a universally understood practice that seems outrageous to us only if we manage to forget all that we may know, of, say, building inspectors in New Jersey. It is not for nothing that boarding a train in Mexico City requires three tickets, two of which must be stamped eight times each by two different stamps, or that cashing a traveler's check in a resort town demands visits to three bank officials.

Drugstore windows on the American side advertise ginseng, "the root of life," as an aphrodisiac. A crayoned sign assures the out of pocket that *sus recetas de "welfare" son bienvenidas.* The last building on the American side shows sex films billed as XXX.

Immediately across the border it is all dentists. Juarez has literally hundreds of them within a few blocks of the Rio Bravo. Signs advise where and when to go for the Rotary luncheon and the "Club de Leones." The border towns are in general the most prosperous places in Mexico. Juarez houses the maids and gardeners, the short-order cooks and whores of El Paso, not to mention the importers and exporters, bankers, moneychangers, and smugglers who cluster along any border. Their countrymen further south are not over fond of those who live along the border, considering them chiselers, hustlers, and cultural bastards, just as they tend to be skeptical about the sufferings of American Chicanos, whose difficulties millions of Mexicans would give anything to have.

But even on the first-class train from Ciudad Juarez down to Chihuahua (fare forty-five pesos, about $2 for 233 miles) certain economic differences are immediately apparent. The ubiquitous luggage is a grocery bag of brown paper or plastic mesh. And not very far out of the station the electric lines and the paving quit, and the thoroughfares become wandering dirt tracks or trash-strewn gullies.

The city of Chihuahua has little to offer in the way of attractions, and, except as the eastern terminus of the spectacular train ride through the mountains to the west coast agricultural center of Los Mochis, would tempt few travelers to spend the night. Like most places in Mexico it has had its share of bloodshed. Hidalgo, the father of Mexican independence from Spain, was executed and decapitated here in 1811, his remains buried in a local church while his head was exhibited about the countryside. Chihuahua was also Pancho Villa's home, and his widow maintains a private museum to his memory at La Quinta Luz, but you must find your own way, for there are no signs, not even on the building itself. Inside you may see the car in which Villa was riding when assassinated, looking like a souvenir from the set of *Bonnie and Clyde*. Senora Villa, who by now is very old, must run the museum as a living, since Villa was never canonized by the state like the other revolutionary figures, and she draws no government pension. It is best not to interrupt her monologue once she has begun it, as she has memorized the whole thing and must start again from the beginning if she stops for a question. At first I thought the Villa museum a perfect memorial to the Mexican past, whose seemingly endless catalogue of plagues, rebellions, massacres, and betrayals one likes to assume are forever history. Then I went to Sinaloa.

Unreported Deaths

Sinaloa, of which Culiacan is the capital, is the richest agricultural state in Mexico, and, with its neighbor Sonora to the north, the site of some of the bitterest and most violent conflicts over land ownership of late last year. One-quarter of the country's food crops are grown in Sinaloa on 3 percent of its arable land. Most of the winter tomatoes eaten in the United States are exported from a narrow strip of irrigated coastal land in the valleys along the Pacific.

In Culiacan they have rediscovered one of history's great truths: the mystery drains from human flesh when you blow holes in it or dismember it with explosives. Last year in Culiacan that discovery was made precisely 2.8 times a day for a brief period in autumn, and over three hundred times during the year. That is surely a nongovernmental peacetime record for a western city with fewer than two-hundred thousand inhabitants.

One of the things they are killing each other for is money. The United States Drug Enforcement Agency estimates that of the $8 million that enters Mexico every day through dope smuggling, 70 to 80 percent comes through Culiacan. In its way the heroin business is as exploitive a form of small-scale neo-colonialism as one is likely to find, dangerous and labor-intensive at the grower's level, with profits multiplying almost exponentially at each step. A kilo of raw opium gum, or goma, is said to bring about six thousand pesos, or three hundred dollars, to the *campesinos* who raise it, and represents a few months of hand labor. The same quantity of gum can be sold to a processor for fifteen thousand dollars once it has been brought down from the mountains, and after refining and cutting has an alleged U.S. street value of one million dollars.

The *pistoleros* are the enforcers, the soldiers in Culiacan's little wars. They drive air-conditioned LTDs, the most luxurious cars available, without license plates to demonstrate their contempt, as well as to tip off the traffic police that they are not to be trifled with. There is no prestige in wasting a traffic cop. Citizens tell stories of having had guns pressed to their heads for honking at intersections, of raped daughters whose avenging brothers were shot dead, of children in the new suburbs along the river terrorized by the children of fathers who kill for a living, of half-hour gun battles in which each side carries off its dead and wounded and the police never show up at all. Officially, it never happened. Unless they are particularly spectacular, like the machine gunning of two municipal policemen on the cathedral square a few

143

months ago, or the fusilade that killed an ambitious assistant police chief a few days after I left, murders are rarely reported in any of the city's newspapers. Questions about arrests and convictions bring derisive snorts from residents, some of whom find amusement in keeping score among the combatants.

Montenegro sometimes goes without his license plates too; he does not wish to be easily identified. He carries a .9 mm automatic pistol in his waistband, a .38 police special revolver in his glove compartment, and keeps a .22 caliber Uzi submachine gun and a few extra clips close at hand. Montenegro is a newspaper reporter who shows his arsenal to anybody who asks, as if by way of announcing to interested parties that he does not intend to go out quietly. A small, almost frail-looking man in his early thirties, Montenegro wears a moustache, tinted eyeglasses, and double-knit suits, hardly the type, it would seem, to be the object of an assassination plot by drug smugglers. A newspaper reporter is small potatoes in Mexico, a kind of petty government functionary, like the mailman. No paper in Mexico pays a middle-class living wage, and certainly not *Noroeste,* Montenegro's employer, whose offices are so festooned with waste paper, broken glass, and sweepings as to make it appear that a bomb has already hit and nobody has noticed. Most Mexican reporters earn their living by collecting envelopes filled with cash from persons in need of good publicity, mostly government and PRI officials and businessmen. Without a payoff it is hard even to make the society page.

Before he took up journalism, Montenegro was a federal agent, and he has a reputation, which he does nothing to deny, as a knower of secrets. As a stringer for several American newspapers he helped originate several of the numerous stories and television news features that have focused international attention upon the drug trade, with the result that the Mexican government is making a U.S. assisted show of cracking down, a nuisance in some quarters, though nobody seriously thinks the trade can be shut off, nor even seriously slowed, short of what would amount to civil war.

Carlos Aguilar Garza stands in front of a wall-size aviator's map of Mexico, holding a pointer. The map, made in St. Louis, divides the western and southern half of the country into three large numbered zones. With the pointer Garza indicates Zone one, of which he is in charge, comprising the states of Chihuahua, Durango, and Sinaloa, stretching from Juarez in the north to Mazatlan in the southwest, an area somewhat larger than California. Zone one is subdivided into smaller alphabetized sectors, and on an enlarged map to his right these sectors are covered with a swarm of colored pins. Each brown pin represents between ten and thirty *plantios*, or fields, of marijuana. The green pins indicate similar concentrations of heroin poppies, the white pins plantations already destroyed. Most of the white pins are located within a few miles of Culiacan, and altogether there are perhaps twenty-five of them. Literally hundreds of the others run in a thick cluster from north to south, outlining the Sierra Madre. Garza agrees to allow photographs of what they are calling "Operation Condor," but only of the map and the back of his head. They may as well call it *Operacion Pato Muerto*, Operation Dead Duck. They haven't got a chance, and while everybody knows it, nobody will say it.

"It is a war," he says, "nothing else. We have four months in which to destroy all this or we will have lost. We must not lose. We are not going to lose."

Gen. Jose Hernandez Toledo nods. According to those sources usually deemed reliable in Mexico, in 1968, when the government sought to avoid the embarrassment of protesting students during the Olympic Games, Toledo commanded the troops who attacked and killed as many as two hundred of them in one night. His assignment here is viewed as evidence that Operation Condor is a serious one. Garza, an Assistant Attorney General in the Justice Department, has command of seventy-three federal agents and fourteen Bell jet-powered helicopters (the *Huey* helicopter gunships of Vietnam) given the Mexicans by the U.S. Drug Enforcement Agency. The general has two thousand five hundred soldiers, teams of aerial photographers, analysts to locate the fields, and agricultural specialists to tell him when the poppies are nearly ready for harvesting and so most vulnerable for spraying. Half of the Bell helicopters have been outfitted with tanks and spray-gun outriggers and thousands of gallons of Gromoxene and Esteron 47M herbicides manufactured by the Dow Chemical Corporation.

145

We have armed ourselves for a press conference at the airport. What started as an exclusive for Montenegro has somehow swelled into a media event.

The helicopters transport us 180 kilometers to the dusty village of Badiraguato in the Sierra foothills, a base camp for Operation Condor, where the party lands in a pasture and makes a loose parade to the headquarters building, together with the village children and dogs. Inside the general holds forth in a whitewashed room filled with the 1,003 weapons confiscated in the first twenty days of the campaign, examining for the cameras a Chinese-made machine gun and explaining that there are enough weapons in the mountains to start a small revolution. He praises Aguilar Garza, who remains nervously off camera, and introduces the governor. A chalk board of statistics is produced, showing the destruction of 960 hectares of poppies, 713 marijuana fields, 100 tons of processed grass, and fifty arrests. The governor urges Sinaloans to quit their lowdown ways and heed the exhortation of Lopez-Portillo, who only yesterday spoke of a revitalized and upright Sinaloa, leading the way in agriculture and industry. In the mountains behind us there are no passable roads, no electricity, no water, few schools or medical clinics. Before the advent of the heroin market, the majority of the 700,000 inhabitants of the Sierra Madre lived on a subsistence level, having no participating role in the money economy of the country at all. To the extent that they know what heroin does to people, they can perhaps be pardoned a bit for not caring very much.

Later that night I went for my walk through the city, looking for an ice-cream cone and a shoeshine. Three hundred murders each year would empty the streets of an American city this size, but, like everywhere else in Mexico, Culiacan teems with street life in the evenings, reinforcing the suspicion that what is going on in this city is not so much an anomaly as it is an intensification of the normal. The day of the singles bar is a long way off, but the erotic tension in the air is almost palpable. In the evening paper "la talentosa actriz Ana Martin" lays down the advanced line from Mexico City: Women's liberation has to do with work, not sex. A woman cannot have the same sex life as a man.

Every theater in town seems to be showing either La Violencia

146

del Sexo or El Sexo de la Violencia. In the bookstore window the main display is an eight-volume set of the Obras Completas de Norman Vincent Peale laid out next to the works of Irving Wallace and Harold Robbins. By the doorway are stacked the real best-sellers in piles four feet high, *Alarma*, *Alerta*, and *La Verdad*, Mexican versions of what the National Enquirer was before it tried to go respectable. On the front page of *Alerta* is a closeup shot of a six-month-old dead baby with a black-and-blue bullet wound through his chest, shot, it says, by his mother's lover to stop him from crying.

La Manzanilla

The village of La Manzanilla, Jalisco, does not appear on any map of Mexico that I have seen, nor does the gravel road that leads to it. La Manzanilla sits in the saddle of a steep hillside in a temperate region about twenty-five kilometers from the southern shore of Lake Chapala, a cigar-shaped thirty-mile-long lake that is the largest body of fresh water in the country, and very near the border between the states of Jalisco and Michoacan.

As things go in rural Mexico, La Manzanilla is a fortunate place. The climate is temperate year round—almost perfect, if what you had in mind was playing tennis or golf. The air at 6,500 feet is bracing and clear; even in midwinter and at this latitude the afternoon sun penetrates your shirt with a pleasant insistence. There is a wet season from June through September; from October through May it is as dry as Southern California. Even in the summer the afternoon temperature rarely exceeds eighty-five degrees; winter nights occasionally bring frost. Towns like Chapala and Ajijic, about twenty miles directly across the lake, are lined with the villas and walled-in ranch homes of expatriated Americans.

From the farmer's point of view, La Manzanilla is far from perfect. The steep hillsides retain little of the water that falls during the summer, and the soil is thin, wind- and water-eroded, and poor in organic materials. What crops are grown are done so for purely local consumption: corn, beans, and chili peppers.

The major source of cash income in La Manzanilla is the United

States. The men of La Manzanilla began spending their summers in California, Texas, and points northward during the *Bracero* program initiated due to labor shortages on American farms in World War II and continued until the early 1960s, when the U.S. Congress, under pressure from organized labor, put an end to it. From March or April through November hundreds of La Manzanilla's men migrate illegally to the "Yunaites" to find work. Most ride in the backs of trucks provided by contractors in Tijuana who charge them one hundred dollars each for the favor. In return the men get not only transportation but jobs, apartments, and forged identity papers, often complete with California driver's license and Social Security card.

When I met him, Willy was at the fork between the gravel road leading father south into the hills and the narrower one that branches off to La Manzanilla. Having little to do at this season, he had that day taken the bus to the lakeside town of Jacotepec about forty kilometers away to buy some household things for his wife and mother, catching a ride back from the paved highway with a pickup load of cows. He was very glad when I happened along, as the last six kilometers to La Manzanilla are mostly uphill, and seven months a year of driving on the Southern California freeways, joined with the idleness of his winters at home, have left him, at twenty-three, a bit stout.

Willy's proper name is Guillermo Barrios Cordoba, but he prefers the nickname when speaking to Americans, as he considers that his boss in California gave it to him out of esteem and affection. "My boss tells me I am number-one weaver" is the way he puts it. Because he knows a couple of hundred words of English, Willy sits at a loom in a nonunion textile factory at three dollars per hour rather than doing harder and dirtier manual labor at the minimum wage or less. He takes every available opportunity to practice his English, asking the word for things he does not know and repeating it several times until his pronunciation is recognizable. His boss, he says, does not know that he is *sin papeles* (without papers), which makes that gentleman very generous with his vacations, as Willy has now worked for him for five half-years. He is very proud to show off his Social Security card and to emphasize that he pays American income taxes. He pays no Mexican taxes on his American income, nor any others that he can avoid, as he considers his government a nest of thieves. "El gobierno wants to get rich and nothing more. They do nothing for us here but take our money."

In fact, La Manzanilla has a new hilltop reservoir and pumping station, bringing fresh water into its homes for the first time, and for the past three years it has had electricity. "All of the men on my street go to work in California," Willy says, indicating an unbroken wall of simple adobe homes crowned with shiny television antennas. In summer there are very few men between the ages of eighteen and fifty in La Manzanilla. By remaining here the average laborer could hope to earn perhaps $750 in a very good year, and in a bad one less than $500. In Orange County he can make that much in a month, and is able to save between $3,500 and $4,000 of his salary to bring home by sharing a one-bedroom apartment in Santa Ana with four other men. "There I can have a nice car—1968 Chevrolet. Here no. There I have heat and air-conditioning and a telephone. Here is one telephone for the whole village—4,000 people." Of course, in La Manzanilla he has no need of a telephone, because everybody he has ever known lives within a ten-minute walk. But Willy isn't buying any of that, and neither is anybody in his family: his wife, his father, mother, sister, and two brothers. When I asked him whether he would move his wife to California if he could do so legally, Willy's mother answered.

"We would all go if we could."

"The whole family?"

"The whole village. Who knows, maybe everyone in Mexico would go."

"Don't you think you would lose a great deal?" I asked. "The village is very beautiful. You have many friends. This is your home."

"We would all go," she repeated. "All of us. There is nothing for us in Mexico."

Willy loves Southern California and will hear no criticism of it, except that he does not understand and is a little bit afraid of blacks. At three dollars an hour and four men in a bedroom, he thinks he is in paradise. He cannot imagine that many Americans, if they could visit his village for an afternoon, would think they wanted to change places with him. He has no illusions about the simple life, having tried it and found it difficult. If he has his way his brothers and his children will grow up to sit in the gutter in Mexico City or Los Angeles and read about babies with bullets in their chests.

Mexico City

Perfumed garden or inferno, the Valley of Mexico is the center of the country: economic, governmental, cultural, and symbolic, it's Paris, it's Washington, New York, and Los Angeles combined. The Aztecs arrived from the north only two hundred years before Cortes came from the east, driving out or enslaving the indigenous tribes in a series of savage wars. In the intervening time they so polluted Lake Texcoco with human waste that it was unfit for drinking. Clean water for the ruling caste of Moctezuma's fortress city of Tenochtitlan came from springs located on the hill of Chapultepec, now Mexico City's most beautiful and pleasant park and the locale of its wealthiest residential districts.

The contemporary moral symbolism of Mexican history extends back only so far as the Spanish conquerors: the conquistador is the villain to the Indian hero. A visitor ignorant of the nastier aspects of Moctezuma's rule could wander half the day through the magnificent Anthropology Museum in Chapultepec without encountering more than the merest hint of the human sacrifices that the Spaniards thought gave them an excuse, so far as they needed one, for slaughters of their own. Many Americans who visit Mexico make the familiar remark about the contrast between the finery of the churches and the poverty of the people. Fewer express bewilderment at the museum, a shrine to deities more universally respected to the north: Science and the State. The newspapers report that air pollution from the six-thousand tons of carbon monoxide and other poisons released into the atmosphere every day in Mexico City kills seventy thousand persons in the valley each year, something like the number, if you are prepared for easy historical ironies and ready to give or take a few thousand, that the Aztecs are thought to have been sacrificing and eating in the years before Cortes arrived. The same geological bowl among mountains that once made the valley floor a swampy lake draining inward from all sides now traps the poisons suspended in the air from the city's 1.5 million automobiles and its heavy industry. At the end of the dry season the dust storms of March and April carry human feces picked up from the slums and deposit them over the city. The destitute and the angry have been migrating here for centuries, but they no longer come in tribes and cannot expect to put the inhabitants to the sword.

An official study has determined that traffic in Mexico City averages seven miles per hour. As most Mexicans drive faster and more aggressively than New York cabbies, accelerating to high speed every time one hundred yards of space opens in front of them, the collective time spent idling and motionless is incalculable. Much of that time is devoted to horn-blowing and the shouting of insults, pastimes that have long since replaced bullfighting as municipal favorites. Mexico City has more than three traffic fatalities every day of the year, and is acquiring automobiles at the rate of twenty thousand each month. It is, in short, a modern metropolis, with all of the outrages and lunacies thereunto pertaining, a demographic and theoretical impossibility that somehow lumbers onward, and is, if you are in banking, medicine, government, law, academia, or publishing—any of the dignified or lucrative middle- and upper-middle-class trades—the only place in Mexico to live. With enough money in Mexico City you can buy anything at all.

Anything, that is, except peace of mind. Mexican homes have walls around them, a custom that came to the country from the Moors. Inside their sanctuaries, Mexicans of means can create the order and beauty that all but the most ceremonial of public places lack. But the walls have been breached by disquiet. There was great and immediate fear of a coup or a popular uprising here last autumn just before Luis Echeverria gave up the Presidency, the most serious worry since the student problems of 1968, when Gen. Hernandez Toledo had helped the government demonstrate just how far it was willing to go to suppress dissent. Mexicans are accustomed to a level of civil violence that would be considered open warfare in many countries—five students and thirty-nine peasants were shot to death by the police in three separate and unrelated incidents in Oaxaca within a week of my leaving there, without causing more than a ripple in the press—but the assault at the National University alienated and intimidated a large sector of the professional and middle classes who had assumed *their* children immune. As Interior Secretary, Luis Echeverria had been directly responsible for that event; after his "Third World" pronouncements he was suspected of megalomania, and a great many people feared that he would find or create a pretext for not giving up his office.

The curious form of democratic dictatorship that Mexico has evolved results in a cult of the Presidency that transcends our own. Even more than Americans, Mexicans are attracted to the mass delusion that their chief of the state has direct control over the nation's affairs, and that whatever happens, for good or ill, is primarily his doing. It is true that during his term the President has extraordinary power—the efficient machinery of the PRI is organized to give him exactly what he asks for. Mexican Presidents are for all practical purposes simply appointed by their predecessors. The congress, labor unions, and campesino, and landowner organizations are subdivisions of the party, and outside of the PRI there is no real politics at all. While there is considerable ideological diversity inside the bureaucracy, a party member who wishes to keep both front feet in the feeding trough does as his leadership requires. It is a commonplace, and quite expected, that the President leaves office as one of Mexico's wealthiest men.

What bourgeois Mexicans have sold publicly they buy back in private irony. In a week in Mexico City, as elsewhere in the country, I rarely heard the government spoken of as anything but a vehicle of self-interest or a large-scale conspiracy to enrich the individuals who run it. A Mexican executive for Volkswagen told me quite frankly that he hoped to make and salt away as much cash as he could before the political collapse that he considered inevitable. Under Lopez-Portillo he anticipated that things would be better soon—for business. Otherwise he thought perhaps Echeverria had the right idea: "We mortgage the country to American banks and then default. Then you take us over. That will be the only solution for Mexico." An American textbook publisher's representative who had been educated in Michigan said that his friends and relatives in the government maligned the new administration for bad theater: "They can't even come up with original scripts. If Carter is for austerity, then so is Lopez-Portillo. When he visited the States, they put it out that he took just six aides and one small piano. Well, he took a 727 full of flunkies and a separate plane just for his wife's luggage, and I know because my uncle saw the flight plans." It is like that. Everyone has an inside story, and all the inside stories add up the same way. Nothing is as it seems, and the graft is always worse than you think. "You want to know what Mexico is about?" the same man said. 'It's 'Fuck you, Jack, I've got mine.' That's the national motto." Asked why he chose to stay he shrugged. "People in the States work too hard. Here if I don't want to come in some morning I just blow it off. Nobody cares."

Mexico makes anguished fatalists out of its most earnest citizens, victims out of the vast majority, and opportunists out of the others.

The fundamental lie, Octavio Paz says in *The Labyrinth of Solitude*, consists in the superimposition of liberal and democratic political ideals upon an economic order that has for the most part remained autocratic, even after the revolution of 1910–17, which had no ideology in the sense we understand it but which seems to have succeeded in the long run mainly in superimposing one landlord class on top of another. As Paz puts it,

> Liberal, democratic ideology, far from expressing our concrete historical situation, disguised it, and the political lie established itself constitutionally. The moral damage it has caused is incalculable; it has affected profound areas of our existence. We move about in this lie with complete naturalness. For over a hundred years we have suffered from regimes that have been at the service of feudal oligarchies but have utilized the language of freedom. . . . Also, the founding of Mexico on a general notion of man, rather than on the actual situation of our people, sacrificed reality to words and delivered us up to the ravenous appetites of the strong.

When people in Mexico mention the strong they usually mean the United States, the holder of patents and bank notes, the merchant of manufactured needs, the exporter of technology and overseer of "favorable climates for business." American corporations who bribe governments in Western Europe and Japan are operating with what amounts to an open field here in the homeland of *la mordida*. Lockheed, General Tire, and several other companies admitted as much in recent U.S. Senate hearings. Many Mexicans, however, assume that the American government will use what power it needs to in order to keep things that way, a suspicion reinforced by the recent news of CIA payments to former President Echeverria. During the boom years of the "Mexican miracle," enormous profits were taken out of the country, but very few taxes were paid and insistent pressure was used to discourage social innovations of any serious kind, as an example of which last year's letter to President Ford from seventy-eight U.S. Congressmen announcing that Mexico was tottering into the grasp of Communism was perhaps only the most ludicrous example. PRI will bring in Communism, I predict, within five years after Texas does.

Corruption itself is not surprising in a developing economy and not necessarily, from the instrumental point of view, very much of a problem so long as bribes are in one way or another reinvested in the economy. Unfortunately, the wealth tends to leave the country in legal or illegal external investments or find its way directly back to the givers of the bribe in the purchase of important luxury goods. In the words of Samuel del Villar, a Harvard-educated political scientist at the Colegio de Mexico, the country's leading graduate institution, "the American attitude is that of the economically rational man: if these people are willing to be shafted, I will shaft them. If I can bribe or force or manipulate them to my advantage, I will. Since we in the United States have a stronger culture, we will shaft them. Now you might do that in Columbia without effect to yourselves. But if you do it in Mexico there will be feedback eventually. Cultural cataclysms do not happen in a moment, so there is a danger you will not notice. But your influence is destroying our culture and in the long run may destroy us politically."

Excesses and Lies

On my last morning in Mexico I went to visit Julio Scherer Garcia, the editor and publisher of *Proceso*. Scherer Garcia had been recommended to me by several persons, Mexican and American, as a particularly eloquent interpreter of his country's dilemma. "Mexico," he said, "is a country that has lost all of its imaginable options because its institutions do not function. We have a saying: in hours the country has lied to itself about years, and in years it has lied to itself about centuries. In this manner we have ended up with the forms of institutions, rather than with the reality. Our congress is not a congress, the unions are not unions, and the newspapers are not newspapers. Form masquerades everywhere as substance. A country like this is almost impossible to organize and it cannot be efficient. Furthermore, in such conditions it is almost impossible to be just."

Scherer Garcia paced the floor of his small office and gestured emotionally as he spoke. As with most Mexicans, it seemed he could speak of his country only with passionate affection or bitterness, having lost touch with the intervening moods.

"Imagine the following circumstances: one day in the Valley of Mexico all of the citizens of the country come together, the rich, the poor, the young and old, the sick and well, the sane and the mad, the blind, the deaf, the workers and the campesinos, the bankers, the policemen, and the crooks. All, all, all. All Mexicans together. We join at the Zocalo in front of the National Palace, and we ask the President to resign. He says that he will deliberate and return in eight days to give us his answer. In eight days he returns and tells us that, yes, he has decided to resign. We cheer and celebrate. All of Mexico has a great fiesta. Then in a few more days we realize that we have no options and no ideas, and we have to go to the Zocalo once more and ask him to be President again.

"I have no idea what will happen. There will be violence; in Mexico there will always be violence. But it would be sterile violence—simple anarchy, because nobody knows what we can do. And in Mexico millions are desperate for food and work." The buzzard may say it was inevitable, but if the Mexican volcano does go off everyone on both sides of the border will hear it.

1977

Politics in the Woods

The Wilderness as Refuge for Ideologies and Lobbyists

> Men nowhere live as yet a natural life. . . . The poets even have not described it. Man's life must be of equal simplicity and sincerity with nature, and his actions harmonize with her grandeur and beauty.
>
> —Henry David Thoreau

> In the beginning, all the world was America.
>
> —John Locke

The word "natural" is on the way to becoming *the* cant term of the decade, replacing "human" as an all-purpose modifier testifying to the moral seriousness of whoever utters it. Now urban as never before (75 percent of us now live in cities, as opposed to 56 percent in 1940), the United States is in the midst of a prolonged rediscovery of things rustic. Country music, once heard only in the boondocks—mostly the Southern boondocks at that—is now broadcast nationwide. Long-abandoned sectors of New England, Appalachia, and the Ozarks have gained population for the first time since the Civil War. Land that once broke the backs of settlers foolish enough to try to make it productive now enriches real estate speculators selling what remaines of Eden.

When it comes to being natural, however, no place compares with California. Nature, in the form of Sierra Club pantheism, was practically *invented* in the San Francisco Bay area. Tranquil-ized wilderness—nicely purged of scorpions, ticks, poisonous reptiles, and lethal microorganisms, thank you—has become the biggest theme park of them all. The theme is not the National In-nocence anymore, as perhaps it was under Theodore Roosevelt, so much as the prelapsarian self. If nature is benign, then by con-templating and merging oneself with it one can rediscover one's own primal integrity. Rather than cathedrals and monuments, we should be about the building of campsites.

Of course pastoralism is nothing new to Americans, and senti-mentality is nothing new to pastoralism. Nor do I wish in my skepticism to be interpreted as calling for the clear-cutting of red-woods and the extermination of whales, harbor seals, and the Tule elk. But concurrent with the growth and dissemination of West Coast Transcendentalism is a parallel and directly related boom in the manufacture and sale of backpacks, tents, pickup trucks, four-wheel-drive units, all-terrain vehicles, and vans. Also, and here comes the insidious serpent, in outboard motors, fishing equipment and licenses, hunting permits, bows, arrows, guns, and ammunition. According to the Fish and Wildlife Service, 25.2 million hunting permits were sold by the various states in 1976, an increase of 6.5 million over 1964. The bosky dells grow crowded these days, often by persons with different definitions of truth and beauty. The man who by meditating seeks Wholeness in the woods ill accords with the gun-bearer hoping to kill for meat. Hence conflict. To a large and apparently growing number of Americans, sport hunting appears as an unnatural, even a barba-ric act. But more of their countrymen are hunting—or buying permits anyway, which may not be exactly the same thing—and since they are living closer together than ever before, these mem-bers of rival tribes tend to want to use the same land for their vari-ous purposes. Things being as they are, that land is often govern-ment land. The dilemma presented by the deer herd at California's Point Reyes National Seashore, then, raises questions that no doubt will become more familiar in time. It is probably fitting that the argument should be jointed in Marin County, that peculiarly blessed community just north of the Golden Gate Bridge that, were such statistics maintained, would no doubt lead the nation in such categories as per capita ownership of bicycles, Cuisinarts, and foreign cars, and be near the top of joints smoked, vegetarian spas, and number of marriage counselors, sex therapists, joggers, and astrologists. As Marin goes, cultural historians of the next century are likely to say, so go the suburbs.

Antecedents exist. What drew my attention to Point Reyes was a conflict over deer hunting on a federal wildlife refuge in—of all places—New Jersey in 1974. There, officials of the Fish and Wildlife Service had proposed a public "lottery hunt" as a means of controlling a deer overpopulation problem in the Great Swamp National Wildlife Refuge in Morris County, about twenty-five miles west of Manhattan. The refuge itself comprises 6,000 acres of marshes and wooded islands and exists because the New York-New Jersey Port Authority considered locating an airport there in the late 1950s, rapidly converting local commuters and real estate developers into what are now called environmentalists.

As hunting was made illegal and all predators save the suburban dog disappeared, the native Virginia whitetail deer began to multiply. From 120 animals in 1964–65, the population had grown to approximately 360 by 1970–71 when the hunt was first proposed. By 1973, the hunt having been delayed in the courts, the refuge management estimated 590 deer. Studies had determined the carrying capacity of the range (the number of healthy animals it could support through a winter without starvation) to be roughly 250. Death by starvation was not only predicted, it was documented. In March, 1974, a researcher from the University of Connecticut came upon two young bucks weighing forty-two and fifty-eight pounds respectively and too weak to walk (normal weight for animals their age would have been at least one hundred pounds); in spite of hand-feeding they died soon after. A search later that year estimated that at least twenty-four animals had died of starvation in the preceding six months.

Nor were the survivors faring much better. Numerous animals suffered virus-induced tumors as a direct result of overcrowding in the competition for food. One doe was found with a grapefuit-sized fibroma on her head that effectively blinded her on one side; another, upon being rescued from a dog pack, was found to have between her legs more than thirteen pounds of tumors, which had prevented flight. Nutritional dwarfism, tapeworms, lung-worms, and hookworm-induced peritonitis were common among animals examined by a state pathologist after a hunt was finally held.

The initial lawsuit aimed at preventing the hunt was brought by an organization called the Humane Society of the United States, headquartered in Washington. (Not to be confused with the older American Humane Association, located in Denver, which is the one that maintains dog and cat shelters all over the country.) Later the effort was joined by the Friends of Animals, a New York-based group whose president is author Cleveland Amory (about whom more later), by the Fund for Animals, housed in Washington, and by an *ad hoc* local group that took the acronym *deer* (for Deer, Ecology, Environment, and Resources, Inc.). Given the evidence in the Great Swamp case, I think one is justified in turning around a question often directed at hunters by their philosophical opponents: How, professing to love wild animals as they do, can so many well-intentioned persons have persisted in so hurtful and grotesque a position for so long and with such passion? Before attempting an answer, I undertook a trip to marvelous Marin, where a similar conflict was being enacted.

A Vision of Paradise

The Point Reyes national Seashore was dedicated in September, 1966, after a sustained period of lobbying and propagandizing by local environmentalists. Just thirty miles north and west of San Francisco and separated from the more populous towns of Marin County by the coastal mountains, the National Seashore presents a vision of paradise as the contemporary pastoral imagination frames it. Geologically older than the adjacent mainland, bounded on the east by the San Andreas fault and Tomales Bay, the park contains roughly 64,000 acres of cliff-girted ocean beaches, fir- and pine-covered mountains, rolling pasture and brushlands, and pristine freshwater lakes. Native blacktail deer, bobcat, fox, badger, skunk, beaver, and even mountain lions exist there in varying numbers, as do some 330 species of birds, among them numerous sorts of duck, swan, pelican, heron, falcon, several species of hawk, and some eagles. Sea otter, seals, and sea lions flourish along the coast; fresh and saltwater fish and shellfish abound. In November and December great herds of California gray whales pass just offshore on their way south to Mexican mating grounds. Even so, a substantial part of the park supports dairy farming and cattle ranching under agreements negotiated with the former owners, at least some of whose families have ranched here since California was part of Mexico. Point Reyes is administered by the National Park Service, which is in turn advised on policy matters by a panel appointed by the Secretary of the Interior to oversee a number of parklands making up what is known as the Golden Gate National Recreational Area, or GGNRA. A traveler would have no difficulty in leaving San Francisco and journeying to the outermost tip of Point Reyes itself without ever leaving government land. The National Seashore receives 1.1 to 1.4 million visitors annually, most of them on weekends during the dry months of April through October, as the weather during the winter is often cold, windy, wet, and foggy, particularly along the Pacific. The surf off Point Reyes is as rough as any in the world, and swimming would be impossible, were it not forbidden.

On the Seashore's southern boundary, and some would say on the cutting edge of West Coast Transcendentalism as well, lies the hamlet of Bolinas. The prevailing ethos of the hamlet has been set forth in Ernest Callenbach's *Ecotopia,* a silly but revealing cult novel about the 1980 secession, nongrowth, and undevelopment of a nation of the same name that includes Northern California, Oregon, and Washington. In Ecotopia, it seems, dope will be legal but automobiles will not, and everybody will have plenty of time to get mellowed out. Most people in Bolinas today think they would like that—the majority of the town's streets are left unpaved, marred by ruts and mudholes in the interest of discouraging speed and outsiders—but they would have trouble with the prohibition of automobiles. Judging from the number and variety of motorized vehicles parked around houses there, they are at least as addicted to the open road as their fellow Californians. What would be more familiar, perhaps, would be the conversation. *Ecotopia*'s heroine talks like this: "'The forest is my home,' she said quietly. 'I feel best when I'm among trees. Open country always seems alien to me. Our chimp ancestors had the right idea. Among trees you're safe, you can be free.'" Even the reviewer for *Outside,* the new magazine begun last year by the publishers of *Rolling Stone* and deriving at least some of its editorial impetus from the attitudes unintentionally parodied above, noticed that the population of Ecotopia was, shall we say, somewhat exclusive.

> The blacks have conveniently seceded to their own private soul cities (where they are permitted, in an incidental flash of realism, to keep their cars); the Chinese are ensconced in a Chinatown "city-state". . . . There are, miraculously, no Chicanos, no Okies, no rednecks, no suburbanites, truck drivers, low riders, Piute deer poachers, gangsters, executives, or currupt politicians—all executed or re-educated, one presumes.

"It's enough," the reviewer concludes, "to make you go out and dynamite pupfish, or have a whale-meat barbecue over a 2,000 year-old bristlecone fire."

Any discomfort one might feel, moreover, about describing Bolinas as if it were a vision out of a bad novel is dispelled by a consideration of the town's history since it became neighbor to the National Seashore. After a nearly disastrous oil spill in 1970 drew their collective attention to the precariousness of their mock isolation from the trials of the modern world, Bolinas residents were shocked to find that the state department of health was annoyed at their pumping raw sewage from their village directly into an adjacent shallow tidal lagoon that separated them from Stinson Beach. Many became exercised when the local Public Utilities District, in California an elective body, proposed an eight million dollar sewer project that would have joined Bolinas with Stinson Beach and increased the likelihood of real estate development. As with the Great Swamp airport in New Jersey, the result was instant environmentalists. Persons previously content to foul their own lagoon became incensed with the idea of releasing treated (and chlorinated) sewage into the ocean. A voter revolt ensued, anti-sewer forces seized control of the Bolinas Public Utilities District. Readers who wish to read the whole story in somewhat gushy detail are directed to Orville Schell's panegyric on the sub-

ject, entitled *The Town that Fought to Save Itself*. In the book Schell
uses the pseudonym of Briones for Bolinas, partly because, he
says, the residents have grown so leery of media publicity that
"we cannot think of anyone who lives here who would be desir-
ous of boosting our town into celebrity status." What he does not
say, of course, is that he may also be acting in self-defense. One
local writer who composed for the San Rafael *Independent-Journal*
a favorable article on Bolinas as a pleasant place to settle had his
house and car vandalized, suffered threatening phone calls, and
was driven out of town for his troubles.

Having defeated the sewer proposal and substituted a much
smaller system on town property, the BPUD discovered the wonders of small-scale totalitarianism. California grants sweeping
powers to its public utilities divisions, in essence granting them
power over all aspects of local government except the police department and the schools. In 1971 the town passed a resolution
declaring "a moratorium on providing its service of water to a
new construction requiring same." In effect, zero growth. To this
date the BPUD has managed to withstand legal challenges to its
authority to mandate such a policy, although a lawsuit filed by a
group that calls itself the Bolinas Property Owners Association,
composed mainly of both the disgruntled minority and of persons who own land in the town upon which they cannot build, is
at the moment winding its way through the federal court system.

Contemporary pastoralism, of course, makes no sense without
antithesis. The sort of "self-sufficient" rural life idealized by latter-
day boosters of mellow "community" like Schell has nothing in
common with the sort of agrarianism that peasants all over the
world are rejecting almost as fast as they can get on buses for
Mexico City or Jakarta; rather it is a product of postindustrial tribalism made possible by the great wealth of the cities. Despite ideology, a town like Bolinas is no more rural, sociologically speaking, and much less self-sufficient than is The Bronx.

To most residents of Bolinas, it seems, San Francisco is The
Beast, representing Power, Complexity, and Compulsion as
against the Freedom, Simplicity, and Laid-Back qualities of home.
"Over the hill" (i.e., Marin County suburbs like San Rafael and
Larkspur), are, if anything, worse. Bolinas so hates tourism that

the Park Service and the California Highway Department have all but given up attempting to place signs indicating the whereabouts of either the town or the southern entrance to the National Seashore. They are destroyed as fast as they can be put up. Not only has the town resisted improving the narrow two-lane road leading into the park (and giving access to about half its acreage), but it has erected a "Road Ends, No Outlet" sign at the last paved intersection before that road winds its way, several miles further on, into the National Seashore. Schell says that 40 percent of those surveyed would forbid strangers from entering Bolinas by car; attempts have been made to blockade the only road. Park rangers and residents of nearby towns like Inverness and Olema speak sardonically of not having a passport to enter Bolinas. Others say they would be more than happy never to set foot or wheel in the village again—so long as the residents were consistent and agreed never to come out.

If the city and its more ordinary suburbs are The Machine, then Bolinas is The Garden: a kind of Walden Pond West. The town motto, one resident says, should be "Don't bum my trip." Almost anything goes, so long as it is not "straight." Okay are denim, fur, nudity, marijuana, hashish, and cocaine. Not a small proportion of the community does a little dealing on the side; some do more than a little; the "Bolinas Border Patrol," listed in the yellow pages, is a vigilante group organized to protect residents' homegrown marijuana plants from marauding adolescents in the critical days before the harvest. Also okay are electric guitars, amps, stereo systems, chainsaws, boats, motorized garden tillers, one's own household appliances, and cars, trucks, or motorcycles. *Not* okay are other people's boats, household appliances, cars, trucks, motorcycles, and other products of the machine age. Also *not* okay is any evidence of industrialism more obtrusive than the town gas station and the power lines bringing electricity into one's own home. Bolinas is the refuge of the contemplative self: factories, time clocks, power-generating plants, and oil refineries are for the despised and ignorant peasants in locations like Oakland and Daly City. Astonishingly, most locals would describe themselves as political progressives.

Quite ironically, as any real estate broker in Scarsdale, Grosse

Pointe, or Santa Barbara could have told them to begin with, one
effect of Bolinas' having raised the drawbridge against tasteless
outsiders has been a rapid inflation of property values. Property
values in the town have doubled and in some cases tripled in the
past five years. Who, after all, would not like to live in a scenic
oceanside community within an hour's drive of San Francisco and
protected from tacky overdevelopment by hundreds of thousands
of acres of state and federal parkland all around? Soon the only
people who will be able to buy in will be rock stars, slumming
movie actors, and renegade holders of trusts. The already tenu-
ous fiction of the village as a gentle, agrarian refuge for souls too
sensitive for the rough-and-tumble of the American marketplace
will become yet more absurd, and then impoverished cranks
who slouch along Main Street will be forced either back into the
city or into similar Freak Refuges elsewhere on the fringes of the
metropolis.

Nature Knows No Steady States

What has all this got to do with the question of hunting wild animals for sport and with the Point Reyes National Seashore? A
great deal more, as it turns out, than it should. Once seen as an
agency of salvation by most area residents, to quite a few the park
has come to represent a threat. With parks come visitors; with
visitors come motels, restaurants, gift shops, and, it was widely
feared two years ago, guns. Even the relatively less righteous
communities of Inverness and Point Reyes Station, which border
upon the park further north, have feared uncontrolled development and made some shift to prevent it, so far with considerable
success. In the *Bolinas Hearsay*, of course, a kind of mimeographed
bulletin-board newspaper distributed around town twice a week,
the issues are starker. Congratulating Rep. John L. Burton, the
district's Congressman, for having got through a bill preventing
the logging of some nearby redwoods, the paper went on to comment that "maybe now he is ready to have his consciousness
raised about *tribal* & *local* control and a new concept in *parks* and
the end of federal *dictatorship*." The parks, in short, should belong

not to the taxpayers who bought and maintain them but to the people who live near them.

Fortunately, Point Reyes' deer problem is not yet so clear-cut as was that of the Great Swamp, although there is reason to believe that eventually it will grow worse. Left alone, nature would have produced a solution in the Great Swamp: starvation on a large scale, epidemic, and a mass die-off that would have reduced the herd to a size closer to what the range could maintain. Unlike some predators—wolves, for example—the Virginia whitetail deer does not stop or even slow down reproduction in reaction to food shortages. In a relatively mild, wet climate like New Jersey's, plant life damaged by overgrazing would have recovered on its own fairly soon, and so long as local residents were willing to tolerate cyclic invasions of their gardens and ornamental shrubs, the overpopulation-starvation pattern might have continued indefinitely.

In Point Reyes the situation differs in several particulars. To begin with, the deer are not native to California, but exotics: European fallow deer (Dama dama), such as populate the game parks of the Continent and Great Britain, and the Asian axis deer (Axis axis) native to India and Ceylon. Several pairs of both species were released by a local physician, with the permission of ranchers and landowners, in 1947, and kept under control, once it became clear that small herds had been established, by hunting. "Back when I was a kid," a member of the Tomales Bay Sportsmen's Association in his early thirties told me, "it was like a hunter's paradise out there. Fishing, clamming, three kinds of deer, cottontails, jackrabbits, duck, quail. The fallow deer were the hardest of all; they were smarter than the blacktails, harder to find."

One reason fallow deer are easier to find these days is that there are a lot more of them. Hunting was effectively stopped in the park by 1970. By the time park resource manager John Aho drew up his first assessment plan in 1975, he estimated that there were as many as 490 of each species on the pastoral lands of the Seashore, and that given their rate of reproduction and the fact that they compete directly for food with cattle and sheep, they were about to become a problem. Both species, left unmolested and with little or no effective pressure from predators, could be expected, Aho found, to double their numbers every two-and-a-half years. Like many exotics the axis and fallow deer do very well in their new habitat, where the grasses they eat are quite plentiful, predators very few, and disease almost unknown. Unlike all native North American deer, which are browsers—feeding primarily on shrubs, bushes, and small trees along forest borders and in clearings (one reason, contrary to popular opinion, why there are millions more of them now than there were when white men first arrived on this continent)—both the axis and the fallow deer are grazers. Except during the dry months of late summer when browse is reduced here and the native deer also graze for a time, the exotics do not compete with them for food. But the exotics do compete directly for food with sheep and cattle. For every two axis or fallow deer grazing on their land, ranchers lose one cow or two sheep that they might otherwise pasture. If nothing were done for ten years, though, the five hundred deer would metamorphose into eight thousand and the ranchers would be out of business. Unimaginable as it may seem—and these are my projections, not Aho's—five hundred fallow deer doubling themselves every two-and-a-half years would become, by 1995, 128,000 fallow deer, or roughly two for every acre of Seashore. Added to the two axis deer who might also be expected to be on hand, not to mention the natives, Point Reyes would have a deer problem even more serious than that of the Great Swamp.

The projection is absurd, but sentimental objections to the killing of wild animals being what they are—especially when those animals are magnificent brown-and-white-spotted (axis) or pure white (fallow) Bambi-like creatures, many with stately antlers—sometimes one needs to flirt with nonsense in order to make a point. Matters in the Great Swamp grew very sad, and still many antihunters were not convinced.

The exotic deer are picturesque, and since they are not nocturnal like the native deer, but graze in the open where many visitors can see them, the Park Service believes they add a dimension to the visitors' experiences. Then, too, a national seashore is not, by statute, the same as a national park or wilderness. Human recreation is held to be one of Point Reyes' most important functions: removing all the deer—providing they can be controlled instead—

would seem an excess of primitivist zeal. Indeed, some question the Park Service's plan to reintroduce the Tule elk to a fenced-off area at the end of the peninsula on the same grounds. Why, after all, introduce another species of large herbivore to an already overcrowded range? But the Tule elk is an endangered species: new habitat betters its chances of survival. And the exotics have not yet occupied the region where the elk are to be placed.

Some would argue that nature's mythical "balance" be restored by reintroducing predators, but that is impossible. The indigenous mountain lions are highly territorial; regardless of how bountiful the food supply, Point Reyes already has as many as will tolerate each other's presence. Wolves need far more room to wander and are incompatible with agriculture and the keeping of domestic animals: while wolves will not attack humans they will run twenty yards to pull down a fat calf before they will run twenty miles to bring an elk or stag to bay. Bears are mostly herbivores and carrion seekers. Once man "unbalances" a wilderness it cannot be restored by fiat, only by near desertion and the passage of a great deal of time. Nature knows no steady states.

The Point Reyes National Seashore is in many ways as artificial a creation as New York's Central Park, and from an ecological point of view, infinitely more complex. The bureaucracy that would manage it according to human tastes is necessarily large. If three species of deer and one of elk are to thrive, if salmon are to return, if the mountain beaver is to increase, if the Bishop pine is to be preserved from gall rust, redwoods grow, the Douglas fir do well, and the pastoral zone not grow up in almost impassable coyote brush; if human visitors are not to start fires, litter, fall off cliffs, and maroon themselves at high tide on remote beaches, the Park Service has to take care of business. Doing that requires federal dollars, which in turn requires good public relations. Like all bureaucracies, therefore, the Park Service is habitually timid. Given essentially the same list of options available to the Fish and Wildlife Service in the Great Swamp case, the Park Service fudged it. After going through the motions of holding public hearings—hearings at which local sportsmen's groups supported a lottery hunting plan similar to the one proposed in New Jersey—the Park Service decided to do the job themselves. Rather than conduct a public hunt or issue rancher depredation permits, an option that was also considered, the bureaucracy discovered the perfect contemporary solution: let the government do the job. The rangers were told to kill the deer themselves.

When I first asked him about it, John Aho was understandably defensive. Although he has not hunted for sport in fifteen years, in the past two he has shot and butchered somewhere between 200 and 225 deer, often pursuing them by jeep. Already disdained as "tree pigs," Aho and his fellow rangers must now bear the additional stigma of assassinating Bambi. "You wouldn't believe it," he says, "but you get inured to it—the gore, the animals dying. It's like working in a slaughterhouse. Because that's all it is, slaughter. None of us enjoys it, and there are some who just can't bring themselves to go out with us. I try to spare them, find them something else to do." Asked if he would prefer a public or lottery hunt, Aho is the good soldier. "I support what the park supports," he says. But as he was given no extra money in the budget to support the deer depredation program and has to allocate time for it among innumerable other duties, he is not reticent in saying that it is less than a success. The axis deer, which run in large herds and can be chased by jeep into the back of a canyon where there is a road they are afraid to cross, have been brought more or less under control. They turn and stampede back into the guns. The others are less easily hunted. "The fallow deer are completely beyond our control now. I would estimate that there are now 1,200 or more within the park boundaries alone. Geographically and in numbers they are far beyond our capacity to manage them." Aho says he does not know what will happen or how far the animals are likely to spread.

While one cannot get anybody in an official position to confirm it in so many words, it is nevertheless clear that the decision to order the park rangers to thin the exotic deer herd—the first operation of its kind and scale the Park Service has ever undertaken—was made primarily in the interest of avoiding bad publicity. "Social controversy," after all, is one of those factors Park Service officials are instructed to assess in making their plans. Then, too, organized groups of sportsmen like the ones who expressed an interest—the Marin Rod and Gun Club, the Tomales Bay Sportsmen's Association, the State Archers Association—are

168

for the most part conservative and law-abiding. No doubt it was feared that many antihunting individuals and groups—serving as they do a higher cause—would not be so tractable. Then, too, given the local sentiment, both organized and disorganized fool-ishness could have resulted if a lottery hunt had been attempted. From the point of view of avoiding difficulty the right decision was no doubt made.

But should avoiding difficulty, in this instance, have been para-mount? From the California Department of Fish and Game's posi-tion, evidently so. A spokesman in Sacramento reminded me that the Bay Area has probably the greatest concentration of antihunt-ing activists in the state, persons who oppose any consumptive use of wildlife at all, and that many well-intentioned city dwellers cannot be got beyond a kind of instinctive sentimental reaction against guns and killing long enough to be reasoned with. "We try not to raise a red flag," he said, explaining why his agency did not press the issue with federal authorities, adding that as hunt-ers comprise a generally misunderstood minority, there is some fear of a referendum making its way to a general election ballot that would ban hunting altogether.

Considerations of class no doubt play a part, too, although per-haps to a lesser extent in prosperous, tribalized northern Cali-fornia than in other regions of the country. I once attended an emotional town meeting in western New England, where a com-bination of academics connected with the local university and property owners from Boston and Hartford tried to pass an ordi-nance that would have forbidden the generally less well-off na-tives from continuing to pursue deer, grouse, and snowshoe hare, as they had done all their lives. Revolutions, I came away convinced, begin from the same passions. Pat Norris, a bowhunt-ing enthusiast who wrote letters and appeared at a public meeting in favor of the lottery hunt at Point Reyes National Seashore, saw it that way: "The whole thing was an absolutely perfect example of bureaucrats trying to run the park system and not having the authority or the guts. Who is on that commission anyway? Old-time politicos and landowners. They represent just one class of people. You can look at them walking in in their three hundred dollar suits and know you've wasted your time coming."

The politics of nature in California has grown so sophisticated, though, that a single earnest individual representing himself is wasting his time if he expects a potentially controversial issue to be decided openly and upon its evident merits. The Bay Area chapter of the Sierra Club, for example, a powerful and well-organized lobbying group, is for the most part antihunting in sentiment, even though the national organization (which has waged fierce internecine struggles over the issue in the past) maintains a different position. Like the National Wildlife Federation, the Audubon Society, the Izaak Walton League, and other broad-based conservation organizations, the Sierra Club believes that sport hunting is a necessary and efficient form of wildlife management in what it calls "degraded ecosystems," which are defined as places in which human activity has had a significant impact. In the matter of the Point Reyes exotics the chapter was opposed to a public hunt on the grounds of safety, the fear that other species might be taken either inadvertently or deliberately, and a concern over precedent: that holding a necessary hunt would put the Park Service in the position of the woman who, having agreed to whore for a million dollars, has lost her ethical leverage when confronted with a smaller offer. So the Park Service, the chapter feared, might be pressured to allow the hunting of ducks, quail, and other game. The concern with purity, one suspects, reveals the true intent.

A Natural Complicity

Ever since taking up the sport of hunting I have been bewildered by the almost theological zeal of persons who object to it on principle. It is no use to argue, in the instance of Point Reyes, that a public hunt of the sort proposed would endanger participants and others less than the automobile travel required to attend; that the Park Service has, after all, been conducting hunts in such areas as the Kaibab National Forest and Grand Teton national park for more than fifty years; or that, if the job could be done safely on a little more than 6,000 acres of New Jersey swamp ringed by suburban development, then probably a way could have been found at Point Reyes' 64,000 acres.

One chooses to argue the issue using examples like the Great Swamp or Point Reyes deer herds largely in the hope of reaching persons who may themselves have no interest in pursuing game, but who are amenable to reason. Admittedly these are special cases, but they demonstrate what can happen in a wildlife habitat—what, in fact, *would* happen in most North American habitats—if hunting were banned. Most sportsmen, myself included, prefer not to hunt at all under such strictly supervised conditions as would apply in the Point Reyes National Seashore. One member of the Tomales Bay Sportsmen's Association who had hunted the area in his youth said he would not take part until the herd had been thinned, and the animals made naturally wary again by the hunt. Shooting a fallow deer now, he thought, would be too much like shooting a cow. A roomful of his companions nodded. Some volunteered, in fact, that they might submit their names to a lottery at least partly out of a sense of public duty. Others said flatly that they could use the meat; for sport they would prefer to drive north.

Such sentiments are not credited by the opposition, for reasons that I did not fully understand until I had been in Bolinas for a few days and had spoken to a woman very active in local affairs who conceded that the park rangers were not fascists, that the deer herd did need to be culled, but that it was, in her opinion, "psychologically cleaner not to have people out there having fun shooting deer." That, at last, is the answer to the rhetorical question I posed earlier about the antihunters who loved the deer there unto death by starvation: it is a matter not so much of loving animals more as of respecting one's fellows less. The literature of the antihunting movement is replete with the attribution to hunters of base and inhumane motives. Cleveland Amory, for example, in a *TV Guide* column, called with tight-lipped humor for a "Hunt the Hunters Hunt Club"; Friends of Animals, the organization of which he is president, speaks in policy statements of the "kill-for-kicks boys" and holds that the "destroyers of . . . life must, in turn, be destroyed—preferably by due legal process."

Amory is the Susan Brownmiller—one is tempted to say the Anita Bryant—of the antihunting movement. His tract on the subject, *Man Kind?*, not only is laden with class and regional bigotry—all Southerners, for example, are depicted as monosyllabic drawling sadists—but fails to make even a passing mention of the sport's more articulate defenders, preferring to prove again and again that many drugstore-rack outdoor magazines and most small-town newspaper hunting and fishing columns are written and edited by persons whose primary talents are not, perhaps, literary. The result, not surprisingly, is much the same as if one were to characterize the romantic behavior of American men by consulting *Hustler* and *Naughty Nylons,* spending a week in Forty-Second Street porn theaters, and examining the rape file of the Los Angeles Police Department. The vilest behavior of backwoods psychopaths—persons who wound, torture, dismember, and burn wild animals alive—is held up as if it were considered normal or even praiseworthy behavior by most sportsmen, as are such pastimes as poaching, road shooting, killing with the aid of airplanes and snowmobiles, drunken littering, and malicious killing of domestic animals. Amory allows his readers to imagine that these activities can best be curtailed by the elimination of licensed and regulated sport hunting. As it is, hunters and fishermen contribute through license fees and the Pittman-Robertson Act—an excise tax levied upon all guns, ammunition, and fishing equipment sold in the United States—virtually all of the money used by the states and the federal government for wildlife management and habitat enhancement.

Not surprisingly, Amory nowhere in his diatribe makes reference to the rather widespread custom of meat-eating. To do so would lead him into absurdity and contradictions. Anybody who eats meat—or, for that matter, wears leather or keeps a dog or cat and feeds it anything other than brussels sprouts—deprives himself of his only philosophically defensible argument against the hunt. Herein lies the telling connection: antihunting zealots and Bolinas ideologues are joined in their mutual desire to purify the self of the World. The positing of the Good in something called nature is, at bottom, a particularly inhumane form of sentimentality: inhumane because it removes a fundamental quality or impulse from the civilized mind of man to a never-never land of childish dream. One cannot, if one wishes to admire the wholeness of natural process, fasten too closely upon the life and death of the individual organism. To come back to the hunt, if one chooses to imagine that the individual rabbit, for example, has a soul, then one must rail against nature, for more than 80 percent of all rabbits die each winter, although the animal's potential life span is several years. That is why rabbits are famous for what they are famous for. Nature's way of solving the riddle of the Point Reyes deer would have taken longer, but the results are nevertheless predictable.

Men kill and men die. One can no more escape complicity than one can walk without touching the ground, whether one chooses to try by purchasing animal flesh out of refrigerated compartments or by converting park rangers into slaughterhouse attendants. Even vegetarians cannot, in the modern world, exempt themselves. How much wheat and corn could Kansas and Nebraska produce with millions of bison eating everything down to the roots? To mow the lawn is to eliminate habitat for small mammals and birds. To drain swamps is to reduce the number of mosquitos—also the number of ducks, muskrat, otter, turtles, and fish.

Just past the argument that hunting is murder lies the related superstition that it is a violent and bloodthirsty pastime that mars the sensibility of persons who indulge in it. The Humane Society of the United States, for example, says that it looks for "a generation of adults who will no longer have any wish, desire, or willingness to kill any living creature purely for pleasure and recreation." The argument is in essence a puritanical one and should be recognized as such. "One does not hunt in order to kill," Ortega y Gasset said, "one kills in order to have hunted." In the death of the beast one rehearses one's own: "Hunting," Ortega argues, "is an occurrence between two animals . . . one the hunter and one the hunted." The hunter cannot exist without the prey, and so, in his way, he loves it. If the hunter were always successful in his quest it would be not hunting but something else—what the park rangers are doing at Point Reyes, perhaps. That is why the sportsman has imposed limits upon himself to prevent the contest's becoming too one-sided. To employ all of one's intelligence and technological advantages against a wild animal is cheating.

If sportsmen's groups spent more time, energy, and money decrying technological abuses and reckless shooting and less time on the lucidrous claim that hunting has some mysterious connection to virility and patriotism, that point might not be so easily lost. I have never been in the company of hunters anywhere, whether in Massachusetts, Virginia, Arkansas, or California—the places I have hunted or spoken to numbers of hunters—where men who exhibit aggressive tendencies and derive obvious pleasure from the killing part of the ritual are not disliked and shunned by their fellows. (There is an obvious and natural limit to man's ability—playing by the rules—to kill game. As any hunter knows who hunts a species in which the season is long enough to make a difference, by the end of that term game gets scarce and difficult to find. The rabbit season where I live, for example, opens October 1 and closes February 15. Anybody who goes hunting after Christmas is in it for something other than killing. By February rabbits become so scarce—and would do so, it is important to note, whether they were hunted by men or not—that it is often hard to find enough to give the dogs a good day's run.) A person seeking sadistic thrills is better off with pro football or stock-car racing. If killing were the point of hunting, most people would give it up out of boredom.

Hunters do have one thing in common with persons who like to take pictures of wildlife or simply to sit in their living rooms, as many antihunters do, and contemplate the *idea* of animals running free. That is the protection of habitat. It is hardly possible to manage a park, preserve, or wilderness to benefit game species without benefiting nongame species as well. Thirty-five species of mammals are legally hunted in the United States; more than eight hundred are not. For birds the figures are seventy-four and over seven hundred. No endangered species are hunted legally, and according to the National Wildlife Federation, no species was ever put on that list by modern (i.e., twentieth-century) sport hunting in this country. Many species have been brought from scarcity or near extinction to abundance through game-management techniques largely financed by hunters' taxes—deer, antelope, wild turkey, elk, and others. More deer by far are killed by automobiles than by all the hunters in Christendom.

The deer is not innocent unless the wolf is guilty. Deer are animals; they have no individual moral natures. To us they are an enigma, permanently other, seeming whole and free of contradiction only because the terms are our own. They live and die as we do, and we are implicated in their fate through the power we have over them. We have humanized our planet to the point where nature itself has grown bureaucratic. In the long run we are likelier to be kept sane by the example of those among us who can join the hunt and tolerate the ambiguity of things than by the childlike visions of half-informed Jeremiahs preaching the omnivorous guilt of others.

1978

Natural Regulation

Truly, it is an epic land, this Yellowstone. The "Jewel in the Crown," the National Park Service calls it—2.2 million acres, an area larger than Rhode Island and Delaware combined, set aside in a landscape of astonishing beauty: craggy, snow-capped peaks, pristine forests, crystalline, trout-filled rivers, thunderous cascades and, in summer, verdant meadows grazed by herds of elk and bison. Established in 1872 during the presidency of Ulysses S. Grant—an administration otherwise infamous for corruption and plunder—Yellowstone was the world's first National Park. Perhaps the first theme park as well. Never mind that the other two salient events in the American West during the 1870s were the hunting to near-extermination of millions of bison and General Custer's disaster at Little Big Horn. Yellowstone endures as a complex and emotionally resonant symbol—an American Eden, if you will. In wilderness, we feel instinctively, lies what remains of our national innocence, an inheritance we cannot imagine losing.

But are we kidding ourselves? Just how, after all, does a wilderness accommodate the more than two million tourists who flock to Yellowstone each summer in cars, campers and recreational vehicles? The answer to the first question is yes, we are—in part deliberately. The policy of the National Park Service, the federal agency charged with this paradoxical task, is to create and maintain "a reasonable illusion of primitive America." Those are the words of the "Leopold Report," written in 1963 by a panel of wildlife management experts appointed by Interior Secretary Stewart

176

Udall and named for its late chairman, the distinguished Stanford University naturalist A. Starker Leopold.

But just what is a "reasonable illusion?" And of whose "primitive America?" Does that mean America before the automobile? Before the white man? Or before man? The document offers remarkably little guidance. What's more, in carrying out this mandate in the 337 public properties it manages, the perennially underfunded Park Service (even former Interior Secretary James Watt thought so) faces myriad difficulties over which it has no control. Many parks, including Yellowstone, face environmental threats from outside their boundaries. Too, the Park Service must make decisions in a political atmosphere charged with the strong feelings of millions of Americans—many organized into powerful interest groups as diverse as the Audubon Society, the Sierra Club, and the National Rifle Association. Among the most bitterly fought issues have always been those involving wildlife. A fundamental question: can one government agency serve effectively as both ministry of tourism and protector of wildlife and habitat?

Most Americans seem to think so. A recent Gallup poll gave the Park Service a 95 percent favorable rating—the highest of any federal agency. But an exhaustively documented book by a scholar and journalist with a reputation for integrity and clear-thinking argues that the Park Service's image of benign competence is an illusion. Alston Chase's *Playing God in Yellowstone* (446 pages, Atlantic Monthly Press, $24.95) is must reading for any literate American who cares for the outdoors. In essence, Chase accuses a Park Service he portrays as tourist-minded, politically timid, and scientifically inept of all but destroying Yellowstone as a wildlife sanctuary—and doing just about everything in its power to hide the resultant ecological disaster from informed scrutiny.

"Those visiting Yellowstone today," Chase writes "will not see what [Teddy] Roosevelt saw. They may encounter elk, bison, and an occasional coyote, but they will see no thousands of antelope, no plentiful sheep or mule deer. They will be fortunate to see a grizzly and will find no black bears . . . no wolves or white-tail deer, and . . . no mountain lion, wolverine, lynx, bobcat, or fisher." Beaver too are all but gone—a fascinating mammal whose valuable fur drew white men to these mountains to begin with, and whose beneficial effect, in a semi-arid landscape, is hard to overstate. As Chase portrays it, the plight of Yellowstone's once abundant bear population could hardly be sadder. Black bear, once synonymous with Yellowstone and almost common in nearby National Forests, are today rare. There is every danger that the mighty grizzly—the very incarnation of wild America—will be driven to extinction within the park by the government's "bear recovery program."

Even more alarming—bears can be transplanted—is the prospect of permanent range damage due to over-grazing by thousands of surplus elk and bison who are literally eating other species out of house and home. Smaller herbivores have nowhere to hide and little to eat. "I would not turn a jackrabbit loose there," a biologist for the state of Montana told Chase "without packing it a lunch first."

So bitterly do Park Service spokesmen resent what they insist is a one-sided hatchet job that the dispute has turned nasty—and personal. "Specious journalism and intellectual dishonesty," fumes Yellowstone superintendent Robert Barbee. "Full of blatant misrepresentations of fact. The premise is ludicrous," says the Audubon Society's Amos Eno, who as a Nixon administration Interior Department official was partly responsible for initiating some of the policies Chase criticizes. Park Service director William Penn Mott, a Reagan appointee, comments "I suppose that's a good way to sell books, to sensationalize, to misquote, to exaggerate." Yet so strongly does Chase, a one-time academic philosopher with degrees from Harvard, Oxford, and Princeton, believe in his book that he sold his ranch on Montana's Smith River—representing his and his wife's life savings—to support himself for the five years it took to write it.

At issue is a wildlife management policy the Park Service bills as "natural regulation." If the phrase itself seems contradictory, the sentiment behind it is of demonstrable appeal to persons whose love of animals far exceeds their grasp of wildlife biology. Conceived in the late Sixties following stormy congressional hearings over the issue of public hunting in Yellowstone, it's portrayed as a "hands off" policy in which something called "nature" is allowed to take its course regardless of human wishes. The idea is that a wilderness like Yellowstone is self-regulating and requires no human intervention in order to reach a stable equilibrium among plant and animal species.

Unfortunately, as scientists outside the Park Service were unanimous and often vehement in explaining, Yellowstone isn't a wilderness in any real sense and hasn't been for at least a century. Why not? In the first place, big as the park is, it's far too small. Secondly, the elimination of predators, human and animal, has so altered the relationship among species that the Park Service's policy has become both a philosophical absurdity and a practical impossibility. Indeed "natural regulation" is based upon principles neither practiced nor accepted by any agency charged with the well-being of wildlife and habitat anywhere in North America—or, for that matter, the world. It was put into effect without preliminary research. That's because, says Yellowstone research administrator John Varley, the policy is itself an experiment, albeit a "controversial" one. Asked how a controlled experiment involving migratory animals can be conducted in a game preserve without fences, Varley contends that "the science of wildlife management is part art. You don't have controlled experiments."

Statements like that from Park Service officials can render outside scientists almost apoplectic. "'The Grand Experiment,' they call it" says Prof. Les Pengelly of the University of Montana's School of Forestry. "Well, they're going at it blind. They never had a tinker's idea of what they're doing, and now they're trapped in their own conniving. The Park Service is like a guy sitting on one end of a branch sawing it off at the trunk. They're not quite through it yet, but they're close. If they want to save Yellowstone, the American people need to learn the rules of the biological game and put a stop to it."

As presently constituted, Yellowstone never was what ecologists call an "intact ecosystem" for large mammals. Before the white man crisscrossed the West with roads, railroads and barbwire fences, ungulate species like elk, mule deer, antelope, and bison migrated out of the snowbound mountains into the valleys to graze during winter. Hunter-gatherer tribes like the Crow, Shoshone, and Blackfoot followed them—setting range fires to

stampede the animals into traps and off cliffs. The elk's most efficient animal predator, the gray wolf, followed too.

But not long after Native Americans were driven from the region, Congress abolished hunting in all national parks. Decades
ago, rangers exterminated Yellowstone's wolves and mountain
lions in the mistaken belief they were doing the herbivores a
favor. But to eliminate predation was, in effect, to remove the top
of the food chain, permanently unbalancing the ecosystem. Assuming that the predators could be restored—much more difficult
than it sounds, for political as well as biological reasons—how
large would Yellowstone have to be to function as an intact ecosystem? "Oh, say a quarter the size of the North American continent," responds Cornell's Richard Root, president of the Ecological Society of the United States.

Elk may or may not be native to Yellowstone. Archaeologists
digging in Indian middens have never found their bones there.
But as the most aggressive and adaptable ungulate species native
to the West, they have been a problem in the park for decades.
Ironically, the same Leopold Report that inspired "natural regulation" warned that too many elk had and could in the future cause
habitat damage and harm to other species. Estimating the "carrying capacity" of the park's northern range at five thousand, it recommended that rangers shoot excess animals in winter and do-
nate the meat to charity. When hunters' groups tried to get in on
the action, Chase thinks, the Park Service came up with "natural
regulation" as a means of defining the problem out of existence.
Officials heatedly deny the charge.

So how many elk live in Yellowstone today? It seems the Park
Service doesn't really know and isn't trying very hard to find out.
The figure given reporters is sixteen thousand. (Park biologists
have made steadily escalating estimates of when the herd would
stop growing. The most recent is 12–15,000.) But that figure represents only a hasty airplane count of the "northern herd" done
in December 1985. It's virtually meaningless, explains Montana
biologist Jon Swenson, who took part in the count, because it isn't
known how many of the animals were browsing in the forest and
thus invisible from the air. Wildlife biologists have methods for
determining these things, but park officials haven't done them

since 1981—the year the count reached sixteen thousand. It seems a curious way to conduct a controversial experiment.

Indeed a hike in Yellowstone's northern range in mid-May showed every plant in sight cropped down to the dirt and the foliage on every tree "high-lined," i.e. stripped bare, to exactly the height a bull elk can reach on its hind legs—even pines and firs, which supply little nutrition and are eaten as filler by animals who can't find anything else. (Making it likely that the number of elk invisible from an airplane was quite high.) It is virtually impossible to find a growing aspen shoot anywhere in Yellowstone Park. Elk crop them as soon a they emerge from the ground. A fast-growing hardwood, aspen provides critical cover and nutrition to just about all plant-eating species—including bears, which, contrary to the popular impression, are mainly scavengers and foragers who hunt live animals hardly at all.

Park spokesmen admit the aspen problem, but say over-grazing has nothing to do with it. They blame drought and a mistaken policy of fire control. (Ecologists now realize that forest fires actually benefit wildlife habitat in the long run.) But thick aspen groves flourish inside a few fenced-in exclosures set up before the advent of "natural regulation" for the purpose of studying vegetation. They end at the fence lines as abruptly as if gardeners had trimmed them with hedge clippers and rotary mowers. Unnatural, responds the Park Service, which has been prevented from tearing down the fences only by protests from area scientists. Aspen also does well in the National Forests which virtually encircle the park—and where ungulate populations are kept in check by hunting. [About twelve hundred Yellowstone elk are taken each year as they migrate out of the park at the so-called "firing line" above Gardiner, Montana—a spectacle rather like a cow shoot criticized by animal rights and hunters groups alike.]

After summer rainstorms, the Lamar and Yellowstone rivers run turbid with eroded topsoil—in a climate in which topsoil forms very slowly. Streams just outside the park run clear— ironic, since the Forest Service, an agency of the Department of Agriculture, draws bitter criticism from environmentalist groups for such sins as clear-cutting, road-building, geothermal drilling, and planned ski resorts near the park. As for fires, Yellowstone hasn't had any since a "let burn" policy was adopted. Elk and bison have eaten the fuel. "The northern range would not burn if you napalmed it," one ecologist told Chase.

What's more, so zealously do Yellowstone officials interpret "natural regulation" that in the winter of 1981–2, when the park's herd of rare bighorn sheep came down with a bacterial infection known as "pinkeye," they did nothing—though the disease is easily cured with eyedrops. (Some local ranchers defied park rules and saved a few rams that way.) Blinded, some 60 percent of the herd starved or plunged to death from cliffs that winter. In 1980, the Mt. Everts bighorn herd numbered 265; by the 1983 census, 38 remained. Montana authorities think the epidemic was caused by poor nutrition due to competition with elk. Sheep outside the park escaped infection. Park rangers who weren't allowed to treat the bighorn were permitted to shoot them to end their suffering.

Rancher Allan Nelson, whose grandfather homesteaded just north of the park in Montana's Paradise Valley, has a cattleman's way of putting it. "I couldn't operate with a management plan like theirs," he says. "I'd go broke. You just can't beat your ground that bare and not suffer for it—just plain common sense tells you that." Herds of ravenous elk migrating into his pastures in winter have forced him to pull his cattle out. "We can get a kill permit from the state," he adds "but who has the heart to go up there and kill five or six hundred head of elk?"

Bison migrating out of the park pose an even greater danger. Many carry brucellosis, a disease that causes cows to abort before coming to term. There is no cure. While it is not clear whether or not cattle can contract the sickness from bison, it is hard to blame ranchers for not wanting to find out the hard way. By law, an infected herd must be destroyed. Yet animal rights groups, in the evident belief that it is possible to treat herd animals like family pets, have supported the Park Service's refusal to eliminate diseased bison because the disease is "natural."

But what does the word mean? As Chase's book does an astringent job of pointing out, "natural" has no firm definition in philosophy or science. It can be invoked to justify almost any wildlife management policy at all. Hence Yellowstone's almost twenty-year old grizzly bear controversy—argued with an ideological fervor normally reserved for issues like abortion and arms control. For at the same time the Park Service decided to stop killing elk and bison, it began to kill grizzlies—more grizzlies than had to be sacrificed to human safety during the first century of Yellowstone's existence. So many grizzlies that Chase is by no means alone in wondering if getting rid of the beasts hasn't been the idea all along, a suspicion met in government circles with outrage and even tears. "I know guys who cry on the phone when a bear dies," says Yellowstone Asst. Chief Ranger Gary Brown. "That these people are accused of conspiring to make the bear extinct makes you physically sick."

For grizzlies, "natural regulation" meant closing the backcountry garbage dumps where the animals had fed since the turn of the century. As Chase points out, the language used to justify the action wasn't at all scientific, but aesthetic and even moralistic. Though scavengers by nature, the grizzlies became "bums," and "garbage hooked"—like so many welfare cheats. Even today park superintendant Robert Barbee speaks of "turning the bears into wild animals before we make them into hogs."

In vain did John and Frank Craighead, the famous naturalist brothers then involved in a ten-year-old project to gather data on the elusive animals, warn that modern man, having driven the grizzlies off their native plains into the mountains to begin with, had usurped much of Yellowstone's choice bear habitat by building roads along the rivers, hotels and marinas on Yellowstone Lake. If he wanted the grizzlies to prosper, they argued, man would have to give something back. While not picturesque, the dumps also kept the aggressive, unpredictable creatures far from roads and campgrounds. Indeed a study done by the Craigheads at Park Service request showed that from 1959 to 1967, the grizzlies had caused just seventeen "bear incidents" involving human injury—none fatal—a period in which more than 11.5 million tourists visited Yellowstone. There hadn't been a bear-caused fatality in the park since 1942, when the war cut tourism (thus garbage) by two-thirds, and rangers had been forced to kill twenty-eight marauding grizzlies—compared to a total of thirteen for the preceding decade. Closing the dumps could make the same thing happen again.

The philosophers won. The scientists and the bears lost. Hungry grizzlies began to show up all around Yellowstone. From six grizzly incidents in 1967, Chase shows, the number jumped to seventy-eight in 1968. Rangers began to kill bears. How many? The Park Service admits 261 "management kills" since 1968—not all by rangers. The Craigheads say 320 would be a truer number. Both figures exceed the estimated 1968 population. To retain their research permit, the brothers were told, they would have to design their experiments according to Park Service wishes, and submit their data for approval before publishing. "It was designed to make us quit," says John. "And we did." Arguing that they were unnatural, the Park Service removed the radio collars the scientists had placed on some bears to track them—thus ending any chance to study the policy's effect. "The biological crime of the century," says grizzly expert Charles Jonkel of the University of Montana.

Ancient history, Yellowstone officials insist. Not so ancient, however, that Frank Craighead's fine book *The Track of the Grizzly*, which includes a chapter critical of the Park Service, may be sold in Yellowstone bookstores—tending to verify what many scientists say is a history of professional retaliation against critics. Asked why, park officials blame a citizen's advisory panel chaired by Alston Chase. (He has since resigned under pressure.) But a *Newsweek* reporter had previously attended a meeting in which the same officials told Chase's committee they'd not yet decided on the book's merits—despite having been asked each year for several years. "The Park Service is essentially destroying Yellowstone," John Craighead says. "Their attitude is 'We're right, by God, no matter what, and we'll do anything to cover up.' They're more than misleading. They actually lie. The ethics of science mean nothing to them."

Spokesmen for the park and the Interagency Grizzly Bear Study Team set up to monitor the animals say there are some two hundred left in the park—though many outsiders doubt the population could possibly be that high. Only thirty to thirty-five, in any case, are estimated to be breeding females. Though IGBST members speak optimistically of halting the continuing decline in the population, they admit that hasn't happened yet. Indeed a 1984 report by the Wildlife Committee of the NPS Advisory Board questioned whether the "Yellowstone ecosystem as currently managed, used, and developed" is capable of supporting a wild grizzly population at all. More recently the same scientific panel has called the IGBST remiss for not investigating the possibility that the killing and partial devouring of three humans in the Yellowstone area since 1968—extremely aberrant behavior for grizzlies—was caused by nutritional stress. Though the odds of being attacked by a grizzly are infinitesimally small, the number of deaths since "natural regulation" began—four—exceeds that of the park's first century.

Prodded a bit, bear managers now admit they are considering importing Canadian grizzlies into Yellowstone's population—even trying to place grizzly cubs with hibernating black bear mothers. Not because the park's grizzlies are otherwise doomed, but for the sake of "genetic diversity." Unless the habitat can be restored, though, first by getting rid of the excess elk and bison, such efforts will very likely prove futile. Chase, who seems to have more confidential sources inside the Park Service than the CIA has moles, hopes that his book will help younger biologists whose careers are not tied to "natural regulation," to kill the policy before the policy kills Yellowstone. But it is a legitimate criticism of *Playing God in Yellowstone* that he fails to spell out what needs to be done. Concerned that his book had a legion of enemies and no obvious friends, Chase admits, he left it all to implication. Which is pretty much the political dilemma that seems to have led the Park Service to try "natural regulation" in the first place.

Having substituted sentimentality and political convenience for science, the Park Service almost certainly requires outside help coming up with a policy that will heal Yellowstone. But the issues involved are not profound scientific mysteries; expertise exists to be tapped. What remains to be seen is whether the American public—from elk hunters to animal rights advocates—can quit squabbling over symbols and demand that the job be done.

1986

Why Teachers Can't Teach

"Fifty percent of DISD teachers fail to pass test," said the headline in the *Dallas Times Herald* last summer, and the wire services relayed the news to much of the civilized world. Poor Dallas. Twenty years in court over desegregation and busing, and now this. Actually, the Wesman Personnel Classification Test was given not to all Dallas teachers but to 535 first-year teachers. Half fell below the score considered acceptable by the DISD—and that standard itself was far from rigorous. The teachers were considerably outperformed on the same test by a volunteer group of juniors and seniors from Jesuit College Preparatory School, a private high school in North Dallas.

Less well publicized, but equally disturbing, was the Houston Independent School District's discovery at about the same time that fully half its teacher applicants scored lower in mathematical achievement than the average high school junior; about a third were similarly defective in using the English language.

Before those whose children are enrolled in districts other than Dallas or Houston congratulate themselves, they should ponder this: every school system in Texas gets its teachers from exactly the same places Dallas and Houston do—the sixty-three accredited teacher-training institutions in the state. Teachers just as poorly prepared are opening school this fall from Amarillo to Brownsville, Orange to El Paso—teachers who cannot read as well as the average sixteen-year-old, write notes free of barbarisms to parents, or handle arithmetic well enough to keep track of the field-trip money.

186

How can this be? Texas spends a staggering amount of money on education—more than half the state budget, or four billion dollars in 1978. And that doesn't include another $397 million in federal funds. What are we getting for our dollars? What happened to the era, not so long ago, really, when teachers were rightfully respected as the best-educated people in the community? And now they can't out-perform high school juniors. How has it come to this?

Everybody has a suspect: integration, segregation, permissiveness, regimentation, the Viet Nam War, drugs, television, divorce, the suburbs, the inner city—everything but sunspots and the phases of the moon. Conditioned by decades of propaganda from professional educators, we indict society, which cannot defend itself. But the educators themselves are largely to blame, and in particular the teacher's colleges, which are their single most harmful creation—harmful both in coddling ignorance and in driving self-respecting students away. Backed by hometown legislators, these colleges have no effective political opposition and are accountable to no one. They turn out hordes of certified ignoramuses whose incompetence in turn becomes evidence that the teacher colleges and the educators need yet more money and more power.

Under pressure from taxpayers and the federal courts, the DISD resorted to the Wesman test because it has learned that the teacher colleges cannot be trusted. Transcripts are a sham; letters of recommendation promiscuous. Certified teachers are pouring out of those sixty-three colleges like the mops and water buckets that overwhelmed poor Mickey Mouse in Disney's *Fantasia*. There is at present a glut of teachers in most subject areas (mathematics and science being an exception due to better opportunities elsewhere), but without some reliable way of distinguishing among applicants, the DISD's surplus of applicants might as well have been a shortage. Hence the Wesman test and subsequent follies.

Troubled and irritated by what the DISD experience seemed to suggest—and versions of it are being repeated all over the United States—I formulated two simple questions and undertook a journey through the wonderland of teacher education in search of enlightenment. Those questions were: How did such incompetents gain Texas teacher certificates? And what on earth did they do in college? Having spent a number of years as a college teacher, I had some idea of what was going on, but the things I found out still took my breath away. The business of teacher education in Texas—as everywhere else in America—is a shame, a mammoth and very expensive swindle of the public interest, a hoax, and an intellectual disgrace. So come along. Until you have been there, you will never quite believe it.

To understand how the teaching profession has degraded itself, you must grasp fully the closed and circular nature of our public educational system and a little bit about how it got that way. Around the turn of the century certain of the pedagogical theories of John Dewey were seized upon by "progressive" educators anxious to reform the authoritarian rote and memorization practices of the time. Dewey was one of America's handful of genuine philosophers, but like many another seminal thinker's, his theories have been misrepresented and wrongly applied so long and widely that today's educational dogma almost parodies the practices he urged. After eighty years Dewey's arguments in favor of student-centered rather than subject-centered approaches to learning have resulted in schools of education that stress method over subject matter to the point that would-be teachers spend all of their time learning *how* to teach. *What* to teach has unfortunately perished in the transition. A now self-evident truth—that a certain amount of pedagogical training beyond mere book knowledge is useful—has been used by the Educationists to create a tax supported empire of cant.

By Educationists I mean the officers rather than the enlisted men—the deans and professors of education, school administrators, the bureaucrats at organizations like the Texas Education Agency and the U.S. Department of Health, Education, and Welfare, the chief beneficiaries, in short, of things as they are. It is very simple: unless and until you have completed basic training as mandated by the Educationists, you cannot teach in a public school. In Texas there is no standard other than the completion of a bachelor's degree with the required number of education courses. As matters stand, no graduate of a TEA-approved teacher-training program, no matter how incompetent, is excluded from the profession. There is no test, no qualifying exam. Nobody else, no matter how learned or capable, is admitted. In order to join the officer class, to become, in other words, anything from assistant principal of an elementary school in San Angelo to director of the TEA, graduate training in education is a necessity. Otherwise there is no use applying.

Compare, for example, journalism. Most of the sixty-three teacher-training colleges in Texas also have journalism departments. Academic journalism is like education in that both are disciplines based upon pragmatic skills; they have no subject matter of their own. As matters stand, however, almost anybody can get a job in publishing or broadcasting if the people in charge think he can write, edit, or perform other necessary skills. Ability to do the thing at hand is deemed sufficient license to practice, and the best judges are assumed to be persons who have shown themselves to be competent. Nobody I know in the trade would *ever* take for granted that a college degree in journalism was on its face indicative of anything except that the bearer had passed a certain amount of time in the proximity of a college or a university. Graduate journalism is mostly for persons who want to be journalism professors; the university, as we shall see more than once, is a world of its own. Most private schools, which are not accountable to the Texas educational establishment, similarly take a dim view of education majors.

Perhaps our ancestors were wiser than we are. Before normal schools grew into teacher colleges and later metamorphosed into universities, basic literacy of the kind the DISD was testing for was not merely expected of would-be teachers, it was required. "No pupil should be allowed in the normal school," reads the 1904 announcement of what is now Southwest Texas State University, "without standing a reasonably fair examination upon the branches taught in the free public schools."

Novels of that period often portrayed the schoolteacher as a figure of fun—a prig, pedant, or old-womanish prude—but never as a dimwit. Learning was respected. But as soon as everyone started going to college, the status of the teacher as the community guardian and source of knowledge was endangered. The profession responded the way of all professions threatened with encroachment: it closed the shop. Since teachers no longer had a monopoly on knowledge, they focused on their one remaining exclusive possession: teacher education. In 1955 the Legislature made graduation from an accredited teacher-training program a prerequisite for a teaching certificate. Like most bureaucratic entities with monopolistic tendencies—the Pentagon comes to mind—the Educationist establishment has three essential and closely related functions besides the nominal one of teaching kids. They are: to grow, to protect the profession from competition, and to ward off outside scrutiny.

Central to all three functions is the establishment and elaboration of dogma. Ask hard questions of almost anyone involved with teacher education—the Texas Education Agency, the colleges and their education departments, the school districts and their teachers—and the chances are the first response will be to kick the problem downstairs. The TEA insists it is powerless to demand competence due to political pressure exerted on the Legislature by the colleges. The colleges insist that they must assume prospective teachers to be literate when they arrive from high schools. High school teachers say they cannot ignore subject matter in their courses to teach skills that should have been mastered in junior high. Eighth-grade teachers blame seventh-grade teachers, and so forth back to first grade, where teachers have no one left to blame but society, which they do. The NEA (National Education Association), the chief proponent of no-fault teaching, urges us in a pamphlet to take note, before deciding who is responsible for plummeting test scores, of the "distractions which characterized American life in the past decade or so." Among the nominees are the war, the draft, riots, corruption in high places, assassinations, and television. The "decade of distraction," we are told, "puts an additional burden on teachers who are asked to provide stability while other aspects of life are in chaos." If everyone is to blame, in other words, no one is to blame.

It is considered rude to point out that all of the above except television have been constants of America's and everybody else's history, and that further disruption outside the classroom may confidently be predicted. Society, moreover, cannot be fired or have its budget cut. All it can do is feel guilty and go to PTA meetings.

The same NEA pamphlet quoted above, written as a response to public concern over declining test scores, urges us to remain philosophical: "While we ask why the scores on college entrance examinations have gone down, T. S. Eliot's probing goes much deeper: 'Where is the learning we have lost in information? Where is the understanding we have lost in knowledge? Where is the life we have lost in living?'" As usual, the Educationists are changing the subject. Eliot was asking a religious question about man's quest for wisdom and his fear of inauthenticity; we want to know about test scores. By quoting him, the NEA seeks a classy way to preserve that most sanctified of Educationist principles, that of the Whole Child. (During the sixties it was called "relevance" but the same thing was meant.) According to that doctrine, so prevalent among professional educators that it is invisible to them much of the time, to insist upon literacy is considered coercive and potentially harmful; secondary matters such as sex education, driver training, drug counseling, and the proper attitude toward siblings are equally necessary. Many of these goals are, of course, worthy. But they *are* secondary. Everywhere but in the education school, that is.

For the Educationists, the doctrine of the Whole Child is a magical balm that washes away their sins. Ask a question about *skills,* and you get T. S. Eliot, transforming the question to one about *values.* Who is a happier and more productive member of the human community, an illiterate peasant or a tax lawyer? Values, of course, are relative. What then is the point of having tests at all, whether of students or teachers? By a marvelous coincidence, the NEA was holding its national convention in Dallas last summer at about the same time the bad news about the DISD teachers was breaking. Hardly ruffled, the nations's largest teachers' organization paused just long enough in its deliberations to pass a resolution condemning competency testing. Should public unrest persist, we may yet hear the NEA citing Ecclesiastes: "He that increaseth knowledge increaseth sorrow."

To be sure, not all teachers agree. The American Federation of Teachers, affiliated with the AFL-CIO, favors competency testing, the Dallas NEA affiliate has no objection, and many teachers I talked with felt the NEA, as one high school teacher put it, "made us look like a bunch of cowardly blockheads." But unless you understand that the NEA was being perfectly sincere, not defensive or cowardly, you don't understand the Educationists' world view in its fullest incarnation. For this I recommend that you read the aforementioned pamphlet, entitled *On Further Examination of "On Further Examination."* Naturally the document contains the obligatory attack on competency tests for cultural bias and the obligatory defense of teachers against charges that they are in any way responsible for whatever may be wrong with American education. But what really caught my eye was the suggestion that competency tests are not just unfair but actually dangerous.

As an example of the NEA's reasoning, consider its reaction to the idea of exit examinations that would ask students to prove, in order to graduate, that they had actually learned what they are assumed to have been taught: "Once we established minimal competencies we tend to get just that—minimal competence. One would hope for considerably more than this." Of course one would. One would also hope for more from the NEA than an assertion so contrary to common sense. No soap.

Equally revealing is the section titled "About the Future." "It is unlikely," the NEA contends, "that eighth-grade teachers would think it appropriate to give a test to one eighth-grade class in 1970 and to another eighth-grade class seven years later and expect the difference in scores to say anything useful. What would such a difference in scores mean? That the teacher is better or worse? That the students have gotten smarter or dumber? That societal values have changed? That our knowledge base is different? Can we, in fact, compare children of one set of circumstances with those of another?" The paragraph closes with a slap at those who "believe that there is a single unchanging standard which can be measured and compared across time," and asks "Is this a realistic assumption?"

To this I can only reply: of course it is. I completed the eighth grade in 1957. There is no question that societal values have undergone considerable change in the twenty-two years intervening, and that the sum of human knowledge is greater than it was then. But the last time I checked, three 9s still equalled 27, nouns and verbs still had to agree, and the nation of Italy continued to extend into the Mediterranean Sea and somewhat resembled a boot. Test results in Dallas, Houston, and elsewhere suggest that large numbers of certified teachers are not capable of passing on such skills and bits of knowledge because they have no command of them to begin with. Educationists are afflicted with a cultural relativism so profound it has become an intellectual disease. The obvious proposition that values are relative has been warped to signify the opposite of what it really means: that some facts and ideas are more important than others. In Educationese it means that they are equally arbitrary. Hence charges of cultural bias, where bias is defined as requiring literacy and the kind of knowledge rarely gained by hanging out on street corners or watching soap operas.

The products of the Educationist monopoly descend upon the colleges and universities, which, like the rest of the bureaucracy, are committed to permanent growth. Having long ago surrendered to the twin deities of egalitarianism and vocational training, colleges and universities have lost control of their own curricula. On most campuses, there is a continuing low-grade conflict between the basic, traditional academic disciplines, in which fundamental intellectual skills are supposed to be taught, and the vocational programs. Job training is winning everywhere—in too many instances a sort of job training that leaves students unprepared for the profession they think they are ready to enter and insufficiently educated to adjust when the jobs don't materialize. Philosophy shrinks almost out of existence, while fashion merchandising advances.

So the catalog grows thicker by the year, and students have a promiscuous choice of courses that are the intellectual equivalent of puffed wheat: one kernel of knowledge inflated by means of hot air, divided into pieces, and puffed again. The vast majority of such courses are graded, if at all, by multiple-choice or true-false exams. In those rare instances where written work is given, grammar, punctuation, and style are seen to be the business of the English department alone. Nobody in most departments really has any idea whether his students are fully literate; very likely he has never asked them to write. (Perhaps that is just as well, given the kind of jargon-laden, semiliterate humbug that is the going thing in far too many disciplines.) American higher education has been drifting in this direction for some time. The public schools, dominated by Educationists, have already been there for quite a while. Very bright students who catch on early or who come from educated families may escape with a few skills; the rest are defrauded into believing they have an education.

When I was in school I always assumed that teachers were persons who had been very good students themselves. Some facts compiled by the Coordinating Board of the Texas College and University System make it clear that such is not the case today—at least, not until they enroll in the school of education, where everyone is transformed into an A student.

Of the 10,120 new teachers who graduated in Texas colleges in 1978, 8273, or roughly 80 percent, attended public institutions. The greatest number, 869, came from Southwest Texas State University at San Marcos. North Texas graduated 648, East Texas 601, Stephen F. Austin 491. Of the larger schools, UT-Austin graduated 690, Texas Tech 623, Texas A&M 453, the University of Houston 362, and so on. In the private sector only Baylor prepares teachers in large numbers, graduating an even 400. SMU was next with 73. Rice graduated exactly 1. The higher a college's entrance requirements and general academic reputation, the lower the percentage of certified-teacher graduates in its graduating class. Smart kids with good high school records avoid teacher training.

Most education majors come from lower-middle- or low-income backgrounds and often from families in which they are the first generation to attend college. I mean no condescension here: I am such a person myself. Those are the facts. Another fact is that entrance requirements at the schools that prepare the largest number of teachers are quite low. To matriculate at Southwest Texas State, for example, one need only to graduate from high school and score 13 on the ACT (American College Testing Program) test, a figure corresponding roughly to a 750 combined score on the Scholastic Aptitude Test (SAT)—far below the average of all high school seniors, and ranking in about the 35th percentile nationally. Anyone who still can't meet what are loosely called the "standards" may attend junior college and transfer to Southwest Texas or any public four-year college after two years of maintaining a C average.

A statistical profile of the Southwest Texas freshman class of 1977 shows that entering freshmen who declared education as their major had the lowest mean test scores of any entering group. Their ACT scores corresponded roughly to an SAT score of 825— still quite below the national average. Reasonable people disagree about whether the ACT and SAT tests measure intelligence or achievement; they probably measure a little of both. What nobody denies is that they are good predictors of academic success.

It is easy to say that higher scores and better grades should be required, but the situation is more complicated: many educators believe we are headed, within a decade, for the worst teacher shortage since the early sixties, particularly in mathematics and the sciences. Short of unforeseeable and quite unlikely changes in the relative economics of the teaching profession, such a tightening of entrance requirements would eventually be self-defeating.

But one needn't be a Phi Beta Kappa to teach elementary school, nor a Rhodes scholar to do an adequate job in a high school classroom. Persons of normal intelligence who have had halfway-decent schooling have nothing to fear from such a test as the Wesman and ought to be able to produce a paragraph free of barbarisms. Unfortunately, most college education programs are even less rigorous than the entrance standards. A recent study at the University of Houston reported that during the spring semester of 1977, the secondary education department awarded A's to 76.5 percent of the students in its courses. Another 13.5 percent received B's, 1.4 percent C's, and the rest were incompletes or withdrawals. No grades of D or F were recorded the entire semester. To show the direction things on campus are headed, in 1966 the grade breakdown for the same department was 23 percent A's, 46 percent B's, and 22 percent C's—not exactly rigorous, but at least defensible.

Think that's an isolated case? Then compare elementary education for the same 1977 semester: 70 percent A's, 23 percent B's, 3 percent C's. But wait: there *was* one D handed out. (One hesitates to think what that poor solitary kid must have done to deserve such ignominy.) Nobody failed. *Nobody failed.* Not one student in elementary or secondary education was too dumb or too lazy to pass. Nobody failed to show up for an exam, nobody failed to hand in his work, nobody just up and disappeared without a trace. Maybe this was a particularly worthy crop of aspiring teachers; maybe they will emerge to reverse the decline of learning in the public schools. But I think I am justified in being skeptical. Nor is there any reason at all to believe the University of Houston is more lax than other schools; it merely had the courage to gather and release the data.

What is the cause of grade inflation? It is simple: all public colleges, and all their divisions and departments, get their operating budgets from the state according to formulas based almost entirely upon the number of students enrolled. Is it any wonder that elementary-education students at Southwest Texas State are allowed no electives whatsoever in four years? The departments get more money by getting bigger, less money by getting smaller. Sufficient shrinkage can lead to loss of jobs. In this atmosphere, academic rigor that caused students to drop out or transfer to a less demanding field of study would be a financial liability. Grade inflation is built into the system; it is a matter of survival.

This is also the key to understanding the puffed-wheat curriculum and the self-perpetuating nature of the Educationist empire. Consider the following examples selected from among the 361 separate education courses listed in the catalog at Southwest Texas. There it is possible to earn three hours of college credit by taking "Materials for Rhythmical Activities," "Administering Leisure Delivery Systems," "Motorcycle Safety and Rider Education," or my personal favorite, a graduate course called "Administration and Supervision of Driver Education." School administrators are drawn almost entirely from the ranks of true believers or hypocrites who will sit in such courses placidly taking notes while fools dissect, categorize, and elaborate upon the perfectly obvious. If you don't believe me, come along to Southwest Texas State University, though stand forewarned that unless you are already quite familiar with what goes on in education departments, much of what you are about to read will seem so far removed from your concept of learning that it will seem a transmission from an alien planet.

I chose to visit Southwest Texas simply because the most teachers are trained there. Among school administrators in Central Texas, where most of its graduates end up, it is regarded as a

196

cut above average, something I had to keep reminding myself as I toured the campus. Walking around on a sunny spring day, I could not help but be struck by the juxtaposition of the institution's monolithic new architecture—hermetically sealed buildings looking as though they were designed to withstand nuclear attack—and the fact that every inch of unshaded grass was covered with roasting young women in bikinis. Judging from what students told me, maintaining a 2.0, or C, average at SWT, which is what is required for entry into the teacher-certification program, seems to be no harder than at the University of Houston or at any of the other schools that produce the vast majority of Texas' teachers.

The School of Education contains five departments: physical education, industrial arts, psychology, education, and special education. It offers twenty-seven different undergraduate and graduate degrees, most of them with specialized options that make a student's choices seem almost exponential. It is now possible—indeed, to get certain kinds of jobs it is mandatory—to secure a degree in elementary education with an emphasis in a specialty like geography, though why an adult would need to specialize in order to stay ahead of a class of third-graders is not explained in the catalog. Since identifying the folly of a semester-long graduate driver education course would be no more difficult than finding a drunk in a roadhouse on Saturday night, I decided to stick to undergraduate classes required of everyone hoping to become certified.

Education 3320, "The Elementary School: Principles and Curriculum," is required for certification and has several sections. The one I attended was team-taught by professors Bob Williamson, director of elementary education at SWT, and Hal Blythe. Both men have doctorates in education administration, and both have been elementary-school teachers and principals.

I asked Blythe whether all, or even the majority, of Southwest Texas State elementary-education majors emerge into their junior-level courses fully literate in basic areas of knowledge. "No, they don't," he said, but added, "by the time they get this far, you can hardly do anything about it." He went on to relate a tale of how, in his first year at the college, he attempted to prevent a student of his who was functionally illiterate from receiving a degree and the automatic teacher certification that goes with it. "Pressure came down from above," he said, "and I was on the griddle. It turned out that he already had a job." Blythe gave the clear impression that he had learned a rueful lesson about the realities of academic power and would be quite reluctant to climb onto the griddle again. He did say the continuing certification of incompetent teachers was, in his words, "a cop-out," but confessed that when the time came to fail or fire those who deserved the fate, "We—and in this case I'm talking about all of us—simply don't have the guts to do it." At the same time, however, both he and Williamson spoke with eager concern about the necessity that elementary teachers, especially, have what the two professors call "human-relations skills," and about their frustrations as former principals with "teachers who could pass paper and pencil tests but who could not relate to people."

Elementary Education 3320, which has no textbook and seems to require no original written work, is clearly aimed at human-relations, not paper and pencil, skills. On the day I attended, the class of forty (thirty-eight of them young women) was divided into three groups of roughly equal size in a large, open classroom. Two of the groups were seated at large tables taking notes from, or drumming their fingertips to, separate recorded lectures of what I took to be of a vaguely inspirational nature. The third group was seated in front of a television monitor watching videotape cassetes of themselves and other members of their group teaching each other various elementary-school lessons. As they watched, they were filling in evaluative forms to be presented to the individual for her private edification. Blythe and Williamson stayed behind them, filling out identical forms and occasionally coming forward to whisper a private note of criticism or encouragement to the student on the screen: face the class, summon students to the blackboard instead of calling for volunteers, involve the quiet students as well as those with their hands always in the air, smile.

Because the students on the tape were not real kids, but college students pretending to be kids, the whole exercise had an air of "let's pretend," like sorority sisters rehearsing a skit for rush week. In an attempt to overcome this problem, Blythe and Williamson sometimes distribute what they call "role-playing cards," which direct the recipients to act up in a childlike manner (is there a card somewhere reading *Urinate in your chair?*), a tactic that, although I did not see it used, would seem likely to make what is already a bit silly become downright absurd. As the spring term was nearly over, I took what I was seeing on the cassettes to be the result of an entire semester's work—which, when I checked the course syllabus, turned out to be true.

I came away with two conclusions. One was that the course was clearly, if not intentionally, set up so that it required a minimum of outside work, kept professors off the griddle on the question of literacy, and was virtually impossible to fail. To give an F or even a C in such a course would be almost impossible without a display of obvious feeble-mindedness or paralyzing stage fright on a prospective teacher's part. Where there is no subject matter, only method, the bad news never gets delivered.

My second conclusion was that enormous amounts of money, energy, and time were wasted by forcing forty students to come to class a couple of times a week for four months. They got less individual guidance and useful experience than they could get in two weeks if, instead of being isolated on a small-town campus and working on their suntans (and the majority looked as if they had just returned from the Bahamas), they were apprenticed after securing honest college degrees to proven and experienced master teachers in actual classrooms with real kids. I asked Williamson if something like that would not make more sense. "You know how I'm going to react to that," he said. "You're talking about my job."

Education 3330, "The Secondary School: Principles and Procedures," is a methods course required for teaching above the elementary level. The dean and the department head commended to me Professor Lowell Bynum, whose doctorate is in secondary education, and who has many years of experience as a band director and a principal at both the elementary and secondary levels. His class was conducted in a room equipped with two walls of one-way glass so observers could watch and listen without disturbing things inside.

On the day I visited his class, again toward the end of the semester, the atmosphere among Bynum's ten or so students—he divides his sections into thirds and meets with them separately—was somewhere between manic and hilarious. Like their counterparts in elementary education, Bynum's charges were spending their hour evaluating videotape cassettes of themselves and their classmates. The tool for this was a mimeographed handout obscurely titled "Refocusing Reteach." Down the left side of the form Bynum had listed six of what he styled "Instructional Objectives for this Teach." Four of those six categories used the word "unique" to describe the quality sought. Another had to do with observing time limits—secondary-school teachers are now advised to change their approach at least three, and preferably four, times each hour, like TV newsmen. The other category dealt with "specific refocusing skills." Bynum seemed to be interested in originality. He certainly got it.

First up was a would-be English teacher who wished to discuss with her classmates the subject of legendary heroes. Or rather, she wished them to name a few. She offered as an example Odysseus. Somebody else mentioned Abraham Lincoln. Luckily for adherents of realism, these role players were not much removed in age or maturity from the adolescents they were supposed to portray, so as would no doubt happen just as quickly in most junior high school classrooms, someone mentioned Roger Staubach and basketball's "Dr. J," Julius Erving. One would hope that the teacher-to-be would have drawn the students out a bit on the difference between literary, historical, and "living" legends, but naming was as far as it got.

Next up was a tennis lesson. On tactics. In a classroom. The putative coach called to the front of the room two students, a man and a woman. The man was introduced as bad-tempered and impatient. She was a steady, dependable, low-key sort of person, good at restraining her emotions. How should she play him? "She should hit the ball real close to the lines to make him blow up," a student volunteered. The coach allowed as how that made a lot of sense, proving not only that tennis cannot be taught in a classroom, but that he couldn't teach it on a court either: the correct strategy in so paradigmatic a case is to imitate a backboard and let the impatient player make all the errors. I never did figure out what specific skills were being refocused by issuing the two students rackets and a ball and having them hit it back and forth at a distance of about four feet, but a good time, I can assure you, was had by all.

A social-studies teaching prospect bunched the entire class into a corner to demonstrate the presumed discomforts of over-crowding. "People in Harris County are getting uneasy" seemed to be the point. More hilarity. Another social-studies trainee did a reasonably funny impersonation of the first woman president holding a press conference. The rest of the class imitated the press corps and asked questions about her private life, most of them containing the kind of guffawing sexual innuendo familiar to watchers of Johnny Carson. A "creative-writing teacher" stressed creativity by spreading out on a desk a collection of small items, most of them from the supermarket, and asking each student to combine any two to make a new product. Thus were invented "coach's liquid pizza" (by the tennis instructor), "spray-on pea-nut butter," and "condensed water." What these students were good at, I began to see, was imitating television skits, since that is where they are getting the bulk of their real education. I began to wonder if I had not wandered into a class for stand-up comedi-ans. Everybody was having a grand time, and why not? Every-body was getting an A, or at worst a B.

One student with hopes of teaching journalism passed around blank sheets of paper accompanied by a list of news stories ranging from ax murders to international treaties and invited her class-mates to cooperate in laying out the first two pages of a "conser-vative" and a "sensational" newspaper, which struck me as the most, and indeed only, useful idea I had heard. It seemed to pro-voke fewer laughs than the others, however, so I feared for the poor woman's grade. The most appalling example from my point of view as a former literature teacher, however, was the TV Col-lege Bowl quiz format invented by another would-be English teacher—appalling not only in its reliance on the tube but also for its revelations about unlettered students. For a five-point toss-up, nobody could name a single work by either Tolstoy or Stendahl. The quiz-master knew one, Stendahl's *The Red and the Black*, but had not read it herself and conceded to her groaning classmates that "it's not well known." For another five-pointer nobody could summon the name of the man who wrote *Lord Jim*. Remember now, we are not talking about real high school students but college seniors, and about college seniors, moreover, who will be in Texas high schools as teachers by the time you read this article, none of whom knew who wrote *War and Peace* or the name Joseph Conrad.

Back to the quiz, William F. Buckley was identified without demur as a senator from New York, not as the brother of James, the real former senator. Apparently the editorial page of the daily newspaper is as remote from the students' consciousness as Napoleonic France. But all is not lost. "Name a novel by Jacqueline Susann" brought a cascade of shouted responses: *"Valley of the Dolls, Once Is Not Enough . . ."* Those are all I know. Several of the students at Southwest Texas State were four titles deep.

Afterward, Professor Bynum got up for a brief set of closing remarks. He stressed the artificial nature of teaching one's peers in front of a television camera, a small group with no discipline problems. He categorized most of what he had seen as "teacher-centered learning" and hoped they would remember there are other methods. "If you end up as one of those teachers who comes in and says, 'Read chapter three and answer the questions,'" he said as a parting shot, "that noise you hear at the window will be me. I'll be back to haunt you." God forbid, I thought, that they should ever ask anybody to read and write. Anything but Jacqueline Susann, that is.

If schools of education were in the business of producing fully literate adult professionals, such nonsense as I have described above would be hooted out of the catalog. Instead, gifted students are forced to choose between certifying to teach and getting a decent education. Who can say how many potentially fine young teachers are lost to public education each year because they have too much self-respect too submit themselves to such play-acting? When both the ambitious and the idealistic are eliminated in large numbers, the incompetent fill the gap. But who is going to change the system? Not the Educationists: "You're talking about my job."

If anything, the impetus is moving the other way, toward more specialization and more education courses, away from basic knowledge. The going thing these days, if you're thinking about getting into teaching, is bilingual education. Accordingly a clamor is rising in the education schools to "upgrade" the degree required from a B.Ed. (or M.Ed.) with bilingual specialization to a degree in bilingual education itself. This will have the dual effect not only of providing yet more courses for an expanded faculty to teach, but of rendering obsolete the credentials of teachers in the field, whose job mobility will be threatened unless they return to school to secure the new degree. And so on. The same "upgrading" has already occurred in such growth areas as special education, learning disabilities, and reading.

With their locomotive rolling along so well, the Educationists never stop to ask about the problem of literacy, and they will either deny that there is a problem or that they have any responsibility for or ability to change it. All those I talked with at Southwest Texas State are sure *their* graduates could not be among those teachers failing basic literacy tests. No one, however, has tried to find out. In that Southwest Texas is not unique: DISD assistant superintendent John Santillo told me that no one from any teacher-training institution in Texas has contacted him to find out how its graduates have done. Several faculty members in education at SWT professed never to have heard anything about the Dallas or Houston competency tests, which must not only place them among the minority of literate Texas adults but, more to the point, shows how little concern or connection they have with how their theories are faring in the outside world. And no wonder: "You're talking about my job."

The self-deception can go to astonishing lengths. In the SWT School of Education's report to the TEA, I learned of a school policy that all prospective teachers must be grounded in "what is [sic] regarded as the basic areas of knowledge." An accompanying letter from the chairman of the English department, which is responsible for twelve hours of this basic knowledge, assures the TEA that Southwest Texas has "put more emphasis on literate writing for all students who are graduated from the University by helping to reinstate a committee maintained by our faculty senate to caretake writing proficiency." Passing over the subject-verb agreement problem in the policy statement and the fact that the chairman of the English department employs a verb "to care-take," that does not exist in the English language, I decided to go to the English department to see if they thought all SWT graduates were indeed literate.

The watchdog committee so proudly described by the department chairman as insuring the literacy of SWT graduates turns out *never to have met.* Three separate complaints about any given student are required before action can be considered. Outside the English department, I was told, the odds are that a junior or senior student at Southwest Texas will not encounter three professors who require written work, much less three willing to turn in a student to a faculty committee for inability to do same. In any event, the committee has had no reason to meet, because no one has ever been referred to it.

At the English department, I asked Professor Lois Haney, the department's liaison with the School of Education, how students are able to get through twelve hours of English without ever learning about such arcana as basic punctuation. Her answer was something I had heard before: "It is a matter of self-preservation," she told me, "not just for the profession as a whole, but for the individual teacher. I'm teaching a methods course for students who will be teaching high school English in a year or two. If I flunked seventy-five to eighty percent of them, what would happen to my job?"

Haney told me a story about a student whose practice teaching she was assigned to oversee in an area high school. When it came time to prepare a unit on Shakespeare's *Romeo and Juliet,* the young woman found herself in some difficulty, as she had never read so much as a line of Shakespeare in high school or college, and when she tried, found she could not make heads of tails of it. She gave in to tears and changed her career plans, a heartening conclusion, actually. Supervising teachers I spoke to in Dallas told me of protracted conflicts with education professors determined not to allow a mere teacher to prevent their young charges from scoring high on their nine weeks of practice teaching, even when the prospects were so ill-educated that the brighter high school pupils reacted with incredulity and derision.

The Teacher Education and Teacher Certification divisions of the Texas Education Agency occupy two identical examples of file-cabinet architecture located along the Colorado River in South Austin, about a mile from the Capitol. Considering that Texas has been investing in public education since 1854, it is a relatively young agency, created during an overhaul of the Texas school system in 1949. In that year the Legislature abolished the statewide elected office of Superintendent of Public Instruction in a futile attempt to divorce politics from education, and created the TEA to oversee both public schools and teacher education. In theory the agency is charged with making sure the colleges produce teachers capable of transmitting knowledge in a classroom. In practice, the TEA is composed of career Educationists who shuttle between the college education departments, the school districts, and the TEA. In terms of being able, or even wanting, to do very much more about teacher competence than shuffle paper, the TEA might as well be in charge of regulating and keeping track of the genealogy of armadillos. Not only does the buck fail to stop here, it doesn't even slow down.

A case in point: the TEA is supposed to set the guidelines for, and approve, every teacher-certification program at each of the state's sixty-three teacher-training institutions. It uses on-campus visits, interviews, and institutional documents the colleges call "self-evaluations" in its deliberations. But the TEA has never rejected a program and never will.

In fairness to the TEA, its futility is not entirely self-imposed. Back in 1974 the agency was showing some faint stirrings of life before then-attorney general John Hill handed down one of the more peculiar rulings to come out of his office. Hill decided that while Texas law clearly allowed the TEA to *approve* teacher-education and -certification programs, it did not let the TEA *disapprove* them. I leave the legal merits of Hill's opinion to learned students of the bar; practically, it left the TEA shorn of power, albeit a power it had never chosen to use. The opinion notwithstanding, I have a hard time envisioning the TEA on a crusade against teacher-certification programs. Dr. Tom Walker, director of the TEA's Division of Teacher Education, told me frankly, "As long as you have decision-making in the political arena, political pressure can determine the decision." Shutting down a college of education would draw the same reaction from the local legislator as shutting down an army base draws from the local congressman—except that the Pentagon packs more clout and once in a while gets its way.

In reality the TEA visitation is an elaborate charade in which the Educationists from the agency visit their soulmates in academia and almost invariably come away agreeing that the only thing wrong with teacher education on any given campus is that further specialization and grander architecture are in order. The TEA visited Southwest Texas State, for example, and presumably could have seen what I saw. It could not, however, have learned anything useful from reading the *1977 Institutional Report to the Texas Education Agency*, a two-volume work containing 1037 loosely bound pages of self-praise. I cannot claim to have perused every word of this weighty document, but I have read a good deal more of it than might be believed, and if there is anything wrong at the School of Education that is perceived by the administration or faculty, it does not surface in the text. The TEA likewise sees, hears, and speaks no evil. On a previous visit to Southwest Texas, the TEA found that the School of Education needed not a spanking (or better, dismantling) but a new main building, a new art building, a new student center, a new industrial arts visual aids facility, a new driver-training range (San Marcos' streets apparently being inadequate), a new gymnasium, and improvements to the university farm, along with several renovations to existing structures. Total cost: ten million dollars. No substantive fault was otherwise mentioned by either party to the evaluation.

If the TEA can do nothing to the colleges, you say, perhaps it can see to the competence of individual teachers? Perhaps it can. At this time, however, the TEA does not have that authority, and the people in charge do not want it. All graduates are assured Texas certification by law so long as they have completed the specific education courses required. Those requirements are listed in detail in a publication of some 243 8½-by-11-inch pages called—and this will give you some idea—*Texas Education Agency Bulletin 753, Guidelines for School Personnel: Certifications, Allocations, and Records, Section 1-Certification, Change* 2. Inside are the courses and degree plans required to earn certification in the many fields in which it is offered; as you can no doubt guess from its bulk, the matter is complicated to a degree one can only describe as insane. In general, the lower the grade level, the more education courses required. Nobody else on campus can pretend to offer the *subjects* taught in second grade; the Educationists have expanded into the vacuum. The same expansion has taken place in any area in which the traditional academic departments on campus have no turf to protect.

In order to teach seventh- and eighth-graders to type, for example, one needs to have had a *College Course* in typing. To teach the same subject in the ninth through twelfth grades, one needs to have had that and twenty-four hours of "business education." Imagine, if you will, what a college course in typing would consist of. Then try to determine how much shorthand and bookkeeping a person would learn in a full year of "business education." Why shouldn't a school district judge for itself whether a prospect types well enough to teach? Included in *Bulletin 753* are copies of the forms sent out by the TEA to tell persons applying for "permanent provisional" certificates why they are deficient. A prospective teacher of vocational education may be lacking in any of twenty-five specific categories, plus "Other." Besides the required courses in Texas and federal government, some of those specific areas are "Aims and Objectives of Vocational Education," "Development, Organization, and Use of Instructional Materials," "History and Principles of Vocational Education," "Human Relations for Vocational Teachers," "Methods of Teaching Vocational Subjects," "Methods and Media for Teaching Vocational Subjects," "Occupational and Educational Information," "Group Organization and Management." Had enough? Then imagine yourself to be a practical-minded and idealistic youth interested in teaching high school shop.

Such tedious, detailed requirements have two fairly obvious intentions: keeping education professors in work and making sure nobody can take his or her training outside Texas, which amounts to the same thing. A more fiendishly efficient program for insuring mediocrity could not be designed.

What about testing for literacy on a statewide level, as Florida will do, starting next year? Mrs. Magnolia McCullough, who is in charge of the TEA Division of Teacher Certification, did not want me to think she was ducking the hard ones, but she passed me along to her boss, Dr. Jim Kidd, who is in charge of both education and certification. Dr. Kidd is very much aware of the problem of competency. Most of our discussion, though, was a waltz around what I came to call privately the chicken and the egg—the chicken being the *what* of teaching, the egg being the *how*. Like all Educationists, however, he prefers talking about eggs to talking about chickens. Current orthodoxy holds that no "paper and pencil test"—a phrase that pops up again and again in talking to Educationists—can determine whether a person will be a good teacher. Now, such a conclusion ought to be obvious. If one could determine a person's ability to succeed in a pragmatic art by administering a written exam, Howard Cosell would wear a helmet instead of a toupee and play cornerback for the Dallas Cowboys.

But if Howard Cosell thought a touchdown was scored by letting the air out of the football, or that a field goal was worth fourteen points, I think one could safely say his usefulness to the Cowboys would be limited. Yet the TEA does not believe in examining applicants for teacher certification because, as Kidd says, "there has been no progress in testing that can establish any positive connection between success on a test and success as a teacher. . . . We could require a B grade average but I'm not sure that would be valid or even desirable."

I did not have the University of Houston figures on hand when I spoke to Dr. Kidd, so I was not able to counter properly. After a few trips around the henhouse we did finally agree that there is probably a connection between sheer ignorance and the inability to teach, but when I left his office I did not get the impression that the TEA would be moving forward on teacher licensing exams anytime soon. The truth is that the education departments have long since carried the day, politically speaking, and that the TEA is not about to begin a pecking party it would surely lose. Despite the odd glimmer of hope here and there—the education school at UT-Austin will start examining the competence of students *before* they enter the major—the system is too far gone to reform itself. Change will have to come from outside.

Between 1967 and 1972 the TEA required the National Teacher Examination of those who planned to certify, never as a condition of certification, but as a fairly valuable indicator to anybody thinking about hiring a given individual of whether he knew what he was supposed to have learned in college. Like the SAT, GRE (Graduate Record Exam), LSAT (Law School Admission Test), and several other tests of their kind, the National Teacher Examination (NTE) is made up, administered, and scored by the Educational Testing Service of Princeton, New Jersey, a nonprofit organization that maintains regional offices in Austin. Some educators will tell you, although not for attribution, that the NTE was given up because blacks and Mexican Americans did so poorly on it. TEA officials deny that, insisting that the instrument was dropped solely because no positive correlation could ever be established between the NTE and classroom success.

As it happens, blacks and Mexican Americans as statistical groups do tend to score worse on the NTE, although as was the case with the DISD's Wesman test, individual members from all groups place from the very highest to the lowest categories. It is a fact of life that Black and Mexican Americans score lower on all standardized instruments as the result of historical discrimination. But historical discrimination is no reason to exempt contemporary students from basic educational requirements, which, after all, are not really very difficult if insisted upon. More and more blacks and Mexican Americans are rejecting the notion that basic standards constitute cultural bias. They realize that the contention can be a form of self-imposed racism as destructive as bigotry. To use the crutch of cultural bias is to load up the schools with incompetents who cannot teach, are fearful of speaking up for themselves and their students, and who validate white superstitions about minority incapacity. The only incapacity really being protected is the Educationists'. Entrance to other professions—medicine, law, architecture, accountancy—is achieved only after passing licensing exams. Why not teaching?

When other states tried licensing exams, the National Education Association's response was predictable. It sued South Carolina for using the National Teacher Examination as one of a number of guidelines for approving or disapproving the certification of teachers. Fortunately, the NEA lost: the U.S. Supreme Court ruled in January, 1978 that the NTE creates classifications on permissible bases—knowledge, skill, and ability—and that they are not used with any intent to discriminate.

The attack on the Educationists' monopoly over the public schools may have already begun. The recent session of the Texas Legislature restored the pre-John Hill authority to disapprove, as well as approve, college teacher-certification programs. The Legislature also partially heeded teachers' pleas to give the profession, not the TEA, control over certification; a new advisory board dominated by teachers will in the future make recommendations on certification programs to the TEA's publicly elected governing board, which still has the final say. Maybe teachers, who covet the status enjoyed by professions like law and medicine, will try to institute licensing tests. Maybe. Experience suggests, however, that they are more likely to seek even more protection than they already have. But Texas teacher organizations have not—as the Classroom Teachers of Dallas' resistance to the NEA position on competency testing shows—grown as defensive as teacher unions elsewhere. Indeed one of the most articulate and forceful critics of the current setup I spoke to was Harley Hiscox, a full-time organizer for the Dallas Federation of Teachers and an AFL-CIO man all the way. "I taught for twenty years in California and had a life certificate," Hiscox says, "and I couldn't get a job anywhere in Texas. I'd have to go back to school for a year at least—full time. I would need the equivalent of another M.A. My wife taught fifteen years in Canada and it is taking her a year to certify. The purpose is not to get better teachers; it's to get more money, more contact hours, and bigger buildings for the colleges."

The monopoly of the education schools must be broken; there must be other paths to certification. Since teaching is a pragmatic art best learned by experience, school districts should establish apprenticeship programs for people who can satisfy the literacy requirements and show a command of subject matter. This isn't 1910, when Texas comprised thousands of tiny rural school districts that needed whatever guarantee of teacher quality the education schools could provide; this is modern, urban Texas, and the school districts are much more sensitive to demands for competence than Educationists who pick their way to class through fields of bikinis. The education schools will never improve substantially without competition. Opening up the profession would not only save money that now sustains the Educationists' empires, but could also help bring into the public schools considerable numbers of persons who chose an education over certification to begin with. It might also go a long way toward restoring the dignity of what is, after all, one of the most decent of professions. Indeed, it is only because there are so many more talented and committed public-school teachers out there than one could possibly expect from the system that produces them—so many who have gritted their teeth and persevered—that one can propose apprenticeship programs over what we have now. Every high school teacher I know at all well, and I know quite a few, would be just as appalled at the goings-on in Education 3330 as I was.

Like all proposals for reform, mine might not work as I envision it. The TEA could subvert literacy standards by setting them so low as to be meaningless. Or salaries could remain so low that schools continue to be outbid for talented people and have to fill slots with whatever they can get.

But I am sure of one thing. We have to do *something*. I believe in public schools, having never attended any other kind at any level. My elder son attends a black-majority urban public school and his younger brother will join him in the fall. Unless I grow convinced that either or both is suffering irreparable brain atrophy, I intend to keep them there through high school. I do not wish that they consort only with children whose parents can afford private schools and whose skin is the same shade as theirs. I also believe that the very future of American democracy is at stake. An illiterate or semiliterate person in our society is a kind of peasant. Peasants may or may not be happier than tax lawyers, but they cannot make intelligent choices in the world we inhabit. Another generation of the same old thing, and even the most egalitarian advocates of the public schools in Texas will come to feel as just about everybody in New York City who can afford private tuition and many who cannot do: public schools were a nice idea for *their* time, but not for their children's.

1979

Repealing the Enlightenment

We must respect the other fellow's religion, but only in the sense that we respect his theory that his wife is beautiful and his children smart.

—H. L. Mencken

The subspecies *Homo Nesciens Arkansas* comprises two distinct varieties: Country, and Country-Come-to-Town. It was ever thus. Back in the bad old days before the invention of polyester suits and communications satellites, however, genuine yokels held all the power in the state we call "the Land of Opportunity." In fact the first Arkansas anti-evolution law was not a product of the legislature. Passed on November 6, 1928, the day of Herbert Hoover's ascension to the presidency, the statute forbidding mention of Godless, atheistic Darwinism in public schools was enacted by popular referendum.

A couple of days before the election, advertisements appeared in newspapers across the state. "The Bible or atheism, which?" read the headline on one favoring the passage of Act One. But more than a hundred prominent citizens, including two former governors and the editor of the *Arkansas Gazette*—most of them from the sinful metropolis of Little Rock—signed another advertisement, urging common sense. Only three years earlier, after all, in 1925, Arkansas's neighbor to the east had convicted John

Scopes for uttering heresies within the hearing of schoolchildren, and in the process had made the word "Tennessee" a synonym for "benighted." The people at large, the second advertisement maintained, were not qualified to pass on the veracity of a theory taught "in every first-class university and college in America, Europe, Asia, Africa, and Australia." It was not the credibility of science that was at stake, but the state's reputation.

Voter turnout was heavy, for not only were science and religion contending on the ballot, but Arkansas faced an excruciating presidential choice. Al Smith, the Democrat, represented both Demon Rum and the Pope of Rome. Hoover, though, was a Republican, the party of Lincoln. Hayseeds emerged from every God-intoxicated hollow in the Ozarks; automobile and mule jams clogged the flat dirt roads of the Delta. Al Smith won the Wonder State, but evolution lost. The vote for banning biological science was 108,991 to 63,406. Only Pulaski County (Little Rock) dissented.

Having made a ritual gesture in favor of the Lord, fundamentalists returned to the sleep of ages. Darwin made little headway in the boondocks, but then neither did any other sort of civilized learning. Most persons capable of reason in those districts found out about evolutionary theory anyway. In Little Rock and the other larger towns the law was ignored, albeit with caution. Acquaintances of mine who grew up in country towns tell stories of science teachers' voices dropping into conspiratorial whispers, of books being slipped to them on the sly as if they were racy French novels. A cruder version of the Moral Majority has been regnant in the Arkansas outback for at least 150 years, after all, without having effected a diminution of freelance sin. Alcohol in drinkable form is still forbidden the rustics across vast swatches of the state. While a federal court in Little Rock wrestled recently with creationism, the school board in Paragould voted not to allow a school prom on the grounds that dancin' leads to drinkin' and drinkin' to lust. Even so, Arkansas leads the nation in teenage pregnancies and ranks high in the incidence of venereal disease. By setting up coherent thought as temptation, Arkansas's anti-evolution law has probably lured as many young Arkansans to science over the years as it has prevented from hearing about it.

Initiated Act One, in any event, remained on the books for forty years with nary a prosecution. It was removed in 1968 by the United States Supreme Court after a Little Rock Central High biology teacher made an issue of it. *Epperson* v. *Arkansas* was the second Supreme Court case involving Central High in little more than a decade. The first, of course, concerned racial segregation.

Know-nothingism in a Lab Coat

Act 590, or the Balanced Treatment of Creation-Science and Evolution-Science Act, as adepts call it, has a more socially acceptable pedigree than the 1928 monkey law. Reporters who came to Little Rock to cover the recent trial about this one's constitutionality found no snake handlers or fulminating barefoot hillbillies. Yessir, folks, with Act 590, country has done come to town. Dress up an ambitious fraud in a suit made of synthetic fiber, style his hair like a health-spa instructor's, give him a pocketful of credit cards, a push-button phone with a "hold" button, electric windows in his late model car, stick a Bible in his pocket, provide a neatly coiffed wife who knows how to make goo-goo eyes at the back of his head for TV cameras, and that man can play the media like a church organ. The statute's very concept of "balanced treatment" derives from, and therefore appeals to, the idea of journalistic fairness taught in the nation's "Schools of Communication." Are there not, after all, "two sides to every question"? Unfortunately that concept, which is shallow enough when dealing with persons holding a post-Enlightenment world view, ill equips a reporter to get at the truth when confronted with persons who do not. Creationists, you see, do not believe that there is or can be a distinction between the sacred and the secular. All ideas to them are religious ideas. Hence they do not hold themselves to the arbitration of facts, evidence, and logic; they reject the metaphysics of science even while claiming its cultural authority.

Neither do creationists believe, accordingly, in the separation of church and state, although they will prevaricate and squirm like sixteenth-century Jesuits when the question is put to them directly. So if the story of the 1981 Monkey Trial strikes you as ludicrous, which I hope it will, do not therefore be deceived into taking creationism lightly. Theirs is a coherent and internally consistent world view. The "scientists" in the movement do science as one does literary criticism, picking among facts and theories for ones that support a preexisting point of view—which in their case is a literal reading of Genesis—and either twisting whatever does not fit, or simply discarding it. Creationism is no more science than is astrology or palmreading; it is William Jennings Bryan's know-nothingism in a lab coat. Creationists claim the designation "scientific" partly as propaganda; but, as with most propaganda, they are their own first victims. Oddly, while not believing in real science, which strikes them as pessimistic, European, and anti-Christian—perhaps even "Jewish"—they believe quite heartily, most of them, in technology and progress. Up to the day of Armageddon, that is. Most would also be shocked to hear themselves described as Social Darwinists, but all are free-enterprise zealots whose views are perfectly congruent with that turn-of-the-century philosophy. And there are a whole lot more of them in California, to come to the point, than there are in Arkansas.

[Evolution is] theory only. In recent years [it] has been challenged in the world of science. If evolutionary theory is going to be taught in the schools, then I would think that also the Biblical theory of creation, which is not a theory but the Biblical story of creation, should also be taught.
—*Ronald Reagan, on the campaign trail in Dallas, 1980*

But the Arkansas experience with creationism is instructive. The sponsor of the "Balanced Treatment" Act was one Sen. James L. Holsted of North Little Rock, a tall, handsome graduate of Vanderbilt University who was at the time president of the Providential Life Insurance Company, a family concern. Creationism zipped through the senate on the last day of the 1981 session, with no hearings and only a few comments from the floor. The house of representatives held no hearings either, having scheduled the bill for a period reserved for "noncontroversial" legislation. Debate consumed all of fifteen minutes, some of which was spent refusing to hear Arkansas's Methodist bishop Kenneth Hicks, who had rushed in vain to the capitol when a member of his flock warned him what was up. The tally there was 69–18.

Better Than the Circus

Arkansans in general are probably no more ignorant than the American public at large, but all the ignoramuses do agree. Political tradition here pardons a legislator who votes on symbolic issues to soothe the prejudices of the fire-breathing element in the dirt-road churches. Arkansas is more than 90 percent Protestant, the hard-shell sects predominate, and ambitious youths yearn to be television evangelists as others wish to emulate Reggie Jackson or Donny Osmond. No sense, runs the usual logic, in stirring people up; the federal courts can take care of it. Then everybody can whoop it up in the next campaign about meddlin' judges thwarting the will of the people, can get reelected, and can continue to work on the truly important business of democracy, like exempting farm equipment from the sales tax or allowing the poultry industry to load as many chickens as can be jammed into a semi-trailer regardless of highway weight limits.

If the reader detects bitterness, that is an error of tone. Traditionally, an Arkansas legislature in session is a spectacle more diverting than any circus, and best of all, it is free. The lawmakers hit Little Rock every two years from such rustic venues as Oil Trough, Smackover, and Hogeye like so many sailors just off a six-month cruise. Any curious citizen may venture of any evening to the saloons where the fun lovers among them congregate, and there be treated to a carnival of boozing, lurching, and panting such as one rarely sees so far from salt water. But there have been no fistfights on the floor this year, spittoons have given way to discreetly handled styrofoam cups, and ironists lament that the diverting spectacles of old are probably gone for good.

Indeed, it appears that many of the legislators mistook the creationist bill for yet another in the series of harmless resolutions in praise of Christianity that they customarily endorse. Others were simply gulled. Had scientists uncovered evidence proving Genesis to be biologically and historically accurate? Who could doubt it? Were atheists and "secular humanists" laboring to suppress the truth? It sounded logical. The legislature was besieged by a well-organized phalanx not of backwoods fulminators but of live-wire "Christian" businessmen and doctors' wives from the newer suburbs of Little Rock. The creationists have laid their traps where the money is: among the semi-educated who, by their prosperity, deem themselves members of contemporary Puritanism's visible elect, but who cling to the childish theology of their fathers because contemporary life has flooded them with a confusion of moral values that will not compute unless the Bible is accepted as a rule book. At the time of the "debate," only the Moral Majority and a local organization called FLAG (Family, Life, America, and God) seemed to know that Act 590 had been introduced at all, much less made it to the floor.

In fact, Act 590 was not written in Arkansas, and there is reason to doubt that anybody here read it all the way through until after it was already law. Senator Holsted got it from an employee of his, who in turn took it from a group of fundamentalist ministers who received it by mail from its author, a respiration therapist named Paul Ellwanger of Anderson, South Carolina. Ellwanger, founder and proprietor of an organization he calls Citizens for Fairness in Education, wrote it with the help of an outfit called the Institute for Creation Research in (where else?) San Diego. The "scientific" godfathers of creationism are Henry Morris and one Dr. Duane Gish, a preposterous buncombe artist about whom more later. The principal legal consultant was Wendell Bird, also of the ICR and author, for those readers who may be tempted to dismiss creationism as a mere regional delusion, of a very long article in the *Yale Law Journal* three years ago that not only posited creationism as a science but proposed its inclusion in public school curricula to "balance" and thereby "neutralize" the teaching of evolution, which it equated with atheism. The University of Arkansas law journal, I am confident, would have rejected Bird's vaporizings out of hand. Not only would the people in charge have recognized the theological underpinnings, but they would have feared for their academic reputation.

Governor Frank White certainly did not read the creationism

bill. A Little Rock bank executive and a graduate of the U.S. Naval Academy, White ran for office as God's own candidate. The Lord, he said repeatedly during his campaign against incumbent Democrat Bill Clinton, had told him to declare his candidacy. On winning a narrow victory in the Reagan landslide, he declared the Deity well pleased. White's equally pious second wife told the press that God had not only introduced her to her second husband, but He had even done a turn as celestial realtor, divinely inspiring their choice of a home. After he signed the bill, White boasted to reporters that Arkansas had assumed the scientific leadership of the known world. White asserted that the new law was undoubtedly constitutional. But when asked specifically about the clause forbidding the "establishment of Theologically Liberal, Humanist, Nontheist, or Atheistic religions," the governor confessed that he was ignorant of the text. His office issued a clarification saying he had been thoroughly briefed, but the aide responsible for keeping track of legislation told the *Arkansas Gazette* that to her knowledge nothing of the sort had transpired. Sponsor Holsted told the same newspaper that "of course" his motives were religious, but, he added, "If I'd known people were going to be asking me about the specifics of creation science, I might have gotten scared off because I don't know anything about the stuff." Democratic Attorney General Steve Clark, in a remark that would come back to haunt him, said he had his doubts the law could be defended.

When the educated portion of the citizenry heard about the law, reaction was strong. There was a near unanimous outcry from the universities, teacher organizations, and the Arkansas Academy of Sciences. Editorial scorn was heaped on the perpetrators by virtually every newspaper in the state. So far have we come since 1928 that editorialists in places like Warren, McGehee, Stuttgart, Searcy, and Lonoke felt free to denounce Act 590 without having to fear burning crosses. The prevailing theme was that the thoughtless bozos of the legislature had again made Arkansas a national joke, just when its image had begun to improve after the damage done by Orval Faubus in the 1957 Central High integration crisis. A Little Rock man had lapel pins made with a banana logo and sold them to benefit the monkey house at the zoo; he raised hundreds of dollars. A series of derisively funny editorial cartoons has appeared in the *Arkansas Gazette* in which Governor White always appears holding a half-eaten banana. Only the *Arkansas Democrat,* the capital's second-string newspaper, involved in a circulation war with the *Gazette* and seeking the lowest common denominator, has defended the law. But then the *Democrat* looks at the world through oddly tinted glasses. Recently the paper devoted its editorial column to the proposition that Franklin Delano Roosevelt was a Fascist. When the American Association for the Advancement of Science pledged itself to resist creationism, the *Democrat* determined it to be an organization of "moral idiots" and "intellectual frauds."

Senator Holsted was prevented from reaping what glory there was to be had from creationism by an untimely indictment for embezzling $105,000 from the family business, but Frank White has got himself an issue. The governor's genius consists of a total inability to be embarrassed. His 1980 campaign was a masterpiece of fraudulent innuendo. Besides the usual denunciations of taxes, Big Government, and welfare cheats—Arkansas has the lowest taxes of any of the fifty states, and thus of the industrial world—White spent most of his money on a series of television commercials showing a minor riot by Cuban refugees housed on a former army base near Fort Smith. Most of the Cubans were black. Had Governor Bill Clinton "stood up" to Jimmy Carter, he asserted, this threat to Arkansas's peace and security could have been prevented.

Whether or not White is the crassest religious hypocrite seen in these parts since Billy Sunday seems to me a question not worth pausing over. Americans overrate sincerity. Morally speaking, it matters little whether a person can't think, won't think, or merely feigns the credulity of a child. In any case, creationism has become so volatile an issue that the governor is welcome to it, should he decide to flog it in the 1982 campaign. Creationism cuts unpredictably across party and ideological lines. As always, the imponderable mystery is how the monkey law plays in the county; White couldn't be elected county assessor in Little Rock. But there are no polls to tell us how many Arkansans favor the law, much less whether its proponents care deeply enough to vote on that basis alone. Many legislators got nervous when they began hearing from their educated constituents, particularly from ministers and churchgoers from nonfundamentalist sects, which have long since given up militant opposition to the visible world, and who believe correctly that antics like those of last year degrade religion rather than advance it. Chambers of commerce anxious to lure new industries, especially of the clean, high-tech variety, found themselves facing embarrassing questions. Some even wondered whether creationism might not hamper the Arkansas Razorback football and basketball coaches in their quest for out-of-state talent. If *that* could be proved, only Jehovah himself could save White from popular wrath. Many legislators said they thought they had made a mistake; there was talk of repeal. But that required the cooperation of the governor, and White stood petulantly firm. If anybody was going to save Arkansas's public school students from necromancy, it would have to be a federal judge. Again.

God Takes the Stand

If one wished to understand why the adult forms of Christianity in America seem afflicted with polite senility while the kindergarten churches bulge with sinners, Little Rock's creationism trial offered many clues. When the American Civil Liberties Union first announced that it would challenge the law and presented its twenty-three plaintiffs to the public, creationism looked to be set up for a quick knockout. Of the twenty-three, twelve were clerics. Their number included not only the Methodist, Roman Catholic, Episcopal, and African Methodist Episcopal bishops of Arkansas but also representatives of the Presbyterians, Southern Baptists, and Reform Jews as well. Here was a perfect opportunity to seize the high rhetorical ground from the electronic fundamentalists. In aligning themselves with an easily exposed religious hoax, the Moral Majority and company would seem finally to have gone too far. To require that a sectarian dogma inimical to most churches be taught *as science* in public schools violates virtually everything sixth graders are taught about Americanism.

But the churchmen blew it, locally at least. They allowed themselves to be muzzled by a platoon of lawyers. Perhaps "muzzled" is a bit strong. Although the trial was political in its essence, the

ACLU conducted it as if it were a corporate merger. In their own pulpits and newsletters, the clergy expressed themselves forcefully and with some eloquence. Bishop Hicks of the Arkansas Methodist Church delivered himself early of a well-written letter to the *Gazette* on the vast presumption underlying fundamentalist bibliolatry: that puny man sets himself up to limit God's power to the dimensions of his own mind. But only a small fraction of readers see the editorial page; Hicks was preaching to the converted. If the churchmen had appeared on the evening news bearing such messages, if they had held regular news conferences and distributed press releases at regular intervals commenting on the trial, if they had put together a paid religious telecast on the subject using some of the very erudite and committed scientists and theologians who came to Little Rock on their own time to testify, they might have dealt creationism a crippling blow. They did not conduct such a campaign. But the Moral Majority and the Institute for Creation Research did. So the fundamentalist line that the trial was a contest between atheism and the Lord went unchallenged, at least in volume and stridency.

The court would never criticize or discredit any person's testimony based on his or her religious beliefs. While anybody is free to approach a scientific inquiry in any fashion he chooses, he cannot properly describe the methodology used as scientific if he starts with a conclusion and refuses to change it, regardless of the evidence developed during the course of the investigation.

—Judge William R. Overton

But that is a cavil next to the brilliant show the ACLU's witnesses made during the trial last December. Arkansans can thank their governor and legislature for provoking a first-rate seminar on science and theology, featuring an array of erudite men and women whose like we would not otherwise have seen in five years of visiting lecturers. University of Chicago theologian Langdon Gilkey made such a forceful witness that he had the fundamentalist preachers who crowded the back of the courtroom nodding and buzzing in agreement when he dissected the language of Act 590

221

to reveal at every turn the unacknowledged authority of Genesis, the very phrase "sudden creation of the universe, energy, and life from nothing" implying not only God, but the God of the Old Testament alone.

Of course most of those preachers are simple souls, not up to the rapid donning and doffing of hats required to maintain that creationism is "scientific" and Act 590's purpose is secular. Unlike many of the state's witnesses, they have never wandered in the wood of materialism and doubt. Evolution is to them an unholy fairy tale whose premises they have never credited for one moment. As for the U.S. Constitution, why, if the Founding Fathers had meant for us to separate God's word from our government, the word "Creator" would not appear in the Declaration of Independence. Only communists think otherwise. When Cornell sociologist Dorothy Nelkin said in cross-examination that she was an atheist, there was a muted gasp in the back of the courtroom. Several heads bowed in prayer.

As the plaintiff's witnesses went on, the courtroom took on most of the aspects not of a religious, but an academic, camp meeting. Except for Moral Majoritarians and creationists taking notes, most of the militant godly among the spectators disappeared, to be replaced by honors biology classes from the local high schools and professors from the Little Rock campuses of the University of Arkansas. Even had I not recognized many of the latter, style would have told: in our corner of the world, as the British reporters on hand rapidly established, creationists go in for synthetic fabrics, styled hair, or toupees, while evolutionists sport khaki, wool, and facial hair.

As an academic camp meeting, the first week of the trial was most inspiring to this apostate English professor. Having years ago wearied of the posturings of most academic literary types, I suppose I had grown more than half dubious that useful thinking was going on anywhere in the academic world. But to hear philosopher of science Michael Ruse of the University of Guelph explain how science both limits and lays claim to knowledge, and to be able to listen to such literate practitioners as geneticist Francisco Ayala of the University of California, biophysicist Harold Morowitz of Yale, Harvard's versatile paleontologist

Stephen Jay Gould, and Brent Dalrymple of the U.S. Geological Survey was a rare privilege. There may be something more to our species after all than the lust for power and things. Thank you, Governor White.

A gorilla, true enough, cannot write poetry and neither can it grasp such a concept as that of Americanization or that of relativity, but . . . in some ways, indeed, it is measurably more clever than many men. It cannot be fooled as easily; it does not waste so much time doing useless things. If it desires, for example, to get a banana, hung out of reach, it proceeds to the business with a singleness of purpose and a fertility of resource that, in a traffic policeman, would seem almost pathological. There are no funda- mentalists among the primates. They believe nothing that is not demon- strable. When they confront a fact they recognize it instantly, and turn it to their uses with admirable readiness. There are liars among them, but no idealists.

—H. L. Mencken

It was hard not to pity Attorney General Steve Clark and his outgunned staff, attempting to show that the creationism law had no religious origins. The record contained letters from the law's author. "I view this whole battle as one between God and anti-God forces," Paul Ellwanger had written. He advised his support- ers to conceal their sacred motives, lest the courts catch on; if they could not forbear witnessing for the Lord when petitioning their representatives, they should reserve the apologetics for a separate sheet of paper.

The text of the law itself betrayed its intent at every turn. Here, for example, is the definition of the law of creationism:

"Creation-science" means the scientific evidences for creation and in- ferences from those scientific evidences. Creation-science includes the scientific evidences and related inferences that indicate: (1) sudden crea- tion of the universe, energy, and life from nothing; (2) the insufficiency of mutation and natural selection in bringing about development of all living kinds from a single organism; (3) changes only within fixed limits of originally created kinds of plants and animals; (4) separate ancestry for man and apes; (5) explanation of the earth's geology by catastrophism, including the occurrence of a worldwide flood; and (6) a relatively recent inception of the earth and living kinds.

In nearly two weeks of testimony, no scientist, whether "creation" or otherwise, could enlighten the court as to the exact meaning of "kind." Creationist Wayne A. Friar of King's College, Briarcliff Manor, New York, said it could mean "species," "genus," "family," or even "order" in which case number four above stands contradicted, since Adam and Eve, Governor White, and Bonzo the Chimp all belong to the order of primates. Friar, who labors at refuting Darwin by comparing the blood-cell sizes of various turtles, said he was still working on the problem of whether or not the shelled beasts constitute a kind. Neither turtles nor tortoises, of course, are specifically mentioned in Genesis 1:11–12 and 21–25, where the concept of "kinds" originates; some, indeed, are "swimming creatures, with which the waters abound," others "animals that crawl on the earth." It is a difficult problem.

Perhaps no more difficult, though, than the problem the attorney general faced in seeking expert witnesses for creationism. Everybody, both in the movement and outside it, cites Henry Morris and Duane Gish of the Institute for Creation Research as not simply *the* authorities on the subject, but in fact its originators. Both, unfortunately, are prolific authors. Putting them on the stand to prove creationism to be a science would be like calling Richard Nixon to testify that politicians never lie. In his treatise *Scientific Creationism*, for example, Morris says:

A. Creation cannot be proved
1. Creation . . . is inaccessible to the scientific method.
2. It is impossible to devise a scientific experiment to describe the creation process, or even to ascertain whether such a process can take place. The creator does not create at the whim of a scientist.

The learned Dr. Gish—he has a Ph.D. in biochemistry from Berkeley—is similarly honest, at least part of the time. In *Evolution? the Fossils Say No!*, he puts it this way:

We do not know who the Creator created, what processes He used, for *He used processes which are not now operating anywhere in the natural uni-*

verse [his emphasis]. This is why we refer to creation as special creation. We cannot discover by scientific investigations anything about the creative processes used by the Creator.

As an article of faith, of course, Gish's is a perfectly sound position and places creationism exactly where it belongs: outside science's claim to know. In a recent letter to *Discover* magazine, though, Gish went further. He was responding to an article attacking creationism's pretensions:

Stephen Jay Gould states that creationists claim creation is a scientific theory. *This is a false accusation.* Creationists have repeatedly stated that neither creation nor evolution is a scientific theory (and each is equally religious).

Yet this same eminence was everywhere in Little Rock during the trial, sitting two rows behind the state's lawyers, passing them notes, indulging in heated colloquies during recesses, and making pronouncements about the indubitable scientific merits of creationism for the television reporters. Indeed, the man's creator seems to have blessed him with a tropism for bright lights and camera lenses.

Despite a definitely simian aspect, which made him the butt of many cruel jokes in the press row, Gish is in fact a masterful artist of the televised debate, that bastard form of showmanship first visited on us by presidential politics. During the trial, good old Jerry Falwell, of Moral Majority and "Old Time Gospel Hour" fame, staged just such a confrontation between Gish and Professor Russell Doolittle, a chemist from the University of California, who was naive enough to think that the winners and losers of such events are determined by evidence and logic. Perhaps in graduate seminars and laboratories they are, but for all of his earnest learning, Doolittle might as well have been trading insults with Johnny Carson. Gish's presentation was timed to the minute and consisted of a premium assortment of half-truths, semifacts, quasi-logic, outright falsehoods, and simple balderdash. All replete, of course, with scriptural authority. In front of the audience of Falwell's Lynchburg church, cheering and whistling to see the infidel routed, Gish was triumphant.

Gish argued, for example, that the Second Law of Thermodynamics renders evolution impossible. How childish of "evolution scientists" to imagine, he implied, that they could push this ludicrous hoax past such a learned and reverent authority as himself. What the cheering faithful do not know, however, is that the Second Law of Thermodynamics states almost the opposite of what Gish says it does. In a closed system, it is true, greater organization of heat energy cannot occur. A closed system is one that energy is not entering from the outside. In an open system, into which energy does flow, increased organization of energy can and does occur. Until very recently, when scientists simply ignored the creationists, Gish and his followers did not trouble to make the distinction, although if the Second Law meant what they said it did, not only evolution but life itself would be impossible. On the "Old Time Gospel Hour" debate Gish even slipped for a brief moment into the Old Time Second Law of Thermodynamics, telling the audience that "on the hypothetical primordial earth, you did not have an energy conversion machine." This is heresy. According to my Bible, God created the sun on the fourth day. Perhaps Gish reads a different translation.

Soon enough, though, he was back on course, acknowledging his critics by maintaining that the very "universe itself is an isolated system." This is why scientists should not debate the man. By the time they got through explaining that a "closed system" in thermodynamics and the "closed universe" hypothesized by some astrophysicists had no more bearing on the matter than a closed checking account on a closed mind, Gish's audience would have swallowed his pun whole and be uttering hosannahs.

With creationism's chief apologists eliminated as potential witnesses by reason of their own past words, Attorney General Clark had no recourse but to call creationists who had published little or nothing. What began in the first week as a fine seminar degenerated into a boring farce with overtones of pathos. That the state's case was incoherent was no fault of the lawyers: it was Act 590 that bequeathed to them the "two-model approach," in turn taken from creationist authors, who in turn plagiarized the notion, as I have suggested earlier, from the "equal time" doctrine that allots television coverage to political candidates in our imperfect world of Republicans and Democrats. Briefly stated, the argument runs like this: "evolution science" posits atheism. "Creation science," while not religious, of course, posits theism. There are no other possibilities. Either there is a God, in which case "evolution science" is falsified, or there is not, in which case . . . But let us not get into that thicket. Suffice it to say, though, that the theory of evolution does not posit atheism. Science agrees to exclude the supernatural, yes. But so do accounting, law, and the rules of baseball. Are we now to have Bowie Kuhn denounced as a godless purveyor of materialistic satanism? Perhaps a creation baseball league will be next.

It was by such incantation that Clark, a handsome man so cleft of chin that he could have been sent down from Central Casting to play the role of up-and-coming Southern moderate, hoped to avoid political disaster. Because a luncheon with Clark had once been auctioned off at an ACLU fund-raiser, the Attorney General was denounced as "crooked" by Pat Robertson, the host of the Christian Broadcast Network's "700 Club," and accused of deliberately throwing the trial. The Reverend Dr. Falwell followed with a similar charge, although the Arkansas Moral Majority confined itself to attacking Judge Overton's impartiality. Even so, Clark is probably safe. Historically, Arkansans have resented outside criticism of their own politicians, and Clark had never sought the hardcore fundamentalist vote anyway.

The "two-model approach" allowed Clark to pretend what creationists pretend: that all evidence against any aspect of any scientific theory tending to support evolution constitutes proof of creationism. Logically, of course, this is like saying that evidence I was not in Little Rock last Wednesday establishes that I was in fact golfing on Mars. Hence scientists were easily convicted of doing science. Does Stephen Jay Gould's theory of "punctuated equilibrium"—i.e., of evolutionary change in relatively rapid bursts, with cataclysms altering the environment—disagree with those of more orthodox theorists who think the process has been more gradual? Very well. Both are refuted and creationism proved. One of the funnier moments in the trial's first week came when one young barrister tried to ensnare the wickedly articulate Francisco Ayala, a former priest with scientific training *and* the equivalent of a doctorate in theology, into admitting the validity of the two-model approach. "Your name," the scientist told the expectant young lawyer, "is Mr. Williams. But my name isn't not-Mr. Williams. The courtroom is full of people whose name isn't not-Mr. Williams." The real Mr. Williams changed his line of questioning. At another point, a state's attorney asked Professor Morowitz of Yale: "Can you tell me the name of one Ivy League university that has a creation scientist on its staff?" Morowitz could not. Neither could he name any other prestigious graduate school or journal that employed creationists. Morowitz added, "I can't give you the name of an Ivy League school, graduate school or journal which houses a flat earth theorist either."

The state's most coherent witness by far was Dr. Norman Geisler of the Dallas Theological Seminary. It was Geisler who admitted, under cross-examination, that besides the two-model theory, he also believed that UFO's were "a satanic manifestation in the world for the purpose of deception." As nearly as I can work it out, Geisler believes that any abstract idea held strongly by any number of people constitutes what he calls "transcendence," and answers his definition of religion. He quoted, as all good fundamentalists do, from something called *The Humanist Manifesto,* and intimated that because there is such an organization, and because a footnote in a Supreme Court decision once classified that organization as a religious one, that all persons who are "humanists" are acolytes of that faith. I shall refrain from insulting *Harper's* readers by letting them work out the syllogism themselves. It is by such arguments that fundamentalist "intellectuals" propose to render the First Amendment tautological and thus useless: if all intellectual positions are equally "religious" in nature, then why bother?

The most profound part of Geisler's testimony was his attempt to prove that the "Creator" of the universe and life mentioned in Act 590 was not an inherently religious concept. After citing Aristotle, Plato, and one or two other classical philosophers who supposedly believed in a God or gods without worshiping them—albeit not as creators of the world "from nothing"—Geisler offered his most thundering proof: the Epistle of James. He cited a line of Scripture to the effect that Satan acknowledges God, but chooses not to worship Him. "The Devil," he said, "believes that there is a God." Whee! If Geisler has not yet squared the circle in his meditations, he has at least, well, circled it. Who would have thought one could prove the Creator a nonreligious idea by means of hearsay evidence from Beelzebub? After unloading that bombshell, Geisler, too, hastened to face the cameras in the courtroom hallway. "We don't rule out stones from a geology class just because some people have worshiped stones, and we don't rule God out of science class because some believe in him." As I listened to Geisler I could not help but recall the words of the Reverend C. O. Magee, a Presbyterian minister who is a member of the Little Rock School Board. "Any time religion gets involved in science," Magee told the *Gazette*, "religion comes off looking like a bunch of nerds. . . . The Book of Genesis told who created the world and why it was created and science tells how it was done." Amen.

After Geisler, the state's case went straight downhill. These witnesses were supposedly learned men, possessing advanced degrees, most of them resident in institutions that purported to be colleges and universities. Some of my own prejudices against academia would have revived, except that this collection of sad sacks, flub-a-dubs, and third-rate hobbyists had been gleaned mostly from the kinds of schools where the faculty must sign pledges certifying their literal belief in the factual inerrancy of the Bible, and were not, in the post-Enlightenment sense, really academic institutions at all. (The Institute for Creation Research requires such a pledge.) Most were like Donald Chittick, a physical chemist from George Fox College in Newberg, Oregon. Chittick spent hours telling the court how fuel could actually be made very rapidly from "biomass" materials. (In the Ozarks, of course, a good deal of biomass fuel has been distilled and drunk over the years.) To Chittick's mind, this proves that the world does not have to be 4.5 billion years old at all. Chittick's most telling point was that the amount of helium present in the earth's atmosphere indicates that radioactive decay has been taking place on earth for about ten thousand years only. That is just about how old creationists say the earth is. Either Chittick did not mention, or does not know, that helium is too light to be held by earth's gravity and disperses constantly into space.

The trial's only poignant moment came during cross-examination of Harold Coffin, a dreadfully earnest Seventh-Day Adventist who spends his time floating horsetail ferns in tanks of water to demonstrate that their fossilized ancestors found standing upright in coal seams hundreds of feet thick could have floated to that position during Noah's flood. Coffin was asked to say how old the earth would seem to a person unaided by Scripture, and considering only the available scientific evidence. Coffin paused for what seemed five minutes before answering, so it must have been at least fifteen seconds. As old as evolutionists claim, he said, about 4.5 billion years.

To his credit, Judge Overton kept his patience throughout, although he did seem to be losing it once with a pompous faculty lounge-lizard type from Wofford College in South Carolina, one W. Scott Morrow, a chemist who claimed to be an "evolutionist," but took it upon himself to testify to the closed-mindedness of "my fellow evolutionists." After more than an hour's worth of plausible generalities about how scientists are slow to accept new ideas, Overton asked Morrow if scientific papers were ever rightly rejected. He said he couldn't answer, as he'd never been an editor. Pressed by Overton for one specific example of a scientifically valid creationist paper's having been rejected, Morrow could not provide one. (Indeed, in the course of the trial the state could not produce a single creationist paper that had been published in a refereed scientific journal anywhere in the world, nor even one that had been submitted.) "Are you saying," the judge challenged, "that the entire national and international scientific community is engaged in a conspiracy?" Morrow replied that he knew a lot of his colleagues in science, and "I know a closed mind when I see one." Afterward Morrow, too, hustled in the direction of the cameras, and told the press that the judge wasn't paying attention and was obviously biased. Then he beat it back to South Carolina, which is welcome to him. Have I mentioned that there was only one Arkansan among the creationist witnesses?

The pro-creationist witness who traveled farthest for the trial, however, was one Dr. Chandra Wickramasinghe, a native of Sri Lanka who teaches mathematics in Wales. Having allied himself several years ago with Sir Fred Hoyle, the notable English astronomer, who seems to have slipped into scientific dotage, Wickramasinghe has collaborated with his mentor on two books that have done very well on best-seller lists in England, *Life Cloud* and *Diseases from Space*. The first book is an elaboration of a science-fiction novel by Hoyle which I read about twenty-five years ago. It posits that life originated in swirling clouds of inter-galactic dust and was brought to earth by a comet. So far the hy-pothesis has not been falsified, but at the moment it cannot be seriously tested either. Wickramasinghe seemed astonished that he would be cross-examined, and devolved from condescension to giggles when forced after protesting that he was being taken out of context to read three paragraphs of *Evolution from Space*. In-sects, the passage said, may be more intelligent than human be-ings, but pretend stupidity because they don't want us to know what a great deal they have on earth. Well, maybe so. Then again, maybe not.

Diseases from Space elaborates on the idea that viral epidemics are in fact visited on us from the great beyond and asserts that viruses cannot be transmitted horizontally from one human being to another. This hypothesis provoked the best joke of the trial. If viruses cannot be transmitted from one person to another, some unknown wag on the ACLU side wondered, then how about the following scenario: a man comes home and tells his wife, "Honey, I've got good news and bad news. The bad news is I've caught herpes. The good news is it came from outer space." As for the creationist notion that the universe is just ten thousand years old, Dr. Wickramasinghe said, "one would have to be crazy to be-lieve that."

A Blow for Theocracies

We are all the poorer for Attorney General Clark's decision not to appeal Judge Overton's ruling that the creationism law is uncon-stitutional. No rationally consequent adult who sat through Little Rock's creationism trial can have expected another outcome. Even the Moral Majority's fulminations were clearly a reaction to the dismal showing the creationist witnesses made. Examined in the light of reason, with evidence honestly given and logically as-sessed, creationism cannot prevail. Unlike a televised debate or a local school-board committee meeting, the trial was a fair fight.

But nothing said that Overton's opinion—and I hope readers will have patience with my pointing out that he was educated at Malvern (Arkansas) High School and the University of Arkansas—would be as cogent and well written as it was. Many of the creationist faithful were privately contacting the attorney general's office here to advise against appeal. They would like to believe they have a better chance in Louisiana, where the local authorities have deputized the Institute for Creation Research's Wendell Bird. Overton dismissed Bird's argument as having no legal merit:

If creation science is, in fact, science and not religion, as the defendants claim, it is difficult to see how the teaching of such a science could "neutralize" the religious nature of evolution. Assuming for the purposes of argument, however, that evolution is a religion or religious tenet, the remedy is to stop the teaching of evolution, not establish another religion in opposition to it. Yet it is clearly established in the case law, and perhaps also in common sense, that evolution is not a religion and that teaching evolution does not violate the establishment clause.

It is equally clear that the state has a "compelling interest" in the teaching not only of biological science, of which the theory of evolution is the fundamental organizing principle, but also of chemistry, physics, geology, and even history, all subjects that would have required "balancing" with creationist gibberish if Act 590 had stood. Where that is the case, the Supreme Court has ruled many times, aggrieved fundamentalists who do not wish to have their children hear what offends them, and wish the shelter of the "free exercise" clause of the First Amendment, are permitted to withdraw their children from science classes or from public school.

Ultimately, the creationists cannot prevail in the courts. Now that the scientific community and the educated public are aroused by the Little Rock spectacle, I doubt that a bill in the U.S. Congress of Rep. William Dannemeyer's (Rep.—Calif.), which would limit funding for the Smithsonian Institution if it refuses to put up creationist exhibits, will get anywhere either. So long as current attempts to limit the power of the federal judiciary are fought back—Arkansas's Act 590 controversy being a textbook example of the political cowardice that has led to courts currently having more power than most of us are comfortable with—we will not have a theocracy in this country, fundamentalist or otherwise. Leave it up to the Arkansas legislature, and in five years we would have an Inquisition.

Creationism was mortally damaged by the Little Rock spectacle. That is why the slippery Dr. Duane Gish now says he thinks state laws mandating its teaching are a mistake; he wants to go back to strong-arming local school boards, as in the past. In fact, the Moral Majority and its politico-religious allies, I believe, will soon be muttering only to each other again. One could not observe the Arkansas Moral Majority head, the Rev. Roy McLaughlin, in action in his modernistic pulpit in Vilonia without speculating that his boyish charm—he looks like a sort of cross between Pat Boone and Howdy Doody—might just be wearing a mite thin. Arkansans may be hotter than most citizens for that old-time fundamental religion, but are they really ready to credit McLaughlin when he says, with unmistakable reference to the clergymen on the opposite side of the creationist case, that "a preacher who does not believe the word of God to be the inspired, inerrant, infallible Word of God . . . is a crook and he ought to resign his pulpit . . . and quit robbing money from God's people"? Even out on the dirt roads, they know McLaughlin is talking about their friends and neighbors. In the long run, Arkansas folks aren't *mean* enough for that.

Before closing, I should bring readers up to date on the activities of two of creationism's hotter enthusiasts. A month after the trial, Senator James Holsted, having repaid the money he was accused of embezzling from his family's insurance company, pleaded guilty to the lesser charge of filing a false statement. As part of the deal with the Pulaski County prosecutor, he resigned his senate seat. Yet he told reporters not to count him out of politics for good. "It's life," he smiled. "A winner never accepts defeat."

Governor Frank White is a winner too. He had considerable trouble fulfilling his pledge to rid Arkansas of black Cubans. By January 1982, though, the government had succeeded in finding sponsors for all but three hundred of them. The Reagan Administration talked of moving them to a camp outside Glasgow, Montana. But January temperatures often reach thirty below zero there. Whether it was the parallels to Siberia or the exorbitant cost of preparing a new site just to fulfill a campaign promise to the governor of a small state Reagan had in his pocket anyway, the idea was dropped. White was getting worried. The awful Cubans had been at Fort Chaffee longer than they were under Democrat Bill Clinton. Far from "standing up to the President," he wrote beseeching letters to Washington, which found their way into the newspaper, reminding him that "my political future" depended upon their removal. Finally Reagan acted. Buses appeared one night before dawn at the gates of Fort Chaffee. The Cubans, all of them impoverished, many physically or mentally ill, some simply retarded, but none convicted of any crimes in American courts of law, were loaded and taken away to Federal prisons. The Arkansas ACLU tried to intervene, but by the time it found out, the Cubans were safely out of state. In the morning paper there was a letter from a lady in Texarkana who said White had committed an obscenity in our names. The *Clarendon Sentinel*, a paper printed so far out in the country it's halfway back to town, reminded its readers of the internment of Japanese-Americans in camps not far from there during World War II. They said White's and Reagan's action filled them with "despair and shame." A few days later White flew off to Washington with a bevy of fundamentalist preachers for a prayer breakfast with the President.

Postscript

Governor Frank White was defeated for reelection in November 1982 by Democrat Bill Clinton, whom he had defeated in 1980. Although Clinton said he would not have signed Act 590 bill and White reaffirmed his stand for it, creationism was not a significant issue in the campaign. Attorney General Steve Clark was reelected, taking 73 percent of the vote against a candidate who criticized him for not winning the case.

1981

Invisible Wars

The Pentagon Plays with Poison

Gas! Gas! Quick, boys!—an ecstasy of fumbling,
Fitting the clumsy helmets just in time,
But someone was still yelling out and stumbling
And floundering like a man in fire or lime.
Dim, through the misty panes and thick green light,
As under a green sea, I saw him drowning.
In all my dreams before my helpless sight
He plunges at me, guttering, choking, drowning.
If in some smothering dreams you too could pace
Behind the wagon that we flung him in,
And watch the white eyes writhing in his face,
His hanging face, like a devil's sick of sin;
If you could hear, at every jolt, the blood
Come gargling from the froth-corrupted lungs,
Bitter as the cud
Of vile, incurable sores on innocent tongues,
My friend, you would not tell with such high zest
To children ardent for some desperate glory, the old lie:
    dulce et decorum est
Pro patria mori.

    —From "Dulce Et Decorum Est" by Wilfred Owen

So what if almost everything serious the boys in the Pentagon have tried to bring off in the last twenty years seems to have been planned by Sergeant Bilko, Major Major Major (no doubt by now General Major Major), and the Wicked Witch of the West? The patriotic citizen is still inclined to leave real madness to the experts. Exterminating nations, after all, is an intimidating prospect; only the most advanced thinkers in the highest places are thought to qualify. My initial interest in the binary-nerve-gas question had been provincial and relatively superficial: after an ICBM silo fifty miles from your home blows up and tosses a ten-megaton H-bomb into a wood because somebody dropped a wrench, you tend to notice when Congress decides to break an eleven-year moratorium on the manufacture of chemical-warfare munitions—a policy affirmed by three administrations and several Congresses—and wants to build the plant forty miles in the other direction.

I wasn't in a panic, mind you. They have been storing nerve gas at the Pine Bluff Arsenal for years. In fact, until President Nixon decided that biological warfare would be almost as dangerous to the offense as the defense and ordered stocks destroyed after negotiating a treaty with the Soviets in 1972, quantities of plague, anthrax, botulism, tularemia, and Venezuelan equine encephalitis were cultivated and stored there. Pine Bluff police had special instructions for handling arsenal employees who caught stray whiffs of the hallucinogen BZ on the production line and began seeing herds of carnivorous elephants where their children used to be.

For the most part, only interested parties, obsessive newspaper readers with good memories, and very serious national-security fans know that there *is* a binary-nerve-gas question, which is part of what finally attracted my attention.

One of the unspoken givens of public debate on doomsday issues is that the rest of us must be solemn when the United States Congress cannot trouble itself to be serious. So what if the September 1980 decision, almost ignored by the press because it occurred during the quadrennial dog-and-pony show held to select the leader of the Free World, was made without benefit of hearings, was intellectually justified by an article read into the record from *Reader's Digest*, and consumed less than three hours' debate in both houses? So what if the quality of that debate made it sound like a skit with Gene Wilder as Chicken Little and Richard Pryor a Henny Penny? No doubt the Russians got the message: "They *bad*, those Russians, but we badder. We real bad, and we be fixin' to get worse. Stand back, you Russians. Watch out! We be mean motherfuckers." Of course nobody really knows what the Soviets make of messages like that, but that is their problem. They had gone pounding into Afghanistan—previously a synonym in this country for the end of the earth—quite as if it were Hungary or Czechoslovakia. Now they would have to pay the price in symbolic gestures.

Once an issue is identified, as binary nerve gas was by its main proponent and the author of the *Reader's Digest* article, Rep. Richard Ichord (Dem.—Mo.), as crucial to "the survival of Western civilization," our civic duty is never to crack a smile. Did Frenchmen smirk at the Maginot Line?

The provincial question that interested me was, why Arkansas? Did the decision to put the plant—to be the country's exclusive manufacturer of chemical munitions—in Pine Bluff augur a sort of inverse pork-barrel approach to unpleasant necessities? Were small, politically insignificant states going to have to choke down what stronger constituencies had the power to resist? Both Arkansas senators, Dale Bumpers and David Pryor—neither a so-called knee-jerk liberal on defense questions—had voted for Gary Hart's amendment to delay funding for six months pending study and full hearings. My congressman, Ed Bethune, a Reagan Republican and former FBI agent, voted against binaries. The then-governor, Bill Clinton, had said Arkansas did not want the plant. Of course the Pine Bluff Chamber of Commerce was gung ho, as was Beryl Anthony, the local congressman, but the former body would back a preemptive strike to exterminate every Godless Atheistical Communist on earth, especially if it meant getting a federal payroll.

My suspicions were unjustified. The binary idea turns out to have had a long bureaucratic half-life within the Army Chemical Corps and dates almost unchanged from the mid-Fifties, when the late Sen. John McClellan was taking care of it and his district. The 155-mm howitzer shells the army plans to manufacture at Pine Bluff are, in terms of performance, theoretically identical to millions of nerve-gas shells it already possesses. "Binary" means simply that instead of containing a live agent, the new generation of weapons—not just artillery shells but bombs, missile warheads, rockets, land mines, and spray tanks—would contain two "nonlethal" chemical precursors that would become a deadly compound only after the weapon was fired. Proponents argue that binary weapons would be much safer to make, transport, and store than current U.S. weapons, because it would not be necessary to load both chemicals into the shells until just before firing. Presumably, too, they would prove more politically acceptable in Europe.

The Marx Brothers' Apocalypse

Readers inclined to doubt my characterization of the proceedings are referred to the *Congressional Record*, both House and Senate versions, for September 10 and 16, 1980, and for May 21, 1981. They should keep in mind that the last time Congress held hearings on the binary issue was 1975; at which time it not only refused to fund the scheme but passed a law, which is still binding, stipulating that the Defense Department may not manufacture new gas weapons until the president submits to Congress a written report certifying that they are needed for national security. Proponents of gas this time alternated invocations of the awesome Soviet might in chemicals with portentous warnings about the folly and futility of negotiating with communists at all. Such practical and factual objections as were raised by opponents—for the most part the same ones that prevailed in 1975—were brushed aside with mutterings about "unilateral disarmament."

My own favorite moment came when Republican senator John Warner of Virginia rose to wonder darkly "who (in the Defense Department) is trying to stop the decision and why?" Reminded that the culprit was then secretary Harold Brown, Warner sat down.

Yet while proponents like Ichord and Jackson invoked binary nerve gas as the only thing that could prevent Bolshevik hordes from poisoning their way clear to the English Channel, they played shrewdly on the 1975 law to assure the dubious that Congress's decision was not critical at all. For a paltry 3.15 million dollars to build the plant and another twenty million dollars to equip it, the United States could be on line and ready to go by 1984 (the Department of Defense has projected total chemical warfare expenditures of between four and seven billion dollars). Since the Carter administration opposed the idea, there would be no nerve gas if the incumbent administration won the election; if Reagan won, it was his baby. Nobody in Congress would have to vote on the issue again.

When it came to the question the Carter administration, as was often its wont, took a walk. It wished neither to be accused of wimphood on national defense nor to fight powerful forces within the Democratic ranks who might win. Candidate Reagan said nothing. Who wants to run on a pro-gas-warfare platform?

"The trouble with the whole thing," says Senator Pryor, a cautiously conservative politician who surprised many by making his antigas position into something of a personal crusade, "is that talking about nerve gas is like picking out your own coffin. Nobody wants to do it at all, and certainly not on the Senate floor." With the skids so artfully greased, it is a wonder Pryor and Sen. Gary Hart's amendment to delay the question and require hearings came as close as it did to passing. It failed 47–46. In the House, the vote was 276–126 in favor of binaries.

Because Sen. Mark Hatfield (Rep.—Ore.) killed the twenty million dollar part of the appropriation in joint committee by threatening to filibuster the entire Defense Department budget in his appropriations committee, the issue came up again last May. It went pretty much the same way, with binary weapons quietly supported by the Reagan administration and winning by a margin of 50–48, despite the defection of conservatives like Pryor among the Democrats and Thad Cochran of Mississippi and Nancy Kassebaum of Kansas among the Republicans.

But if the congressional debate was often unintentionally comic, nerve gas itself is not. Next to nuclear bombs, nerve gas is as serious a weapon as the swarming imagination of man has conceived. Should a full-scale chemical slugfest break out between NATO and the Warsaw Pact countries, the dread scenario that all binary proponents invoke, only the mind of God could comprehend the slaughter that would ensue. Nerve gas kills everything with a nervous system that is not equipped with a protective suit and a gas mask: women, children, cats and dogs, rabbits in the fields, and birds in the trees. One good lungful or as little as a drop on exposed skin of the colorless, odorless, tasteless gas blocks the action of the enzyme acetylcholinesterase at the nerve endings. Every muscle in the body contracts and cannot relax: victims are said to be "stimulated to death." Outward symptoms are intense sweating, mucus clogging the bronchial passages, loss of vision, simultaneous and uncontrollable vomiting and defecation, convulsions, paralysis, and, finally, inability to breathe. The fortunate die in minutes; victims who get smaller lethal doses may linger for hours.

If this stuff comes down, brothers and sisters, millions of European civilians, pets, farm animals, and adventitious earthworms will be stone dead and rotting on the ground. Since nerve gas is quite closely related to the organophosphorous family of insecticides, the flies that alight on their eyes could have contamination problems.

The military literature on the subject refers to such an eventuality as "collateral effects." The soldiers on both sides, you see, will be buttoned up tight in their masks and protective suits or zipping around in airtight tanks and armoured personnel carriers executing battle plans.

Well, maybe not zipping, exactly. The point of shooting gas, assuming both armies are fully equipped defensively (gas is unique as a weapon of war in that near-total passive defense is theoretically possible), is to afflict your opponent with what Lt. Col. Charles H. Bay, writing in *Parameters,* the journal of the U.S. Army War College, calls "nightmare drag." Protective suits are hot, uncomfortable, and awkward. Both the heavy rubber Soviet models and the more dashing and lighter NATO suits, made of synthetic fibers impregnated with activated charcoal, inhibit communication (Russian gas masks, in fact, make no provision for enlisted men to speak, just officers), impede dexterity, and prohibit eating and excretion. The Russian gear can be worn for only a couple of hours—less than forty-five minutes at more than seventy degrees—before a soldier must remove to a gas-free area and have his suit and weapons decontaminated so he can disrobe before he passes out. Characteristically, perhaps, the NATO suits are disposable; after about six hours our boys will have to climb out and get another from the quartermaster. In a continually contaminated environment, combat maneuvers could come to resemble a ghastly game of musical chairs: the apocalypse played by the Marx Brothers.

But I was speaking of civilians, their kith, kin, and kine. Here is the same Lieutenant Colonel Bay on the subject: "collateral effects, *if one is really concerned about them* [my italics], may be minimized through the careful application of target-analysis procedures and definitive rules of engagement." Like almost all military enthusiasts of binary weapons, Bay is a career man in the Army Chemical Corps, a branch the Pentagon tried to abolish after Vietnam but which has always had powerful congressional supporters. His current command is the Tooele Army Depot in Utah, where 40 percent of America's existing stockpile of nerve-gas weapons is kept. (The rest is at Pine Bluff, Rocky Mountain Arsenal near Denver, Ft. McClellan in Anniston, Alabama, Johnson Island in the Pacific, and various other locations.)

Tooele is not too far downwind from the army's Dugway Proving Ground, where, as readers may recall, 6,400-odd sheep perished in March 1968 when a badly designed aerial spray tank put twenty pounds of nerve agent VX into the ambient breeze at a somewhat higher altitude than target-analysis procedures called for. For fourteen months afterward, the army resolutely denied its responsibility. The dead sheep had been grazing over a two-hundred-square-mile area at an average distance of thirty miles from the target. Definitive rules of engagement, indeed. Statistically speaking, two hundred square miles of West Germany may be expected to contain about 128,394 citizens, although most would not, presumably, be eating grass. No wonder nobody else in NATO wants to have anything to do with nerve gas, whether binary or otherwise.

The more I succumbed to the dread fascination of nerve gas, the more I began to suspect that there were no experts on the subject—or at the very least none who hadn't a career stake in promoting the binary idea. Colonel Bay's article was not unique. Like the politicians who had echoed them in Congress, most writers on the subject simply ignored the substantive arguments of people who remained doubters; they suppressed evidence clearly within their ken and elevated speculation and *a priori* assumptions based on quite dubious political theology to the status of un-

241

deniable fact. Was it possible, I began to wonder, that the unthinkable remains unthought?

I began compiling great lists of factual and inferential questions to ask, and essayed a visit to Washington, where, like a humble Gulliver in the Grand Academy of Lagado, I walked miles of corridors visiting the resident experts in their variously appointed cubicles, politely discussing the unspeakable in tones more reasonable than most men use to talk about baseball or the vagaries of women. By the end of a week I was more bewildered than when I had begun. My questions were multiplying, yet I found myself meeting the sublime and authoritative calm of persons who—although they couldn't answer my queries—nevertheless assured me that everything was under control. Without exception, every believer in the necessity of binary weapons whom I met was at pains to assure me that the Soviets intend to conquer the world by force, have nothing but cold-blooded contempt for our sniveling pieties, and are exactly on schedule. If you are a patriot and a man, it is strongly implied, you must leave off asking and begin believing.

When they are held so firmly, such views can be intimidating, if not to one's own opinions, then to the prospect of further conversation. Anybody who lives in Arkansas and who is not a religious fundamentalist learns the futility of arguing about faith. But I am a skeptic, so I went on to Baltimore, where I met with Saul Hormats, whose name I was given by a "nameless government official."

Hormats was for thirty-seven years an army employee, and before retiring in 1973 he had been at one time director of development at the arsenal in Edgewood, Maryland. In that capacity he oversaw the creation of the current generation of nerve-gas weapons, as well as of the gas masks and protective equipment now in use. He was at first reluctant to speak, but I said I was worn out with political theology and wanted to know, in the simplest way of putting it, whether nerve gas—its horrors aside—was still a useful weapon. Assuming it was, was a new generation of binary weapons needed or not? Was the 155-mm artillery shell planned for manufacture at Pine Bluff the weapon of choice? And, given positive answers to all of the above, would the weapons work?

For readers who lack the patience for the detailed considerations that follow, the answers to my questions were, in order, no, no, no, and probably not. "What happened was that when you asked those questions about wind and weather, topography, and logistics," Hormats said, shortly after I'd come in the door, "people you were talking to had not thought of them before, let alone of the answers, in terms of live firings. You can only go so far with computer simulants of the vagaries of weather, terrain, and target. We'd be fielding an untested weapon system. There is no hard military experience for these weapons."

In other words, the big development in nerve-gas warfare since we quit making the weapons in 1969 is the prospect of an open-ended defense budget. It has to be spent; the people who can figure out how are judged by their rhetoric.

The Most Gruesome Weapon

The history of chemical and biological warfare is long, but except in a metaphorical way has relatively little to offer students of nerve gas. Indian accounts describe the use of smoke screens and toxic fumes as much as four thousand years ago; Thucydides tells of Spartans besieging Athens with the aid of sulfur dioxide clouds made by burning sulfur and pitch. Christians burned poisoned rags to ward off Turks during the Crusades, and poisoned weapons have been used around the world times out of mind. In North America, it is recalled that Lord Jeffrey Amherst, hero of song and fable, sold to Native Americans blankets infected with smallpox, thus weakening their resistance during the French and Indian War.

The modern era of chemical warfare, though, began at the Ypres salient on the Franco-Belgian border on April 22, 1915, when the Germans released 168 tons of chlorine gas from canisters simply opened in a light wind along four miles of British, French, and Canadian trenches. They achieved total surprise, allegedly killing five thousand men immediately and generating as many as twenty thousand casualties. "Try to imagine," wrote a later student of the subject, "the feelings and the condition of the

243

French colonial troops as they saw the vast cloud of greenish-yellow gas spring out of the ground and slowly move downwind toward them, the vapour clinging to the earth, seeking out every hole and hollow and filling the trenches and shell holes as it came. First wonder, then fear; then, as the first fringes of the cloud enveloped them and left them choking and agonized in the fight for breath—panic. Those who could move broke and ran, trying, generally in vain, to outstrip the cloud which followed inexorably after them." So vivid and terrifying were the accounts written by journalists who visited the trenches not long after that news of the attack was printed in England almost uncensored—a rarity in the carnival of lies that passed for reporting during that war. Even if it conveyed news of a defeat, the anti-Hun propaganda was too good to resist. (German sources consulted by Frederic J. Brown in his excellent study *Chemical Warfare: A Study in Restraints,* however, claim that five thousand deaths are many more than actually occurred.)

In any event, the use of gas proved indecisive. Apparently quite surprised by the effectiveness of chlorine against a totally bewildered and demoralized enemy, the Germans were unprepared to exploit their temporary advantage by pushing through the corpse-littered front for a breakthrough. What came to be called the Second Battle of Ypres ground on for another month, cost one hundred thousand total casualties to participants on both sides, but moved the front hardly at all. The memory of that first sneak attack, however, has colored civilized attitudes toward chemical warfare ever since.

Military historians agree that the pattern first seen at Ypres continued throughout the war. The Allies developed a crude gas mask and retaliated in kind six months later, with the prevailing westerly winds in their favor. A tactical seesaw tipped throughout the conflict, as protective equipment, experience, and training rendered troops relatively immune first to one gas weapon, then another, then yet another. The combatants used collectively between thirty-eight and fifty different toxic agents between 1915 and 1918, and delivered them through a variety of increasingly sophisticated weapons. By the end of the war, about half the German artillery shells were filled with mustard gas, by far the most effective of the agents at producing casualties because it burned the skin and persisted on contaminated surfaces for days. In fact, the highest incidence of burns among British soldiers was on the genitals and buttocks of those who relieved themselves on a contaminated ground.

The overall effect, however, was stalemate. One important British history of the war relegates gas to a footnote: "Gas achieved but local success, nothing decisive; it made war uncomfortable, to no purpose." Of twenty-five million military casualties in that war just over 1.3 million came from gas, and only a small percentage of those were fatal. Civilian casualties seem to have been relatively few; due to the static nature of trench warfare, civilians were rarely close to the battlefield. Due to uncertainties of climate and delivery, gas was almost never used in the First World War on attacking troops, only to "soften" resistance before assaults on fixed positions. Of the military casualties, it is worth noting, about a third were Russian.

Yet regardless of its ultimate ineffectiveness as a weapon, gas came to stand in the public mind for all that was gruesome about World War I. "To the military," writes Frederic Brown, "it represented the encroachment of science which was corrupting the expertise and honor of their profession; to the civilian, it symbolized the ruthlessness and inhumanity of modern war." Never mind that the triumph of technology over chivalry and individual human courage in 1918 might more properly have been awarded to the machine gun—on the Russian front German commanders complained of stacks of bodies so high in front of their positions that gunners could no longer see. The machine gun had been around for some time, and was an extension of a weapon that was understood and accepted. Gas was insidious, sneaky; perhaps too, some have speculated, men have a primordial fear of suffocation that makes the prospect of breathing poisoned air more horrible than other ways of dying.

A treaty to ban both chemical and submarine warfare was negotiated at the Washington Conference on Limitation of Armaments in 1921–22, but the French balked at the submarine provisions and it never took effect. In 1925, however, the Geneva Conference for the Control of the International Trade in Arms—

today the very title has an almost absurdly optimistic ring—accepted an American draft resolution on gases: "Whereas the use in war of asphyxiating poisonous or other gases, and of all analogous liquids, materials or devices, has been justly condemned by the general opinion of the civilized world . . . prohibition shall be universally accepted as a part of International Law."

As treaties go, the Geneva Protocol is weak. It has no machinery for enforcement, provides no penalties for violations, does not apply to wars that involve nonsignatories, and has never banned the testing and manufacture of chemical weapons. Although just about all countries with a chemical-warfare capacity ratified the treaty shortly after it was written, many did so with the reservation that they agreed to renounce only first use and would retaliate in kind if attacked.[1] Ironically, the United States, to its own and Vietnam's later rue, did not itself ratify the treaty it wrote until 1975—it fell victim to a strong lobbying campaign in the Army Chemical Warfare Service and the chemical industry. Despite all those weaknesses, however, all the Geneva Protocol has ever done is work; no signatory has ever attacked another with gas.

Perhaps, in the great cosmic account book, it will be written that the German attack at Ypres was a beneficence. Among the victims of gas warfare was one Corporal Adolf Hitler, who was temporarily blinded and conceived a hatred for gas warfare that he carried with him almost to the last bunker. In the end, Albert Speer says, Hitler ordered a suicide attack on the advancing Allied armies with the nerve-gas weapons German scientists had discovered during the war, but by then his dementia was apparent and the task too complicated to be carried out. The German high command, which had been as ill prepared for gas warfare as were the other belligerents in 1939, ignored him. Current proponents of a new generation of American nerve-gas weapons make much of mistaken German intelligence reports, which supposed that the United States, having discovered DDT, also knew how to make nerve gas. Richard Ichord's *Reader's Digest* article maintains that only the fear of retaliation in kind dissuaded the Nazis from using nerve gas, and other propagandists of the cause cite him when the subject is deterrence. The truth, of course, is far more complex, and the assumed American capacity seems to have had relatively little to do with it.

In fact, none of the belligerents in World War II was prepared for the offensive use of gas. The British issued thirty-eight million civilian gas masks in 1937–38, but more as a means of arousing popular understanding of the German threat than from the real fear of gas attack. One reason Germany did not invade the south coast of England after Dunkirk, amazingly enough, is that it feared the British command might resort to mustard gas on the beachheads, and it was weakened by a shortage of gas masks for the horses used to haul munitions. The American refusal to take gas seriously seems to have been relatively typical: "Dislike of gas," writes Brown, who had access to the archives of the combatants, "was based upon more than instinctive fear or distrust. There was also the question of effectiveness. Many officers wondered if the costs of employing poison gas on the battlefield were not greater than the tactical rewards. Problems of operating in a toxic environment, unsolved at the end of World War I, were for the most part still unsolved in 1939."

Among those problems were enormous logistical difficulties, since gas substitutes for no other weapon but adds huge complexities of its own: decontamination; the prospect of mass casualties, many of them civilian; and communications disruptions while wearing masks. Given the budget constraints of the era and the need for such basic weapons as rifles, tanks, trucks, and airplanes, chemical warfare was slighted. There was also general resentment within the armed services toward the insistent propaganda efforts of the Chemical Warfare Service.

In the end, Brown shows, numerous factors, among them the airplane's ability to take retaliation to an opponent's homeland— whether by gas or other means—exerted a moderating force:

> Each nation assumed that tactical employment of chemical weapons would escalate to strategic counter-city exchange. And fears of strategic retaliation precluded serious consideration of tactical use. . . . Poison gas was a weapon too technologically demanding and psychologically disquieting to be assimilated by the military profession. It was an unacceptable anachronism, born too early out of a unique marriage of science and war.

Allegations of gas warfare have been relatively common in the years since the adoption of the Geneva Protocol. They are often made by obscure groups fighting larger powers and seeking outside support. Documented instances are much rarer. Mustard gas was used by the Italians in their glorious campaign in Ethiopia, by the Japanese against the Chinese between 1936 and 1943, and by the Egyptians against South Yemen tribesmen in the mid-1960s. To binary proponents, these instances are clear proof that nations that cannot retaliate with gas are invariably its victims. A bit of paring with Occam's razor, however, shows that what all the victims have had in common was an inability to retaliate at all.

Gas Stratagems

Given the popular horror of gas, readers may be surprised at one traditional line taken by Chemical Corps stalwarts. According to Maj. Gen. H. L. Gilchrist, an early exponent, speaking just after World War I: "[Gas] is not only one of the most efficient agencies for effecting casualties, but it is the most humane method ever applied on the battlefield." Actually, there is some support for at least the second part of Gilchrist's apologia. Mustard gas—which came into use quite late in the war—produced forty incapacitating casualties for every death. Which of us, indeed, would not prefer to languish in a hospital with embarrassing burns than to be dismembered by high explosives or stitched across the gut with .50-caliber machine-gun bullets?

The invention of nerve agents, however, changed everything about gas warfare except the rhetoric of its proponents. Brig. Gen. J. H. Rothschild of the Chemical Corps puts the question another way in his 1964 treatise *Tomorrow's Weapons.* "Why is it," the general asks, "that we accept methods of war which will burn a man to death, or blast off his limbs or part of his face, and leave him blind or mindless, yet say that gas or biological warfare is unacceptable? . . . an excellent case can be made for toxics as the most humane weapons of all." Thomas Dashiell, the Pentagon's current staff specialist for chemical technology and overseer of binary weapons, takes a similar line. Writing in the house organ,

Invisible Wars

Defense/81, Dashiell dismisses distaste for gas warfare as a product of misunderstanding. "A closer examination of casualty figures from World War I, where approximately seven percent of chemical casualties were fatal, belies the view that chemicals should be thought of as weapons of mass destruction." What Dashiell neglects to pass on to his brethren in arms (or behind desks, as the case may be), is that the nerve gases currently stockpiled by the United States are more poisonous than mustard gas to an almost exponential degree. VX, for example, the persistent nerve agent that killed the sheep at Dugway, has two thousand times the toxicity of mustard gas when absorbed through the skin, and is almost three hundred times more deadly when inhaled. One cannot begin a rational discussion of a nerve-gas conflict without knowing that.[2]

But then Dashiell's specialty, as a subsequent journey to his cubicle made clear, is not rational discussions of fact. Here is his summary, in the same *Defense/81* article, of our national record on chemical questions: "The present United States . . . policy has been essentially unchanged through the course of history: we will not initiate chemical warfare using lethal or incapacitating chemicals, we will continue to seek an effective and verifiable ban on production, stockpiling, and use of chemical weapons, but in the absence of such a ban we will maintain a chemical warfare capability to deter the use of chemicals against U.S. or Allied forces. . . ." Sounds appropriately firm, yet idealistic, does it not? Exactly as one would have an American policy, in fact. Unfortunately, however, the historical part is sheer nonsense.

Dashiell's first evasion is perhaps understandable from the bureaucratic point of view. In order to make any sense at all on a contemporary battlefield in a war between technological equals, gas has to be seen as a tactical weapon. Not even in the bowels of the Pentagon are there many who think the United States needs any weapon of mass destruction to compete with nuclear bombs, especially one that doesn't work when it's raining. The second whopper, though, cannot be explained as anything other than deliberate propaganda. Most officers now serving can be counted on not to have read the *1956 Army Field Manual*, which pointed out that:

249

The United States is not party to any treaty now in force that prohibits or restricts the use in warfare of toxic or non-toxic gases, of smoke or incendiary materials or of bacteriological warfare. . . .

The Geneva Protocol . . . has been ratified or adhered to and is now effective between a considerable number of states. However, the United States Senate has refrained from giving its advice and consent to the ratification of the protocol by the United States and it is accordingly not binding on this country.

Neither are they likely to have plumbed the depths of the *Congressional Record* in 1959, when Rep. Robert Kastenmeier of Wisconsin introduced a joint House-Senate resolution reiterating the national policy to be one of no first use, as Dashiell describes it, which had last been stated by President Roosevelt. Kastenmeier was responding to "Operation Blue Skies," an intensive propaganda and public relations drive then being conducted by the Army Chemical Corps on behalf of chemical and bacteriological war. The Defense Department opposed the resolution in a letter dated March 29, 1960. Such declarations, the DoD held, "might apply with equal pertinency across the entire spectrum and no reason is conceived why biological and chemical weapons should be singled out for this distinction." The State Department tendered its opposition to a policy of no first use two weeks later, as follows:

We must recognize our responsibility to our own and the free world's security. These responsibilities involve, amongst other things, the maintenance of an adequate defense posture across the entire weapons spectrum which will allow us to defend against acts of aggression in such manner as the President may direct. Accordingly, the department believes that the resolution should not be adopted.

The resolution failed, and in November of that year the State Department made it official: "The President thus remains free to determine American policy on the use of such weapons in any future war." There is no use opening a chicken-and-egg inquiry into who is responsible for what part of the arms race, but it bears mentioning that the Soviet Union's great interest in the defensive aspects of chemical war, which it makes no effort to conceal, began just about the same time the Chemical Corps budget began to grow.

But if they are unaware of the ancient history of American policy, most of Dashiell's readers ought to remember Vietnam. As it is now unfashionable to dwell upon the particulars of that conflict, I shall pass over them quickly. Suffice it to say that without presidential knowledge or approval the United States and South Vietnam secretly initiated the use of three gases early in the war. These were the tear gases CS, the less powerful CN, and an agent called DM, or Adamsite. Although it was used far less than the other two, DM may be lethal under certain conditions, particularly to the very old or young, and was listed under military regulations as not for use "where deaths are not acceptable."[3] When the newspapers first printed stories about gas use in March 1965, Secretary of State Dean Rusk said, "We are not embarking on gas warfare in Vietnam." It was his understanding that nonlethal agents were to be used only for riot control, in order to avoid "artillery or aerial bombs that would inflict great damage upon innocent people." The national and international outcry, however, was sufficiently great to cause the use of gas to be suspended for a time.

It was not a very long time. By October of the same year Gen. William Westmoreland had received permission to use tear gas "when it will save lives," and for the next few years Vietnam became a Chemical Corps playground. All manner of ingenious devices were employed to protect the innocent, from "Mighty Mite" blowers to force gas into tunnels and bunkers, to helicopter drops of large quantities of gas just before B-52 bombing runs. At the same time, some with especially long memories may recall, the United States declared war on Vietnam's plant life, guilty of both sheltering and feeding communist Vietcong. Millions of acres of forest and croplands were defoliated with the herbicides 2, 4D and 2, 4, 5T or "Agent Orange," which came advertised as harmless to all but politically unsound trees and rice paddies. It was called Operation Ranch Hand; its slogan, according to Seymour Hersh in the *New York Review of Books,* was "Only We Can Prevent Forests."

On August 19, 1969, President Nixon sent the Geneva Protocol to the Senate for ratification, having renounced bacteriological-warfare weapons, an act of "unilateral disarmament" for which he has perhaps received insufficient credit. At the same time he sent along a letter from Secretary of State Rogers reserving the right to retaliate in kind if attacked with lethal gas weapons and claiming that "the Protocol . . . does not prohibit the use in war of riot-control agents and chemical herbicides. Smoke, flame, and napalm are also not covered." Some months later, after the completion of hearings, Sen. J. W. Fulbright, chairman of the Senate Committee on Foreign Relations, wrote the president to ask for reconsideration:

We note that the use of herbicides in Vietnam is now being discontinued. It would appear that their actual utility in Vietnam has been marginal and that the corp destruction program may well have been counterproductive. . . .

Testimony on the question of tear gas . . . presented the following conclusions:

1. The military value of riot gas is very low.

2. Our overriding security interest in the area of chemical and biological weapons is to prevent the proliferation and use of biological and lethal chemical weapons.

3. Our use of riot gas in war runs directly counter to this fundamental interest.

Taking note of an 80–3 vote in the U.N. General Assembly to the effect that riot gas and herbicides *were* prohibited by the Protocol—only Australia and Portugal voted with the United States, while most allies abstained on legalistic grounds—Fulbright went on to suggest that "the military cost of giving up tear gas and herbicides (appears) relatively low and that the United States position could therefore properly be dominated by 'decent respect for the opinions of mankind'" and the Protocol ratified without reservation. The Nixon administration never replied.

In December 1974, however, the Ford administration dropped the reservation after Defense Department studies concluded that the chemical operations in Vietnam had indeed been useless. The Senate quickly ratified the Protocol by ninety votes to none, and President Ford signed it in January 1975, almost exactly fifty years after Americans had written it. United States policy had once again become what Thomas Dashiell assures his readers it has been all along. Coupled with an announcement early in 1974 by Nixon and Brezhnev to the effect that the United States and the

Soviet Union would open joint talks aimed at producing a total chemical-weapons ban, this was bad news indeed for the Army Chemical Corps. Having failed to deliver on its extravagant promises in Indochina, the Corps was once more stigmatized in the words of one high-ranking officer, "as a legion of the damned," a low-prestige outfit in which one might bury a promising career. The prospect of a treaty, moreover, threatened extinction. Nothing would do but a massive Soviet threat.

Toxic Scenarios

A newcomer to the world of nerve-gas scholarship cannot but notice that it is exactly that: academic, even pedantic. Since nerve gas has never been used in combat, the literature on the subject is necessarily theoretical. As in art criticism and the garment trade, fashions change. When General Rothschild wrote his book in 1964, the memory of mounds of Chinese corpses before American machine guns in Korea was fresh, and the presumed enemy was the communist hordes of all Asia. Accordingly, and quite accurately, Rothschild stressed that:

Toxic agents are area weapons. Both chemical and biological agents, when released into the air in finely dispersed form, will travel for long distances on the wind. Chemical agents will cover only tens of square miles, possibly a hundred square miles, in a single attack, but biological agents can blanket hundreds of thousands of square miles.

Toxic agents are search weapons. When released into the air, they move with the wind, and, as they move, they penetrate shelters, buildings, dugouts and other types of fortifications, seeking enemy personnel. . . .

Protection for toxic agents is difficult. A properly devised attack either can release the agent sufficiently far upwind from the target, so that little warning that an attack is in progress will be given to the target population. When odorless, colorless agents . . . are used, target personnel either will have a difficult time knowing, or will not know, when to mask or take other protective measures.

But since Nixon and Henry Kissinger have played the China card, the going thing is now European war. Scenarios have accordingly grown more precise, like Colonel Bay's. Rothschild's cruder formations, accurate though they may be, have simply disappeared down a memory hole.

What is most striking about the contemporary pedantry—and it is worthwhile emphasizing that Rothschild and more recent theoreticians are talking about *exactly the same weapons*—is the almost absurd bloodlessness of the genre, as if the Third World War, should it come, will be fought according to the rules of "Risk." Except as sentimental icons that need protection from the enemy, whose motives are so diabolical as neither to require nor to admit of rational analysis, civilians do not exist. Such contingencies as rain, wind, hills and valleys, temperature inversions, panic, mutiny, shells that don't fire at all or that misfire, truckloads of new protective suits stuck in the mud or delivered to a company that needed *masks*—all highly likely to screw up the plans of anybody using nerve gas as a weapon of war—are not permitted to intrude upon the elegance of the scenario. Amoretta Hoeber, cited by all proponents of binary weapons as *the* expert on the subject, sits coolly in her securely locked office at Systems Planning Corporation, just upriver from the Pentagon, and says that hostility to gas warfare is an irrational dread that dates from "the Middle Ages and the view of chemistry as witchcraft."

It is a "morality bias," according to her, which conditions American and European attitudes, a bias the Soviets do not share. Feelings such as rage, terror, racial hatred, the desire for revenge of NATO allies should the Russians initiate gas warfare, and the enemy's consequent need to fear nuclear retaliation, seem to Hoeber topics not worth considering. War-game scenarios, one is told, rule out a tactical nuclear response. People who think otherwise, she chides, are guilty of "lowering the nuclear threshold"; ironically, when she is not plumping for binaries, Hoeber writes articles on winning nuclear wars in Europe. "In a European war," she says, with great firmness, "civilians are going to get killed no matter what you use. Chemicals will make it worse, but probably no worse than nuclear." In any event, she insists, the West is so far behind the Soviets in nuclear weaponry as to be practically defenseless.

There is no question that the Soviets have a chemical-warfare capacity, and probably a significant one. Just how great it is, how willing and likely the Russians are to use it in Europe, and whether the United States should replace its own quite formidable capacity with a new generation of binary weapons, are what the fight is about. At almost every turn, though, a humble petitioner seeking straight answers from proponents of the weapon encounters evasion.

How large is the Soviet offensive capacity? "You run very quickly into classified material on that," says Pentagon spokesman Maj. Lee DeLorm. "It's not like counting missile silos. But I can describe it adjectivally as 'vast.'" In her study "The Chemistry of Defeat: Asymmetries in U.S. and Soviet Chemical Warfare Postures," Amoretta Hoeber quotes "press reports" that claim the Russians stockpile as much as seven hundred thousand tons of gas. Although she admits the evidence for that quantity is "not conclusive," it is the only number she uses in her summary argument, and it was widely touted on the Senate floor. If that figure had even the remotest possibility of being accurate, "vast" would be an understatement. Our own current 155-mm artillery shells weigh one hundred pounds each and contain six pounds of live nerve agent. Using a conservative ten-to-one ratio of hardware to gas, that would place the total amount of Soviet chemical munitions at seven million tons—roughly fourteen times as much as all the stockpiled munitions NATO has in Europe.

The current American supply of nerve-gas artillery weapons, we are told, totals roughly 150,000 tons, which works out to about three million projectiles. That is enough, according to Rep. Clement Zablocki, chairman of the House Foreign Affairs Committee, to allow fifty divisions to wage chemical warfare for one hundred days, by which time, of course, very few animate creatures in Europe would be left to fight over. In his brief appearance before the Senate Armed Services Committee last year, Defense Secretary Brown warned that little credence should be given to numerical estimates of Russian weapons. Face to face, Hoeber concedes that the seven hundred-ton figure assumes that every Soviet plant capable of producing organophosphorous poisons has made nothing but nerve gas day and night for years.

"I don't believe there's hard evidence to support any number," she says. "The intelligence community hasn't looked for it. In the whole Western intelligence community there are probably no more than ten people whose specialty is chemical warfare." Translation: nobody has the foggiest idea what the Soviet capacity is because nobody outside the world of True Believers really thinks it matters.

There is no evidence that the Soviets have made any new munitions since treaty talks began with the United States in 1976, although Hoeber cites Alexander Haig, in an old interview in *Stars and Stripes*, as saying that they have. Nobody says they are making or contemplating binary weapons, because nobody seems to know if they can.

Proponents tend to play fast and loose with troop numbers as well. On the floor of the Senate, Senator Jackson spoke of 80,000 chemical troops, giving the Russians a forty-to-one advantage over the United States. Hoeber says there are 70,000–80,000 men under the command of one General V. K. Pikalov, a gentleman so ferocious of mien that binary sales teams sent out from the Pentagon to deal with dubious senators have been handing out 8 × 10 glossies of him as part of their pitch. Where these figures come from is a mystery. An unclassified 1980 report from the Defense Intelligence Agency lists the Soviet numbers at 50,000, and makes clear something for which one has to search in the fine print in the contributions of proponents: *All 50,000 are trained entirely for defensive purposes and are not combat troops at all.* Their tasks are detection, decontamination, and evacuation of casualties, nuclear and biological, it should be emphasized, as well as chemical.

Moreover, the Defense Intelligence Agency report makes clear, the Soviets have been organized in exactly this manner since World War II, and are said to believe that their defensive readiness and offensive capacity influenced Hitler not to attack them with gas. Much is made of the collective-protection apparatus found on Soviet tanks and armored personnel carriers captured by the Israelis during the 1973 war, but the drum beating has more to do with the Chemical Corps dilemma during that period than with anything new those systems represent. Among other drawbacks, the systems don't work very well—to protect riders inside an armored vehicle from nerve gas would require a virtually hermetic seal—and soldiers riding inside cannot get out and reenter without contaminating the interior.

In testimony at previous congressional hearings, Defense Department spokesmen, by their refusal even to consider collective-protection systems, all but admitted that the Russian ones are less an advantage than an effort to make up for the awful quality of their cumbersome suits and masks. Rather than organize as a separate branch, as the Soviets do, the American approach is to have fifteen soldiers, in each company of 100–130 troops, who have among their duties chemical and nuclear defensive responsibility. How many offensive chemical soldiers do the Soviets have? If anybody knows, nobody is telling.

Almost all the other evidence marshaled by advocates of binary systems to establish the Soviet threat is purely rhetorical. One cannot read very far into the literature, for example, before coming on the 1977 congressional testimony of Lieutenant General Cooksey, then deputy chief of staff for research, development, and acquisition, U.S. Army:

> Chemical warfare would almost certainly be employed by the Soviets in the event of a tactical nuclear war in Europe, because if a strategic exchange did not result from tactical use of nuclear weapons it would obviously not be provoked by chemicals. The more important question is whether chemicals would be employed by the Soviets in a non-nuclear attack. The answer is quite probably yes. The Soviets are so immersed in chemical weaponry, tactics, doctrine, equipment and personnel, and so much of their training centers around the use of lethal agents that it would be odd, from a military standpoint, if they did not employ them. . . .
>
> Chemical warfare, to the Soviet leadership, is just another means of winning. This form of warfare holds for them none of the disgust and fear with which it is justly regarded in the West.

The general's authority for this opinion, of course, is himself. Hoeber goes so far as to introduce a translated Soviet document that she says proves the point. According to one Colonel A. Steblinin, no doubt the Slavic counterpart of Colonel Bay:

> Chemical weapons—toxic chemical agents (TCA) and the technical equipment used to deliver them in combat—can be used in modern wars. Their use, for example, has been officially sanctioned by the U.S. command in southeast Asia.

How's that again? That is all of it. Does it say gas *can* be used, *will* be used by the United States (the Defense Intelligence Agency report on Soviet defensive capacity says they believe their enemies might use toxic weapons despite the Geneva Protocol), or what? Without context and an annotated translation, I fail to see how it means anything at all. For Hoeber, though, it is the clinching bit of evidence.

Or consider the following Hoeberism, introduced by way of accounting for military doubts about gas:

The problem of skepticism about utility again has exacerbated the U.S. propensity to mirror image; because much of the relevant U.S. community does not believe CW weapons have military utility, the Soviets are viewed as rejecting an effective role for such weapons. Thus, according to this rationale, attention need not be paid to either offense or defense preparedness.

If nerve gas has no military usefulness, of course, a mistaken Soviet notion that it does is of no consequence as far as the United States offensive capacity is concerned. Defense against gas, which we shall look at in a moment, has nothing whatever to do with the decision on binary munitions.

So what have Pentagon officials been doing in the last ten years in between parading up to Capitol Hill to look authoritative for the cameras, and warning of the Soviet determination to reunify East and West Germany through chemical assault? Very little. "A massive non sequitur" is the way one Senate staffer describes the army's refusal to take seriously the consequences of its own rhetoric. While constantly calling for a very expensive binary-munitions program, the army has done next to nothing to equip soldiers with adequate defensive gear or to train them in its use. In 1979, for example, the army cut its already meager budget for protective suits by one third in order to spend the money elsewhere. Hoeber says she thinks Congress would have appropriated more money for defensive equipment if the Pentagon had asked for it, but that "they're too busy pushing paper over there to get it done. Advocating CW is not the way to get your next star. It is unpopular and not considered the way to get ahead."

But the enthusiasm of Brig. Gen. Gerald C. Watson, commander of the Army Chemical Warfare School at Fort McClellan, Alabama, should not be lightly dismissed. In the midst of a recent interview with the *Birmingham News* in which he touted the "humanitarian" wonders of binary nerve gas, Watson revealed that he has requested permission to use real poison gas in training soldiers to protect themselves against chemical warfare. Current training using smoke and tear gas, he says, is not realistic enough. The general may have something there. Last year an ABC film crew taping a "20/20" segment on gas-warfare training of American troops in West Germany, watched an unexpected temperature inversion send a cloud of tear gas back through the barracks, forcing a hasty evacuation, and then through a nearby village, where several inhabitants had to be hospitalized afterward. Had it been nerve gas, the Germans might take gas more seriously than they do. Increased realism should do wonders for enlistment, too.

Then there is the matter of decontamination. Much has been made of the elaborate Soviet decontamination equipment—although the pictures in the DIA report show that their vaunted lead in this area consists of tank trucks with hoses that could just as well be used for mosquito control, and the TMS-65, an obsolete jet engine bolted to a truck frame that blasts equipment with hot exhaust and decontaminating solution. Although some observers doubt that the TMS-65 can actually do the job, in theory a tank can be decontaminated by such means in less than one minute.

The American plan is rather more involved, as the following colloquy between Rep. Larry McDonald and Gen. Frederick Kroesen, then commander in chief of the U.S. Army in Europe, makes clear. Senator Pryor dug it out of the *Congressional Record* and read it on the Senate floor during the 1980 debate:

> *Mr. McDonald:* Do you have any rapid washing process, or do [you do] the decontaminating process out in the field?
> *General Kroesen:* The manner we are pursuing it right now in Europe, sir, is to have identified for unit commanders the locations of all available washing facilities, such as schnellwasch stations, automobile drive-in washing facilities.

Should tank commanders run short of change, another congressional staff member describes what he saw on a visit to Fort Hood, Texas: "a half-million-dollar tank, and our decontamination equipment was a guy in heavy boots with a bucket and a goddamn

$1.49 K-Mart mop, swabbing it down. And they were proud of it!"

The legislative history of the binary idea makes it quite clear that such gestures toward an improved defense posture—and everybody on all sides of the binary issue agrees that a sound defensive posture is essential—have come about mainly through congressional prodding. "No one explains how a defensively inferior force can counter a defensively superior force simply by retaliating in kind," Democratic Rep. Donald Fraser of Minnesota told binary proponents as long ago as 1974. As yet no one has, and until now the new munitions have been held hostage to improved defense.

But the army isn't ready to use nerve gas offensively either, and except for allowing the Chemical Corps to publish manuals now and again, doesn't seem to be getting ready. All but a very small amount, stored on American bases in West Germany, lies in remote spots in this country, where it is alleged by proponents of the new system to be deteriorating rapidly and growing obsolete. According to a GAO report made in 1977, however, "little has been done to maintain the stockpile in a serviceable condition or to restore the unserviceable portions." Whole lots, the GAO says, have been declared useless because of minor container rust and similar cosmetic defects. "Using anticipated approval of the binary program as a reason for not maintaining the stockpile is inconsistent with sound management," the report concludes. Offensive gas-warfare training is not now and has never been on the curriculum at the Army War College.

In sum, concluded a team from the Stanford Research Institute under contract from the Defense Department in 1977, while

There are statements in testimony, in field manuals, in CW studies and in war games which purport to show that CW has a high utility and that it could be a decisive factor in future battles. . . . the long-standing low state of both defensive and offensive CW capabilities in U.S. forces belies that conclusion. The low priority assigned to CW would be inexplicable if that were true.

Even so, the researchers concluded that the Pentagon had better get on the stick defensively and continue, out of prudence, to maintain a deterrent capacity.

I can see only four possible conclusions a skeptical citizen might draw from such a pattern of hysterical inaction:

1. The army is, collectively speaking, as dumb as a brontosaurus in a snowstorm;

2. The people in charge know or suspect that binary nuts within the Chemical Corps and its attendant civilian claque are making wild overstatements both of the Soviet threat and NATO unpreparedness, but keep mum out of the bureaucrat's instinctive inclination for mutual back-scratching;

3. Binary weapons are neither desired nor intended for Europe at all, but are recognized as having anti-guerrilla possibilities that will kindle a spark of hope in such military dictators and beleaguered oligarchs in the third world as may attract the support of the United States;

4. All of the above.

The Russians' Last Resort

"Here is the very worst thing that could happen," Saul Hormats told me over an omelette in his Baltimore apartment. "Let us suppose that the Russians are determined and unprincipled monsters. Their first move would be to put all their forces on full gas alert. Then launch an attack against a surprised Allied force. All hell would break loose. All historic precedents show that surprise attack would be devastating to us. There would be a very large number of casualties, widespread panic, in a word: chaos. We would be facing a complete military disaster.

"But counterattack in kind," he continued, "won't work. The wonderful attribute of chemical warfare—that's a hell of a word, wonderful—is that it's always more effective against old people and children than adults. And it is almost useless, militarily speaking, against an enemy who is prepared. Retaliation in kind would be a symbolic gesture that would hurt only our Allies' civilian population. You don't respond to a horror like a nerve-gas attack with a symbolic gesture. Once they use chemicals, the war isn't a game-room exercise. Scenarios aren't worth a damn. If they use gas, it's for real."

But the time for gas, Hormats thinks, is over, like the time for crossbows and catapults. "Maybe," he says, "the Soviets are monsters. But I don't think they are fools. If there were a war in Europe and they were winning, why should they do it? The risks are incalculable, unthinkable; they would be risking the survival of their civilization—and for what? They wouldn't be out to poison all the French and German people, they would be out to win. Gas isn't going to be a deterrent or a determining factor in the war that would follow a chemical attack. The Russians, or anybody else, would go to it only as a desperate last resort, and then only if they are convinced we'll respond only in kind. I concur with Reagan and Haig one hundred percent. If we must go, we must go for real. If there is going to be a next war, I want us to win it.

"I have a 'morality bias' that says it's immoral to respond to a devastating Soviet attack with a symbolic weapon. What use is a weapon that will kill all the old people and leave the Russian soldiers alive?

"Going ahead with binaries," Hormats continues, "sends a completely wrong signal to the Soviets, one that Reagan doesn't want to send, and that is that we're not serious. Four, five, or seven billion dollars that will be wasted are trivial compared with that."

Even if he is wrong, Hormats contends that the Chemical Corps is vastly overstating its problems with the current weapons. There are some, like the "weteye" series of bombs—many of which have been stockpiled, believe it or not, in the Rocky Mountain Arsenal, located in the suburbs of Denver and in the flight path of the city's commercial airport for many years, despite howls of protest—that probably ought to be destroyed. But the "bigeye" binaries that the Chemical Corps wants to replace the "weteyes" with have been on the drawing board for fifteen years and are not close to being ready for production. The artillery shells the Corps wants to make are not really capable of becoming obsolete as long as they are maintained at all, and the effective life of the nerve-agent loads can be extended for at least twenty years by the addition of a stabilizer, if easy tests show that is necessary.

Even so, Hormats maintains the tactical claims being made for gas weapons are ludicrous. At best, "gas is a weapon of hope. This stuff about micro-meteorology is cant. It doesn't work. The

262

uncertainties of gas artillery fire are at least an order of magnitude greater than with any other weapons system." Producing a paper napkin, he sketched out an enemy defensive position, then surrounded it with dots representing nerve-gas shells. "The only way to make sure you've covered them is to surround the targeted area with gas and hope you've achieved surprise, which, in retaliatory attack, of course you haven't." With standard high explosives, especially the fragmentation cluster bombs now available, far more predictable results are possible. He agrees that the tables produced in *Scientific American* last year by Harvard biochemist and chemical-warfare expert Matthew Meselson and English expert Julian Perry Robinson are accurate, and perhaps even conservative. The tables show that to cause 30 percent casualties among a platoon wearing gas masks but not defensive clothing, more than 1,300 155-mm GB shells would be required. At one hundred pounds each, that would come to sixty-five tons' worth of shells. Since the same figures apply on both sides, it is clear why defense is so important. The gas cloud produced from such an assault—even more would be required under less favorable weather conditions—might drift as far as sixty miles in whatever direction the wind took it.

That much was a confirmation of my own suspicions. But what really took my breath away was Hormats' assertion that binary artillery shells might not, and probably would not, work. The existing nerve-gas shells, he says, were merely an adaptation of already existing munitions. Even so, it took a great deal of testing and tinkering to get it right. In the Fifties, literally thousands of test rounds were fired at the Dugway facility in Utah. "You can have a gas cloud that burns up, if the reaction is too hot or forms too high off the ground and dissipates. Having a poison isn't the same thing as having a weapon. If it's more than six feet off the ground, it's no good. Or it might not form at all.

"And the binary rounds are not a simple change from other rounds. There's a whole new design involved. You need engineering data on cloud size and shape, rate of formation, yield, droplet-size distribution, persistency, etc. You need static and dynamic tests in statistically significant numbers. Simulants and computer models won't do. These would have to be live tests. You just have to keep testing and testing until you get it right. How many out of 1,000 rounds are going to be duds, and what happens to the gas when you get one? How much is agent, how much waste? If you don't do all that, you're going at it blind with World War III hanging in the balance. Where in the world are you going to do it? My God, the governor of Utah would send in the National Guard."

So there you have it, Armageddon fans, the ultimate cold-war weapon: billions of dollars and whole hurricanes of political and bureaucratic huffing and puffing for an outmoded form of mass murder that isn't needed and probably won't work. Of course, Thomas Dashiell, while admitting that the 155-mm shells are not needed as badly as he says bombs are—"there are other systems in R & D, it's more of a circumstance than a well-thought-out thing"—maintains that simulant testing will work, and proved it with a stream of jargon and acronyms I was not quick enough to write down.

Amoretta Hoeber remains consistent: "I would argue that there is no reason why they shouldn't be test-fired, at least a couple of rounds. If it doesn't work, we'd have a problem." Pentagon public-affairs spokesman Maj. Lee DeLorm, who serves as an artillery officer when not guiding inquisitive reporters through the labyrinth, did the best performance as Good Soldier, though, when I put the question to him: "You've got to have confidence. People who don't understand the technology have a hard time. I didn't have a lot of confidence in my wife's microwave oven, either, until she used it."

A Gesture for Sanity

One can get giddy contemplating a doomsday weapon that seems, in the final analysis, almost a joke; but in truth, the whole binary debacle seems to me absolutely symptomatic of the prevailing confusion in America about what we are up to in terms of "national security." Congress is prepared to go to the rhetorical wall and spend billions of dollars in order to protect Europe from the Russians, by manufacturing a weapon no European country will allow us to store on its soil. (The French, alone in Europe as always, are said to have a chemical capacity of their own.) The German position is particularly firm. In a 1970 white paper the West German government said:

In 1954, the Federal Republic of Germany renounced the production of biological and chemical weapons. She does not carry out any research or development conducive to the production of such weapons. The Federal Republic neither possesses nor does she store any biological or chemical weapons; she does not seek possession of, or control over, weapons of that kind, she has made no preparations for using them, does not train military personnel for that purpose, and will abstain from doing so in the future. Any allegations to the contrary, as occasionally made to the public, are false.

That position remains as stated. The European objections, moreover, are more than moral and have little to do with fear of peacetime accidents. What they fear, as well they might, is that they may become a backdrop for the feverish scenarios cooked up by half-baked ideologues with a career interest in eschatological daydreams. This is not to impute all wisdom to the worldly Europeans and wicked innocence to the brute Americans. It is simply to observe, with Dr. Johnson, how wonderfully the prospect of hanging tends to concentrate the mind. Were it a question of defending Atlantic City or Long Beach, nerve gas would have been out the window long ago.

For exactly that reason, the Soviets, with their long history of fighting wars on their own soil, have a clear self-interest in negotiating a chemical-warfare treaty; only the preposterous inversion of the actual world order that obtains in this country whenever an issue like nerve gas is bruited about could obscure something so obvious, or, rather, make even the firmest patriots and anticommunists nervous lest they seem "soft." Nobody is supposed to notice that the Soviets are surrounded by powerful enemies who can march into their territory on foot, while the greatest economic and military machine on earth has a hemisphere all to itself (with the exception of one small island). In order to maintain one's manly posture in the world, one has paradoxically to abandon everything one has learned as an adult and evaluate the Bad Guys through the eyes of a child. The Russians not only represent the quintessence of evil—and the very pressures I am speaking of here make me hasten to say that I think the Soviet government perfectly capable of using nerve gas, if it could do so with impunity—but they *know* that they are Bad and we are Good. Our government, of course, would never think of such a thing. Good Guys don't attack Bad Guys just for being Bad. They wait until the Bad Guys do something really mean, and even then they always fight fair. And why not? Don't the Good Guys always win?

I do not wish to be inflammatory or to call up old and buried controversies, particularly not ones interred since 1945. But so extreme is the national self-preoccupation that it requires from most of us a serious effort of the imagination to conceive that the world does not see us as Senator Jackson does. The bilateral talks between the United States and Russia on the subject of nerve-gas weapons have been in progress since 1976. The same binary proponents who use the Afghan allegations to confirm their suspicion that the Soviets plan to use nerve gas in Europe also say that their participation constitutes a cynical ruse designed to lull the West into unpreparedness. For both statements to be true would require extraordinary stupidity on the Soviets' part; they can squat on Afghanistan indefinitely without resorting to gas.

Both nations have agreed in detail to the kinds of chemicals that would be banned—it is a complex matter, since many have non-military uses. For quite some time the tough nut has been verification: how each will know the other isn't cheating. At last year's session, the Soviets agreed, at least in principle, to the idea of on-site inspection, which is a very hard one for them, sneaky, secretive buggers that they are. There is a considerable distance yet to go, but many reasons—among them the great dangers and manifest uncertainties of anybody's starting to shoot nerve gas around—to think that an acceptable treaty can be negotiated. If President Reagan really wants to show how Good, and in Richard Pryor's sense, how very *bad*, we are, he will sit on the report he has to submit to Congress before binary weapons can be made, and will indicate to the Russians that the United States wants a treaty. If the two nations cannot agree to get rid of nerve gas, with all its dangers and absurdities, he might well say, there is no point in bothering to try for nuclear arms reductions. He can make a gesture in the direction of sanity for exactly the same reasons Richard Nixon could recognize China and ditch biological war.

Nobody on earth would be mad at him except the Army Chemical Corps.

1981

Notes

1. Countries signing the Geneva Protocol with no reservations, thereby renouncing even retaliatory use of gas, include NATO members: Norway, Denmark, West Germany, Greece, Iceland, Luxembourg, and Turkey.

2. Had it not been for allegations of Soviet use of nerve gas in Afghanistan, it is doubtful last year's appropriation would have passed in the Senate. Of that allegation the best that can be said is that it is highly dubious. No physical evidence has been produced and alleged eyewitness accounts differ. State Department spokesman Matthew Nimetz told the House Foreign Affairs Committee that it was about a "fifty-fifty" proposition. Defense Secretary Brown spoke in Los Angeles of "mounting evidence that the Soviets are using incapacitating gas—and some that they may be using lethal gas," but said there was no hard evidence to prove either. Earlier, Edward M. Collins of the Defense Intelligence Agency told the House committee that "there is no confirmation at all that they have used chemical weapons." Bruce C. Clarke of the CIA, asked about the common perception based on rumor, replied: "I don't see anything wrong with letting that rumor run."

Saul Hormats has been following the allegations closely from the beginning. "I am one of the few people presently involved in the controversy who has been exposed to nerve gas," he says, "and have experienced an array of symptoms. I am absolutely certain that nerve gas has not been used by the Soviets in Afghanistan."

Just before this article went to press, moreover, the State Department presented what it called "significant, although preliminary" evidence of the presence of mycotoxins—organically produced poisons not indigenous to Southeast Asia—on one leaf-and-stem sample collected in Cambodia, near the Thai border. The release of this report followed by one day Secretary Alexander Haig's charge in a Berlin speech that the Soviets are guilty of chemical warfare, although the document itself makes it quite clear that the origins of the poisons are conjectural. The Russians, of course, deny everything. Neither the names nor the titles of the people responsible for the report, in what *The New York Times* described as an "unusual move," were made public.

To anybody familiar with the pattern of charges and countercharges in this smarmy business, just one obvious conclusion emerges: nobody seriously believes any longer that nerve gas has been employed by the Russians or their nasty pals, either in Afghanistan or in Southeast Asia. Whether that change of mind has more to do with the evidence or with the already assured funding of our own binary program cannot even be guessed at with the facts available.

Should these latest charges prove to be anything more than propaganda, the Russians will have been not only inhumane and duplicitous but also very dumb. Organically produced toxins are covered in the 1975 biological-warfare treaty. To have produced them as weapons of war, or to have supplied them for such use, much less to have actually used them, would be a direct violation of that treaty and would no doubt result in the cessation of *all* serious arms negotiations for some time to come.

The most cogent comment on the subject was made last year by Harvard biochemist Matthew Meselson, perhaps the leading academic expert in this country on chemical warfare, in testimony before the House Foreign Affairs Committee. He was speaking of the Afghan charges: "What we have . . . is the worst of both worlds. If the unconfirmed allegations of the use of poison gas are false, continued doubt serves only to erode the existing restraints against chemical warfare and to undermine the basis for effective arms control. If the allegations are true, our inability to document them prevents us from having much impact on the actual course of events."

3. DM reacts with water to form arsenical compounds that can be fatal. Very likely it, or something like it, accounts for the persistent reports of nerve-gas use by the Vietnamese against Hmong tribesmen in Laos. People familiar with nerve-gas symptoms say they are not among those reported by refugees, but that the drinking of water after an attack of DM could account for them. By the end of the war North Vietnamese troops had the capacity to use gas and did use it.

Postscript

After enjoying a considerable vogue among conservative political columnists of the sort who question the loyalty of anybody who questions the wisdom of any new weapon system at all, "yellow rain" was proved by Harvard's Matthew Meselson to consist of the excrement of bees, and eventually vanished from journalistic shortlists of Soviet atrocities.